Florence Whiteman Kaslow
and Associates

Foreword by JULES C. ABRAMS

Supervision, Consultation, and Staff Training in the Helping Professions

Jossey-Bass Publishers

San Francisco · Washington · London · 1977

SUPERVISION, CONSULTATION, AND STAFF TRAINING IN THE HELPING
PROFESSIONS
    by Florence Whiteman Kaslow and Associates

Copyright © 1977 by: Jossey-Bass, Inc., Publishers
                  615 Montgomery Street
                  San Francisco, California 94111
                        &
                  Jossey-Bass Limited
                  28 Banner Street
                  London EC1Y 8QE

Library of Congress Catalogue Card Number LC 77-82919

International Standard Book Number ISBN 0-87589-353-8

Manufactured in the United States of America

JACKET DESIGN BY WILLI BAUM

FIRST EDITION

Code 7753

The Jossey-Bass
Social and Behavioral Science Series

Foreword

Supervision, Consultation, and Staff Training in the Helping Professions comes out of the rising tide of interest in the whole problem of staff training, supervision, and consultation in the general context of educating students, fledgling therapists, and other mental health professionals. The fifteen chapters explore most of the important problems involved in the process of supervision and training, processes utilized to deepen and broaden the skills of experienced clinicians and other human services personnel. In this book, leaders in clinical psychology, psychoanalysis, sociology, psychiatry, marriage and family therapy, and social work introduce some novel perspectives and help us broaden our horizons. A hard look is taken at both the practical and theoretical issues involved. While not all of the problems are solved, this book goes a long way to delineate the basic issues and to present alternative ways of coping with problems; as such, it is of foremost importance to the whole system of competent and effective education.

As psychotherapy is practiced today, there exist no standards of training, functions, or responsibility about which mental health professionals generally agree. It is not surprising, therefore, that there is even greater disagreement and variance regarding issues of supervision and training. The divergence of opinion is manifested in this book; paradoxically it becomes, at the same time, one of the book's great strengths. The authors boldly and definitively offer the best of their specialized wares as they speak to such controversial issues as the changing role of paraprofessionals in service delivery, the psychoanalytic approach as a supervisory model, and the pros and cons of individual and group supervision. The book contains excellent and vivid descriptions of a wide variety of supervisory techniques. While some of the ideas expressed will stir up many dissenting opinions, there can be no controversy over the fact that there are many gems of wisdom here that can be applied concretely and specifically to the supervisory and consultative process.

While the more traditional approaches are discussed carefully, this book breaks new ground in considering some novel perspectives. There is a good deal of new material—particularly in the areas of supervision of marriage and family therapists, criminal justice personnel, and the role of the private practitioner as supervisor and consultant.

All in all, this is a very timely and stimulating book, rooted firmly in a sociohistorical perspective, on supervision, staff training, and consultation. As we all recognize that the social demand for *well-trained* therapists far outruns the available supply, we can see how very crucial the need is for this kind of reference for anyone who trains in this complicated province of mental health practice.

Philadelphia   JULES C. ABRAMS
September 1977   *Professor and Director of*
                                     Graduate Education in Psychology
                                  Hahnemann Medical College and Hospital

Preface

The fields of human service, mental health, and social service have seen a rapid expansion and proliferation in recent decades. From a basic core of three professions—namely, psychiatry, psychology, and social work—the human service fields now also draw staff members from psychiatric nursing, mental health technology, marriage and family therapy, and counseling and guidance. As the numbers of students, trainees, and new staff members have multiplied, they have been deemed to need either supervision, staff training, or consultation—sometimes all three—to increase their knowledge and augment their skills. Yet there is not a great deal of literature that synthesizes what is known about these three interesting, varied, and vital processes and the techniques that comprise them. Thus in 1971 some of the current authors came together to try to fill this gap, and *Issues in Human Service: A Sourcebook in Supervision and Staff Development* was published (Kaslow and Associates, 1972). Although *Issues* is still timely and relevant, additional information is needed in this polyglot, mammoth arena of supervision, staff training, and consultation. Therefore, another book was planned, one which could either stand on its own or serve as a companion to the earlier volume. The chapters contained herein are all original, written expressly for this book.

Since it had become obvious that the need for such a volume existed in all the major human service disciplines, the intent was to address it to a multidisciplinary audience. Thus the authors are drawn from psychology, sociology, psychiatry, social work, and marriage and family therapy, and the chapters reflect their different professional perspectives, adding depth, breadth, and controversy.

Part One is devoted to presenting the history and philosophy of supervision and consultation. In the first chapter, Kutzik sets a backdrop by offering a scholarly sociohistorical analysis of consultation and supervision in the medical field in England and the United States. The ancillary professions of pharmacy, nursing, and physician's assisting also receive attention in this carefully documented chapter. His evolutionary exposition of supervisory and training principles in the field of social work is equally erudite; he chronicles the early origins of these two processes in the charity organization societies and the settlement houses, moves through time to discuss the development of schools of social work as the field became professionalized, and goes on to point out that social work leaders and administrators often fostered prolonged dependency of staff members through perpetual supervision. In the past two decades, avant-garde social workers have challenged the need for ongoing hierarchical supervision; peer supervision and voluntarily sought consultation have become more prominent. Kutzik ably brings us to the present as he looks at current dilemmas caused when the National Association of Social Workers decided to admit people with bachelor's degrees into the professional organization, thereby conferring professional status on them and enfranchising thousands of workers who needed more and different kinds of training.

The evolution of consultation and supervision in psychology has some elements of medical philosophy and methodology, particularly insofar as private practice is concerned. Yet in agency settings it bears some resemblance to social work supervisory practice while permitting more latitude for the therapist and less fostering of long-term dependence.

The historical theme appears again in several later chapters as necessary background for understanding how and why a particular form and substance of supervision and training has evolved in marital and family therapy (Chapter Ten), in community mental health centers (Chapter Thirteen), and in private practice (Chapter Fourteen). The origins of each are shown to have separate but intertwined roots, and these glimpses of the antecedents of current practice are illuminating.

Finch (Chapter Three) lodges supervisory and training functions that occur in agency and institutional settings in the larger organizational context. To be unaware of the organization's structure, function, hierarchy, and philosophy is to be naive and to feel baffled. The agency's mandate and the administrator's expectations have a strong influence on the atmosphere in which service delivery occurs. The broad, sweeping principles that Finch sketches are dealt with more specifically in Chapter Thirteen, on community mental health centers, when the spotlight is focused on how the goals of this movement and the press for community involvement have affected organizational structure, staff patterns, and consequently what constitutes acceptable supervision and staff development. A novel pathway, in some ways the antithesis of Finch's theme, is explored in Chapter Fourteen on private practitioners, in which Cohen establishes that those who wish to be free of bureaucratic constraints and regulations often eventually seek out voluntarily some sort of supervisory or consultative arrangement and enter into a professional accord around accountability.

Each of the authors had free rein to write from his or her particular perspective. Therefore all shades of opinion are expressed—ranging from the orthodox analytic stance on the importance of carefully structured one-to-one supervision so ably articulated in Melchiode's chapter on psychoanalytically oriented individual supervision (Chapter Eight) and in Abroms' brilliant treatise (Chapter Four) on supervision as metatherapy (in which Abroms makes an analogy between the parallel processes of therapy and supervision and analyzes the essence of the trainees' personal and professional development as it unfolds in supervision) to the other end of the continuum, represented by Richan (Chapter Six) in his profoundly nonanalytic discussion of training lay helpers in human services. Richan, like Gitterman and Miller (Chapter Five) in their description of the supervisor as educator, conveys that the supervisor's mandate is to educate (or administer) and that supervision that verges on or encompasses quasi therapy is an infringement on the worker's private domain. Since Abroms and Melchiode are psychiatrists and Richan, Gitterman, and Miller are social workers, these divergent positions may well reflect prevailing attitudes and value orientations as they have historically evolved in each of these fields as much as they reflect the philosophies, experiences, and perspectives of the several authors.

Psychiatric residents tend to seek as much precepting as they can line up—sometimes competing for a weekly hour with a highly respected professor-therapist—and in some programs they desire and are permitted multiple supervisors for different cases and different treatment modalities. The ramifications of the psychiatric ethos in medical settings are most apparent in the interdisciplinary community mental health centers, where students and junior staff often "shop around" for topnotch supervisors. Conversely, graduate social work students tend to be assigned a specific supervisor, who oversees their work on all cases. Thus they are often locked in, in a totally encompassing fashion, with one supervisor. Efforts to seek counsel or input from other staff are perceived as resistance to and circumvention of supervision.

The supervisory pattern to which psychology students are exposed tends to depend on how much of their education and field practicum takes place in a medical setting or primarily psychological facility in contrast to a social work-dominated agency. The attitudes of students are shaped by the supervisory patterns they have been exposed to: The graduate psychiatrist or psychologist seeks consultation, when need be, from a valued elder in the field or from a colleague; the social worker, resentful of too tight and controlling supervision—eager to move out from the dependent, one-down position he or she has felt was superimposed for too long—often longs for the day he or she can be unsupervised.

Richan (Chapter Six) eloquently presents the status, role, and dilemmas of paraprofessionals or lay helpers, and the issues involved in their training and supervision. The scene is quieter and less tumultuous in the late 1970s than it was in the mid and late 1960s. The paraprofessional is less controversial now; that he or she is a permanent part of the helping panorama is now an accomplished fact. But the division of responsibility is not always clear, and it is in the muddy overlap areas and in the fear of being co-opted that identity crises and territorial conflicts still arise.

Many clinicians graduate and quickly find that the marvelous programs they dream of launching or expanding will never take flight if they do not seek and find funding. Thus, writing proposals for grants, a function for which many helping professionals have not been equipped, is one they must undertake soon after graduation. Royster (Chapter Seven) makes a major contribution in delineating what the procedure and content should be in training staff members for grant proposal writing—an area rarely covered in the literature.

Part Two, on supervisory and training techniques and processes, moves from the historical and philosophical to the theoretical and technical—the "how to" that many practitioners want. Melchiode's straightforward and sensitive essay on individual supervision, which is apt to leave the reader wishing to have a supervisor like Melchiode, is followed by a wide-ranging, integrative chapter by Kaslow on the relatively new bailiwick of supervision in marriage and family therapy. The reader will find not only a discussion of techniques but also a helpful appendix that lists degree- and non-degree-granting training programs. Abels does a whimsical presentation, cleverly using an analogy to a Sufi tale, as a unifying theme in Chapter Nine, on group dynamics and group supervision. By using excerpts from records that reveal mediocre supervisory practice, Abels pushes the reader to think about better ways of working with trainees and to assess what kind of rationale undergirds our own supervisory behavior. Coché offers a rich, crystal clear exposition on the methods and techniques of training group therapists; since a good deal of his material describes an actual training program in a psychiatric hospital as a prototype, the flavor of reality is in every page (Chapter Eleven).

Part Three progresses from methodology to specific settings in which supervisory and training activities occur. Two burgeoning fields that service hundreds of thousands annually receive attention. The problems and possibilities in criminal justice settings are handled by Brodsky, an eminent correctional psychologist (Chapter Twelve). He speaks of supervising correctional officers, people without graduate degrees and often also without undergraduate degrees, many of whom would fit into the paraprofessional category described by Richan. Yet these people, like psychiatric aides in hospitals, are the front-line personnel who spend the greatest amount of time with the inmates or patients. Therefore, their close contact makes their role a critical one, and they are in need of the preparation, stimulation, and encouragement that can be derived from a supervisor and/or staff trainer. In Brodsky's chapter, the organizational dictates that circumscribe practice, as described by Finch earlier, come alive with new meaning. Brodsky also discusses the supervision of prisoners and the urgency of treating them with respect and dignity. This last is a recurring theme, whether one is dealing with the supervision of students, as Melchiode and Abroms do; of staff members, as Finch, Royster, Coché, and others do; or of offenders, as Brodsky does. All are in a sense underlings, yet their humanity and integrity must be accepted and fostered, and there are ethical guidelines for dealing with people for whom the supervisor carries grave responsibility.

The spotlight in Chapter Thirteen, on community mental health, falls on interdisciplinary supervision and its attendant advantages and disadvantages. Moving in a very different vein, Cohen explores the functions of the private practitioner as consultant, educator, and supervisor—in some ways going full cycle back to some of the early roles traced by Kutzik that private physicians fulfilled, in other ways highlighting recently evolving activities.

The book concludes with a projection into the future. Crystal ball gazing is fun and full of surprises—but it is also an essential ingredient in offering speculative suggestions as to the directions in which a field should advance.

One additional note on the main thrust of the book. We are dealing with *supervision* of various categories of people: (1) students and trainees in formal graduate and professional educational programs, (2) workers in special institutes and in private arrangements, and (3) paraprofessional and professional staff members in agencies as they attempt to master new knowledge and add additional helping and clinical skills. Attention is also paid to the panorama of activities that carry the label *staff training*—an activity that usually occurs in groups and may be voluntary or mandatory. We also delve into the role of the *consultant,* an expert hired to work toward resolving specific problems and improving programs or interpersonal relationships, who, unlike the supervisor, does not have a direct line of authority over consultees. Sometimes the techniques utilized in one process are quite similar to those used in another process; they are definitely not discrete, and at times the separation is only arbitrary, made for the purpose of achieving clarity. Yet each has distinct features, which should become apparent as one reads carefully. They all are based on imparting information, attitudes, and values and on improving skills, but they differ regarding elements of authority, accountability, and the nature and purpose of the relationship. Each is a process or set of activities shaped by the desired end point or objective and the setting in which it occurs.

Since each author was free to write in his or her own style, the handling of sexist references to *he* or *she, his* or *her* is not always uniform, despite efforts to bring about similar nonsexist terminology. No sexist connotations are inherent or implied.

In *Supervision, Consultation, and Staff Training in the Helping Professions,* we make no effort to be internally consistent. To do so would distort reality; consensus does not exist in the human services today. If it did, innovative supervisory endeavors would not be under way. Even the nomenclature varies from author to author and profession to profession—as, for instance, in referring to the professional as *therapist, helper, clinician, practitioner, enabler,* and *service deliverer.* We hope that this collection of viewpoints succeeds in drawing together existing knowledge in the field of supervision, in teasing out the implications, in reaching new conclusions, in formulating new directions, and in stimulating the reader to use supervision effectively. If so, the goals of the authors have been realized.

The preparation of this volume required the assistance of a number of people. I wish to express appreciation to the contributors, who worked so diligently to write original chapters of high quality and to meet deadlines while teaching and rendering social and clinical services. The freedom that they all extended to me to edit the drafts was a support, as was their continuing belief in the importance of this book. I would also like to express my gratitude to my secretary, Jean Riling, who patiently typed the manuscript and offered encouragement.

Finally, the deepest thanks go to my husband, Solis, and our two children, Nadine and Howard, for their patience, understanding, and cooperation during the long nights and weekends when I sat in the office writing and editing and for all their playful chiding to hurry up and finish "the book."

Philadelphia   Florence Whiteman Kaslow
September 1977

Contents

Contents

The Authors

FLORENCE WHITEMAN KASLOW is associate professor of mental health sciences and chief of the Forensic Psychology/Psychiatry section at Hahnemann Medical College in Philadelphia. She is currently editor-in-chief of the *Journal of Marriage and Family Counseling*. She also has a private practice in individual, marriage, and family therapy and is a staff trainer and consultant for numerous agencies and institutions.

Kaslow received her A.B. in 1952 from Temple University, her M.A. in 1954 from Ohio State University, and her Ph.D. in 1969 from Bryn Mawr College. The editor of *Issues in Human Services* (1972), Kaslow has also contributed chapters to numerous other books in the areas of special education, consultation, and forensics and has written over twenty-five articles. She supervises psychiatric residents and candidates for master's degrees in family therapy and doctorates in psychology and is an approved supervisor for the American Association of Marriage and Family Counselors.

The numerous professional organizations in which she is active include the Philadelphia Society of Clinical Psychologists, the Pennsylvania Psychological Association, the American Psychological Association, and the American Psychology-Law Society. Among other honors, she has been named an outstanding Liberal Arts Alumnus by Temple University.

She is married to Solis Kaslow, and they have two children, Nadine and Howard. She enjoys theatre, ballet, music, tennis, and traveling with her family.

PAUL A. ABELS, Ph.D., is associate dean and professor, School of Applied Social Sciences, Case Western Reserve University, Cleveland.

GENE M. ABROMS, M.D., is professor and director of Residency Training, Department of Mental Health Sciences, Hahnemann Medical College and Hospital, Philadelphia.

STANLEY L. BRODSKY, Ph.D., is professor, Department of Psychology, University of Alabama, and editor of the journal *Criminal Justice and Behavior*.

ERICH COCHÉ, Ph.D., is clinical psychologist and director of Psychological Services and Research and Psychology Internship Program, Friends Hospital, Philadelphia.

EUGENE COHEN, M.S.W., is social work coordinator of Mental Health and Behavioral Sciences, Veterans Administration Hospital and Out-Patient Clinic, Philadelphia.

WILBUR A. FINCH, JR., D.S.W., is assistant professor, School of Social Work, University of Southern California, Los Angeles.

ALEX GITTERMAN, Ed.D., is associate professor, School of Social Work, Columbia University, New York.

ALFRED J. KUTZIK, Ph.D., is associate professor, School of Social Work and Community Planning, University of Maryland, Baltimore.

GERALD A. MELCHIODE, M.D., is associate professor and director of Medical Student Education, Department of Mental Health

Sciences, Hahnemann Medical College and Hospital, Philadelphia.

IRVING MILLER, D.S.W., is professor of social work, School of Social Work, Columbia University, New York.

WILLARD C. RICHAN, D.S.W., is professor and former associate dean, School of Social Administration, Temple University, Philadelphia.

EUGENE ROYSTER, Ph.D., is senior scientist and project director at Abt Associates, Cambridge. On leave as chairman, Department of Sociology, Human Services, and Anthropology, Lincoln University, Oxford, Pennsylvania.

Supervision, Consultation, and Staff Training in the Helping Professions

CHAPTER 1

The Medical Field

Alfred J. Kutzik

This chapter presents a frame-work for discussing consultation and supervision in the helping professions by relating them to the norms and context of professional practice, by defining and differentiating them, and by describing their prototypical development in medicine.

The relationships of professionals to those they help has always received great attention from the professions; however, the relationships among professionals have generally not been of much concern. Understandably, the latter have been most attended to during the formative stages of the professions. Once what are considered appropriate relationships have been established, they have practically never been reexamined. Only in those rare periods of major change in a profession, when the traditional mode of interaction among its members no longer adequately fulfills the functions of supporting and advancing the practitioner and the profession, do these relationships become a matter of concern. We are now at such a point in most of the helping professions, including those which are the focus of this book: clinical psychology, psychiatry, and social work.

It has long been recognized that modern society has increasingly placed professional practice within organizational settings. In the case of the older, well-established professions, such as medicine, the change from predominantly independent practice to more collaborative forms in institutions ranging from hospitals to multiple partnerships has changed the pattern of relationships among their members. It is not only that the traditional "two-party arrangement: the professional and his client . . . is not the prevailing arrangement" (Hughes, 1965, p. 10). More pertinent for the present discussion has been the concomitant change, noted by Hughes and others, in professional-nonclient relationships, specifically those structured into the organizations in which most professionals practice. "Historically . . . the free professions (law, medicine, ministry) tended to be free from organizational restraints. For the most part, they worked alone with individual clients, were oriented to their own sets of norms, and were free from responsibility to an immediate employing organization. This . . . has been changing rapidly" (Abrahamson, 1967, p. 7). The contradiction between the older, predominantly self-controlled mode of interaction among established professionals and nonclients (professionals, paraprofessionals, and nonprofessionals) minimally involved in independent practice and the newer, more other-controlled mode of interaction in the necessarily cooperative practice within organizations has led to concern among leaders and students of the professions, for this is viewed as a conflict between the basic professional norms of autonomy and collegiality and the basic bureaucratic norms of organizational hegemony[1] and superordinate-subordinate authority.

> One of the essential attributes of the professional role . . . is autonomy or self-control by the professionals themselves with regard to the development and application of the body of generalized knowledge in which they alone are expert. On the other side, it is an essential requirement of an effective formal organization which is devoted to the coordination of a variety of activities necessary for the realization of some specialized goal that the

executive maintain adequate control over all those persons in the organization responsible for carrying out these subsidiary activities. Whereas professions find the pattern of "colleague control" most suitable, the required pattern of authority for formal organizations is "superordinate control." The former consists of control by peers, the latter control by superiors [Barber, 1965, p. 25].

Barber suggests several ways in which conflict between these opposing norms can be minimized, based on the relatively limited experience of professionals working within host organizations. Like most students of the subject, he largely overlooks the ways of doing this that have been developed, in the course of lengthy experience, by those whose professions originated within organizations of their own, such as nurses and social workers, and he also overlooks the ways in which their situation differs from that of "free" professionals such as physicians.

These new professions, developed during the past century, are also now undergoing major change, necessitating changes in the relationships of their members among themselves and with their collaborators.[2] But their situation is practically the reverse of the older professions' situation. Having evolved within organizations, members of the new professions have been socialized into accepting organizational hegemony and hierarchical authority, as well as limited autonomy and collegiality. This traditional (for them) orientation conflicts with the current trend toward greater autonomy and collegiality among social workers and nurses, who in recent decades have attained a higher level of professionalization through lengthened and strengthened professional education.

Their different orientations to the same problem have become increasingly apparent as new and old professionals have been forced—by a combination of factors, ranging from the high degree of professional specialization, to the intractability of clients' problems, to the efforts of a single professional discipline—to collaborate to an unprecedented extent in providing professional service.

While they differ greatly in orientation, the solution to this problem is generally seen by both new and old professionals as a simple one: If there is a conflict between professional and organizational norms, the latter should be minimized if not eliminated.

However, this simplistic solution not only underestimates the degree to which those who participate in organizations must conform to group norms but also disregards the negatives involved in professional autonomy and collegiality and the positives involved in organizational hegemony and control—both of which have led to professional practice taking place in organizations. It also assumes that these contradictory sets of norms necessarily conflict and that, if they do, this is problematical.

The following discussion is based on very different assumptions. It is here assumed that, despite the inevitable strains and possible conflict,[3] both sets of norms are essential for the provision of professional services and that both should be part of the helping professional's value orientation, store of knowledge, and repertoire of skills.[4] Another assumption is that a major source of conflict between these two useful approaches is their frequent misuse, one being incorrectly applied where the other is called for. More specifically, it is assumed that the principal ways in which the two approaches are put into practice are the familiar activities of consultation and supervision and that what is being advocated here is their skillful differential use. The following discussion is intended to demonstrate that both supervision and consultation are indeed part of professional practice and to contribute to better understanding of their appropriate use through analysis of historical and contemporary experience of them within the helping professions.

Because of evident constraints and for heuristic purposes, this analysis is largely confined to the medical and social work professions, in which, respectively, consultation and supervision are most developed. Since psychiatry typically follows the "medical model" in nonpatient and patient relationships and since clinical psychology combines the psychiatric and social work patterns in this regard, discussion of medicine and social work is assumed to be relevant also for these other professions. (The next chapter discusses the development of supervision and consultation in social work.)

Consultation and Supervision Defined

Before embarking on this analysis, it is necessary to define *consultation* and *supervision*. Despite the familiarity with these activities by most professionals and laypersons alike, the precise meaning of these terms and the precise nature of the social mechanisms they denote are not general knowledge, or they would not be so frequently confused. Such confusion largely derives from the fact that, within a professional context, consultation and supervision are superficially similar: They are relationships typically involving two helpers sharing knowledge and skills to help one of them better help clients. However, the structure, functions, and modes of operation of these mechanisms are very different.

Consultation is a time-limited relationship of professional peers in which the consultee voluntarily seeks the advice of the consultant regarding a specific case or problem and decides whether or not to take this advice; supervision is a continuous relationship of an organizational superior and subordinate—supervisor and supervisee, respectively—in which the latter is required to report regularly to the former on the state of his or her work and the supervisor provides direction that the supervisee is bound to follow.

Going beyond a case to a problem is a departure from normal medical consultation that is defined in a recent authoritative work as: "A deliberation between two or more physicians concerning the diagnosis and proper method of treatment in a case." Our definition incorporates the medical one but reflects the broader scope of consultation in the newer professions exemplified by the following definition of mental health consultation: "A process of interaction between two professional persons—the consultant, who is a specialist, and the consultee, who invokes the consultant's help in regard to a current work problem with which he is having some difficulty and which he has decided is within the other's area of specialized competence" (Caplan, 1970, p. 19). Similarly, "consultation in social work" has been defined as "a professional method of problem solving involving a time-limited, contractual relationship between a knowledgeable expert, the consultant, and a less-knowledgeable professional worker, the consultee . . . concerned with problem definition and problem solution for the purpose of strengthening the consultee in his designated professional role functioning by increasing his knowledge and skills, modifying his attitudes and behavior to solve specific work problems, or, more generally, to enhance his work performance" (Rapoport, 1971, pp. 156–157). Like Rapoport, most previous discussants view social work consultation as carried on by "outside" consultants who are usually specialists, but the existence of nonspecialist consultants among regular agency staff is noted in the literature (Austin, 1960, p. 585; Kutzik, 1972, p. 114; Pettes, 1967, p. 19).

The term *supervision* is not included in current medical lexicons, although it is used in medical and psychiatric education for the relationship of students and interns to their clinical practice instructors, a usage that has been adopted by clinical psychology. While such "supervision" largely conforms to our definition in regard to structure and mode of operation, it does not conform in another essential respect: Its function is to educate the student, not to help improve service to patients. Since its objectives are different, the focal concerns, techniques, and evaluative criteria of practical instruction differ fundamentally from those of actual supervision. Despite disuse of the traditional term in recent decades (as this discussion will show), supervision has always existed in medical practice and is prevalent today, as physicians and psychiatrists oversee the work of other professionals and technicians engaged in health care. Similarly, social work supervision is generally defined in the literature as an educational process, for example, as "the method of transmitting of social work knowledge and skill in practice from the . . . experienced practitioner to the inexperienced student or worker" (Burns, 1965, p. 785). However, it is just as generally acknowledged that this educational "supervision" is always combined with administrative supervision (Towle, 1963, p. 413; Kadushin, 1976), the latter conforming to our definition in all respects. A few social work theoreticians agree with our position that only this administrative process should be considered supervision (Miller, 1971, p. 1494; Hanlan, 1972, pp. 48–50).

While consultation and supervision may be differentiated in a number of other ways, it is the structural differences between them that underlie and largely determine their other characteristics. Consultation is not merely a professional relationship because it involves professionals; it is an institutional mechanism of the particular profession(s) involved that requires equal professional statuses of consultant and consultee, on the assumption that this ensures the professional soundness of their collaboration on behalf of the client. Similarly, supervision is not merely an organizational relationship because it involves organizational staff; it is built into the hierarchical structure of the organization in which the supervisor must have a higher and the supervisee a lower status. While this has always been more or less understood, it is often forgotten.[5] This has recently been brought out in a discussion that notes that in community mental health "consultation can be differentiated from supervision on the grounds that . . . the consultee has no administrative authority for the work of the consultee . . . and the consultant has no organizational power relationship with the consultee" (Bloom, 1973, p. 17).

In light of these essential differences between them, consultation and supervision are here considered to be not only different but opposite "ideal types" of collaboration among helpers to combine their knowledge and skills for the purpose of improving service to clients. As with all ideal types, these are never found in a pristine state but in amalgams of varying proportions. Nevertheless, since elements of one or the other inevitably predominate, the knowledge- and skill-sharing collaboration between helpers in any given situation can be characterized as consultation or supervision.

Medical Consultation and Supervision in England

Historians have shown that in the seventeenth and eighteenth centuries, when medicine as a modern profession was founded, consultation became better institutionalized and more widely practiced by physicians than ever before (King, 1958, Chap. 1). However, it has been overlooked that supervision then also became prevalent among medical practitioners.

Consultation was already common among physicians in Europe by the thirteenth century. However, its norms were uncertain, and the consequent difficulties it caused physicians led many of them to avoid consulting. This is reflected in the statutes of the Guild of Doctors and Apothecaries of Florence, which required that consultation be initiated by its members in difficult cases (Riesman, 1935, pp. 231–232). Similarly, in France an early stage of development is evident from the opinion of one medical authority at about 1300 A.D. that "the patient should be warned against consulting more than one doctor at a time, although the doctor himself may call in some of his colleagues for consultation," while another advised physicians to avoid being consultants by "feigning an illness or some other likely excuse," the reason being suggested by the further advice that "if he [the consulting physician] accepts their [the attending physicians'] demands, let him make a covenant [contract] for his work and make it beforehand" (Bullough, 1966, p. 98).

Such uncertainty as to the norms and the very need of consultation was even greater among the handful of less well-trained and organized physicians in England from the thirteenth to sixteenth centuries.[6] As late as 1420, there was an attempt by the physicians (and surgeons) of London to establish a professional association, which, among other things, proposed to require its members to consult with one of the city's three leading physicians in "desperate or deadly" cases (Carr-Saunders and Wilson, [1933] 1964, p. 67).[7] However, it was a century before the Royal College of Physicians of London was granted its charter and two centuries before consultation became a normal, well-regulated practice among English physicians.

One can recognize the characteristics of consultation at its modern-day best in the well-documented case of the fatally ill heir to the British throne in the year 1700. When consultant Dr. John Radcliffe joined the two attending physicians, the collegiality of their relationship was such that his account reads "we ordered" various prescriptions and procedures. That the drugs and blistering agreed on by consultant and consultees may have hastened the demise of the patient is beside the point. What is relevant here is that Radcliffe did not blame his colleagues nor they him in a case involving the death of a crown prince. This is an outstanding example of the noncompetitive pooling of knowledge, skill, and responsibility among professional medical peers that was, by then, a widespread practice governed by traditional norms. Demonstrating this and providing some idea of the manner in which consultation took place is the following excerpt from "The Dispensary," a satirical poem of the time by Samuel Garth, M.D. (1709, p. 39):

> . . . grave *Physicians at a Consult met;*
> *about each Symptom how they disagree*

and how unanimous in case of Fee.
and whilst one Assassin *another plies*
with starched civilities,
the patient dies

Such an obviously expensive mode of practice was limited to patients from the upper socioeconomic strata. A very different kind of "consultation" took place in connection with the treatment of the less affluent and poor. The latter were regularly cared for not by the few, high-priced physicians but by the numerous apothecaries, who not only filled prescriptions for physicians but also had the right to prescribe and thereby to practice medicine on their own. They charged only for prescriptions—treatment was free. These unschooled, apprenticeship-trained apothecaries constituted the largest number of medical practitioners of the period.[8] Since English law made it a felony if a patient died in the course of treatment by an unlicensed practitioner—that is, anyone but a university-trained member of the Royal College of Physicians—when an apothecary's patient took a turn for the worse, he would of necessity involve a physician as a "consultant." Even if the disparate professional statuses of the participants in such "consultation" were not known, that something other than consultation was taking place is evidenced by the fact that the physician's fee was paid for by the apothecary. Ordinarily, the physician would see the patient in the latter's home, charging the apothecary a guinea per visit. But sometimes this considerable expense was reduced or avoided by other forms of "consultation" that can more readily be recognized as supervision.

A fee was avoided through "consultation" by mail. This was an accepted professional practice during the seventeenth and eighteenth centuries, whereby a practitioner would request the opinion of an eminent physician on the basis of a letter describing the case. Occasionally the letter writer was another physician, so that this was indeed a form of consultation. However, he was often an apothecary who was not in a position to reject the proffered "advice."

Another form of so-called consultation was even more clearly supervision. Since there was not always a response via the mail, a reliable form of paid "consultation" evolved that was far less expensive than the physician's visit to the apothecary's patient. The physician would be visited by the apothecary, listen to or read a report of the case, and, without seeing the patient, give his "advice" on the proper course of treatment, charging the apothecary half or less the customary fee for a bedside visit.

Any doubt that such relationships between physicians and apothecaries were supervisory is removed by Thomas Percival's authoritative *Medical Ethics* ([1803], in Leake, 1927, p. 112), which has a chapter on consultation among physicians and a separate one on "the conduct of physicians towards apothecaries." As King observes, the latter "emphasized that the relationship was one of the superior to the inferior. . . . Even though he has confided in the apothecary, the physician should nevertheless inspect, from time to time, the apothecary's drugs and should instruct him in the particular conduct of various cases" (King, 1958, p. 259).

The relationship of physicians and apothecaries finally changed to one of equality and their supervision to actual consultation only when apothecaries achieved the status of physicians. Having been legally recognized as general medical practitioners by the Apothecaries Act of 1815, in the next several decades apothecaries were able to become physicians by obtaining acceptable professional education at the new private and nonelite university schools, such as London's University College (founded in 1827). It was, of course, common practice for these general practitioner physicians to call on their more experienced or specialized colleagues for consultation in difficult cases.

While freely "consulting" with apothecaries, eighteenth-century English physicians did not consult with a good number of bona fide physicians who had graduated from Scottish medical schools, which the Royal College of Physicians, consisting exclusively of Oxford and Cambridge graduates, held to be inferior. This was rationalized by the fact that lax regulations at some Scottish schools permitted them to be used as diploma mills by absentee students, but it was unfair to their regular students, particularly at distinguished institutions such as the University of Edinburgh. Since English physicians were then "consulting" with English apothecaries, their refusal to consult with Scottish physicians evidently involved national prejudice. Whatever the reason, clearly consultation was reserved for those recognized as qualified members of the profession.

As the nineteenth century progressed, consultation between graduates of Scottish and English schools of medicine developed. These physicians would not consult with self-appointed "physicians" who had no medical school education. More important, the orthodox majority organized in the medical societies would not consult with actual physicians, whatever their educational or other professional qualifications, who were considered to have an unprofessional, unscientific theoretical orientation guiding their practice. Chief among these were the "homeopathic" physicians, who followed Hahnemann's theory of the efficacy of miniscule dosages of drugs. No professional relationship of any kind, above all consultation that was understood to assume acceptance of participants as qualified and ethical practitioners, was permitted between regular and irregular physicians.

Although the number of technical and professional groups involved increased greatly during the nineteenth century, relationships between qualified physicians and nonphysicians involved in medical practice was not considered problematical. All of these, without distinction—and without dissent—were viewed as properly subject to the physician's supervision.

The norms of consultation and supervision in British medicine remained essentially unchanged until recent decades. These were expressed in the 1927 code of ethics of the General Medical Council[9]: "Any registered medical practitioner who by his presence, countenance, assistance or cooperation, knowingly enables an unqualified or unregistered person . . . to attend, treat, or perform any operation upon a patient in respect of any matter requiring professional discretion or skill . . . or otherwise engage in professional practice as if the said person were duly qualified and registered, is liable on proof of the facts to have his name erased from the medical register. The foregoing do not apply so as to restrict the proper training and instruction of bona fide students, or the legitimate employment of dressers, midwives, dispensers, surgery attendants, and skilled mechanical or technical assistants, under the immediate personal supervision of a registered practitioner" (in

Carr-Saunders and Wilson, 1964, pp. 516–517). That the earlier section of this clause on "unqualified assistants" refers to consultation ("advice") with irregular physicians is made clear by its reiteration in another clause dealing with "association with unqualified persons." This is further clarified by the 1902 "Rules as to the Ethics of Medical Consultation" of the British Medical Association (which remained in effect into the 1930s), which specifies that, in addition to otherwise unethical physicians, "It is the duty of a practitioner to refuse to meet in consultation: (1) An unregistered person [and] (2) A practitioner whose exclusive profession of any peculiar system of treatment would render consultation futile" (1964, p. 519). While the former of these categories patently refers to un-qualified physicians, the Aesopian language of the latter refers to homeopathic and other unorthodox practitioners.

While generally indicating who among medical practitioners are barred from consultation with qualified, orthodox, ethical, and licensed physicians, the General Medical Council's code specifies that certain technicians ("dressers," "surgery attendants," and "skilled mechanical or technical assistants") and professionals ("dispensers," "midwives")[10] may be "legitimate[ly] employ[ed] . . . under the immediate supervision of a registered medical practitioner" (1964, p. 517). The remarkable omission of nurses from this list is not accidental. What accounts for the absence of these classic "hand-maidens" of physicians from among those whom the latter may supervise was the new level of professionalization reached by nursing by the time this list was drawn up. An authoritative 1933 study found that British nursing had "undergone a profound transforma-tion" since the first training schools for nurses had been established less than a century earlier and their first professional association begun in 1887. It notes that "Until lately . . . the nurse worked under the direction of the doctor and there was little element of cooperation. While the nurse must continue to work under direction, the tendency is towards cooperation, which is made possible by higher training" (Carr-Saunders and Wilson, 1964, p. 121). This trend of the new professions away from working under supervisory "direction" toward consultative "cooperation" with physicians and the trend in medicine toward consultation with new professionals, together with increasing supervision of nonprofessionals, is even more evident in the American experience.

Medical Consultation and Supervision in the United States

There were only some 400 medical school-educated physicians in the United States by the 1780s when their earliest professional associations were formed. But consultation was already customary, as indicated by the fact that its regulation was a major function of these medical societies. They promoted and facilitated consultation among their members while excluding nonmembers from this lucrative area of practice. As in England, these unschooled nonmembers constituted the great majority of the medical practitioners of the time, estimated at well over 3,000. Unlike those in England and other European countries, they were not apothecaries but apprentice-trained "physicians" and a few untrained self-appointed ones. Their exclusion from consultation with regular physicians differentiated nonprofessional from professional practitioners.

Medical consultation here did not have to undergo the gradual development it did in Europe. Given the English ethnicity of nearly all physicians and the general intellectual dependence of pre- and postrevolutionary America on England, it followed the pattern that had been evolved in the "mother country." In fact, after 1803 the codes of the U.S. medical societies were all based on Percival's crystallization of British experience, with its detailed attention to the ethics and etiquette of consultation. These were so stringently adhered to by the more highly professionalized that the record of an 1837 case involving eminent practitioners shows the attending physician being overruled by no less than three successive consultants and abiding by their decision although convinced it would result in harm to his patient (Rothstein, 1972, pp. 47–48). But not all members of the developing profession were so observant of the ethics of consultation. In fact, Daniel Drake, one of the consultants in the 1837 case, had five years earlier noted that consultation was a major "source of difficulty in the profession" because of the competition generated between the consultant and attending physician for the confidence and patronage of the patient, his family, and friends (Drake, [1832] 1952, p. 98). Troublesome as it was, the continuation and expansion of consultation shows that its positive effects on most physicians and the profession itself outweighed the negative ones. This is reflected in the code of ethics adopted by the newly founded American Medical Association (AMA) in 1847, whose "most important section concerned consultations" (Rothstein, 1972, p. 171). It explicitly encouraged them, rationalizing that "consultations should be promoted in difficult or protracted cases, as they give rise to confidence, energy, and more enlarged views in practice." In performing such functions for the patient and practitioner, consultation simultaneously performed the important function for the profession already alluded to, namely the isolation and (by the mid nineteenth century) the elimination of unqualified practitioners.

The AMA code's article on consultation presented these various functions as interdependent: "As in consultation the good of the patient is the sole object in view, and this is often dependent on personal confidence, no intelligent, regular practitioner, who has a license to practice from some medical board of known and acknowledged respectability, recognized by the association, and who is in good moral and professional standing . . . should [have] . . . his aid refused in consultation, when it is requested by the patient. But no one can be considered as a regular practitioner or a fit associate in consultation whose practice is based on exclusive dogma, to the rejection of the accumulated experience of the profession, and the aids actually furnished by anatomy, physiology, pathology, and organic chemistry" (Cathell, 1895, pp. 214–216). The reference to dogma, coupled with rejection of medical tradition and scientific disciplines, indicates that this passage was primarily directed against homeopathic physicians. Despite the strong AMA stand, consultation increased between the latter and orthodox physicians, who were nearly all members of the AMA. This was particularly true in the New York City area, which was a center of homeopathic practice. In 1882 this eventuated in the Medical Society of the State of New York dropping the restrictions against such consultation and in the society's expulsion from the AMA. Among the arguments by the opponents of the New York society's decision was the charge that the reformers wanted to "break down the barriers that . . . pre-

vented them from coming into certain consultation fees that homeo-
pathists might throw in their hands," noting that most of those in
favor of the change were specialists, that is, actual or potential
consultants. That discussion of this issue brought out the function of
consultation in conferring professional status on participants can
be seen in a passage from a contemporary "best-seller" on medical
practice:

> Do not refuse to consult with foreign physicians,
> doctresses, colored physicians, or any other regular prac-
> titioners. . . . On the other hand . . . refuse to extend
> the hand of brotherhood to anyone belonging to a party
> or association whose *exclusive system,* narrow creed, or
> avowed or notorious hostility to our profession, prevents
> him from accepting every known fact and employing all
> useful remedies. . . . When called in a case in which the
> medical attendant [irregular physician] cannot do this,
> you cannot agree with him, and must let his retirement
> be one of the conditions on which you will assume charge.
> . . . [In] a pressing emergency . . . temporarily set aside
> ethics and etiquette, and . . . unite your efforts—head,
> heart, and hand—with those of your chance associate.
> Treat him with courtesy, but studiously avoid formal con-
> sultations, or private professional dealings, or whispering
> conversation with him, or any other act that might imply
> association in consultation [Quoted in Rothstein, 1972,
> pp. 299–300].

Arguments and sanctions notwithstanding, consultation with
homeopathic physicians increased until in 1903 the AMA code of
ethics was revised to eliminate all restrictions on consultation among
licensed physicians. This still prevented the latter from consulting
with chiropractors, naturopaths, and osteopaths. In states where
osteopaths have since been licensed, some consultation between them
and regular physicians has developed. However, reflecting the continuing differential in professional status of the two groups, this
has generally been a one-way process, with regular physicians being
consulted by osteopathic physicians but the former consulting regularly trained orthopedists.

Because of the specialization of medicine, during the past century consultants have typically been and are today almost always specialists. However, the typical modes of consultative practice during the first and second halves of the century are quite different. The earlier predominantly solo practice, the consultant traveling to the home of the patient to confer with the attending physician—as his or her professional predecessors had done since the Middle Ages—has almost disappeared. Although in very different form, the solo aspect of it continues when the ambulatory patient is sent by the attending physician to the office of one or more consultants and returns to the attending physician after the latter has received their reports, which he or she takes into account in arriving at a diagnosis or treatment plan. However, the extent to which this is solo practice may be questioned, since often the consultant's office is located at the hospital with which he or she is affiliated. Frequently the consultant is called on for an opinion as a hospital staff member, examining the patient and conferring with the attending physician in the hospital. This model has become so prevalent that most large hospitals maintain a consulting staff of specialists who have no other duties. In fact, today, here and in Great Britain, unless otherwise qualified, the term *consultant* designates a specialist who is a member of the consulting staff of a hospital (Stedman, 1966, p. 359; Davies, 1969, p. 17).[11]

At the same time, in the past half century there have been secondary but significant developments in medical consultation outside of hospitals and even outside of medicine. This has largely taken the form of the involvement of medically trained psychiatrists as consultants to psychologists and social workers in child guidance clinics and family service agencies since the 1920s and in the community mental health centers of the past two decades. While the traditional role of public health physician has always had a consultative, "advisory" component vis-à-vis nonmedical professionals such as educators, physicians have been more clearly involved in extramedical consultation in recently organized multiprofessional programs dealing with problems that are only partly medical. Exemplifying this are programs that deal with child abuse in which pediatricians collaborate with psychiatrists, psychologists, nurses, social workers, and lawyers (Kamerman and Kahn, 1976, pp.

173–174, 177)', in a peer relationship much of which takes the form of consultation, the physician being sometimes consultant and sometimes consultee.

As in England, the development of medical consultation in the United States is far easier to trace than that of supervision. It is even more difficult to discern in the formative period of the American medical profession prior to 1850, since there were no socially sanctioned low-status medical practitioners such as apothecaries that physicians could supervise.

However, in the colonial period the unschooled "physicians" who served as practitioners for the low-income population must also have been supervised by physicians under the guise of "consultation." Otherwise such consultation would not have been so forcefully prohibited by the medical societies of the late 1700s. In the early 1800s, as medical societies proliferated, they barred these "physicians" not only from consultation but also from any other collaborative relationship with regular physicians, including supervision. Of greater import is the fact that in late colonial and early republican America there were a large number of reputable medical practitioners who did not have full professional status and who could therefore be supervised by physicians, for during this period American medical students exclusively "learned by doing," by practicing medicine under the supervision of a physician. Analogous to the pseudo-consultation of apothecaries in England, the education of most medical students in eighteenth- and early nineteenth-century America was actually supervision. This education of individual students by individual preceptors unconnected with medical schools is universally understood to have been a form of apprenticeship training. But it is not understood that apprenticeship is a form of supervision. In fact, it is one of the most intensive forms of supervision, for the "master" not only at regular intervals but continuously directs the work of the subordinate, whose status as apprentice depends on compliance with this direction. Apprenticeship conforms to the pattern of supervision in all respects except a particularly essential one: Where is the organization of which supervision must be an intrinsic part and whose maintenance and advancement is its reason for being? It is the master's business, in the case of medical apprenticeship, the physician's practice. It is this "organization" with, typically, only two staff members of unequal status in which the mechanism of supervision coincides with the entire "organizational" structure that made the apprenticeship of student physicians in early America practically ideal-typical supervision.

Since this was the only form of medical training prior to the late 1700s, when the first American medical schools were established, it is not surprising that "many practicing physicians in the colonies took on apprentices and functioned as preceptors" (Kissick, 1971, p. 204) nor that this continued well into the nineteenth century. But, reflecting both the opposition to such nonprofessional training by the growing number of medical school-educated physicians organized in professional societies and the rejection by medical students of intensive, extensive, and expensive supervision that did not enable them to attain full status as physicians, it became far less common by mid century. In fact, in the early nineteenth century there was a pendulum swing in the other direction as low-standard entrepreneurial medical schools proliferated in which mass lectures with no practice instruction whatsoever sufficed to provide a diploma that became a generally accepted credential by the medical societies. On the other hand, the curricula of the university-based medical schools, which gradually increased in number after 1800, included both clinical and classroom instruction.

At first these schools hired preceptors from among the many physicians experienced in providing such training and, later in the century, from among capable practitioners. As the teaching hospital became an integral part of medical education, there evolved the present system of unremunerated clinical instruction by outstanding practitioners who are rewarded with "hospital privileges" and teaching appointments in conjunction with paid clinical instruction by attending physicians on the hospital staff. While, reflecting its historic origin, the clinical instruction of medical school students is called *supervision,* it is not a supervisory but an educational process, since its objective and the main concern of both instructor and student is the latter's education. Yet the similar "educational" relationship of interns and residents to their clinical instructors is essentially supervisory, since the provision of hospital service is considered the primary responsibility of both instructor and student. This is brought out less by the fact that the instructor has traditionally been called *supervisor* than by the fact that interns and residents are considered and generally called *house officers* of the hospital. That this "educational supervision" of novice practitioners is, despite educational components, predominantly a combination of apprenticeship and administrative supervision is evidenced by the different positions of the supervisor and supervisee in the organizational hierarchy of the hospital.

In addition to such special time-limited supervision of partly trained and novice medical practitioners, physicians have regularly supervised others involved in providing health care. One need not dwell on the patently supervisory relationship of physicians and technicians, ranging from the surgical assistants of colonial times to contemporary inhalation therapists. However, the "supervisory" relationship of physicians to nonmedical professionals with whom they have traditionally collaborated in hospitals and clinics requires scrutiny.

As noted earlier in relation to Great Britain, nursing has long been moving from a strictly supervisory to a more consultative position vis-à-vis the medical profession. Despite this trend, particularly in recent years, the century-old pattern of the subordination of nurses to physicians still prevails. This is brought out by a 1962 study of the authority structure of the nursing service of a hospital in which the physician was placed at the top of the five-tier hierarchy by most of the participants in the four lower levels ranging from head nurse to nursing assistant. Although nurses were supposed to be supervised by nurses in the next higher level, many at each level considered the physician to be in charge and to be their actual supervisor (Pearlin, 1962).

If a similar study were made of hospital social workers, it would reveal a very different set of relationships, reflecting a pattern going back to the turn of the century. While the earliest social worker-physician collaboration (around 1890–1905) was supervisory, it has since increasingly become consultative. The charity organization society agents who were on occasion assigned to hospitals and clinics in the 1890s to check on the veracity of poor applicants for free medical care were supervised in this task by those who administered the facilities, including physicians. This was to be expected, for these charity workers were not professionals, despite their aspirations, since the first schools of social work had not been established yet. Graduates of social work schools who were employed on a full-time basis by hospitals after 1905 to perform a full range of social work services as well as to verify patients' financial resources were increasingly less supervised and more consulted by physicians. This tended to vary with the emphasis placed by the particular hospital on providing social services or checking financial resources, as exemplified, respectively, by Massachusetts General Hospital and (Boston's) Berkeley Infirmary. It also varied from physician to physician, depending on their view of the professional or technical role of medical social workers. Many physicians saw these invariably female staff as a new kind of nurse and related to them accordingly. As social service departments were established in hospitals in the ensuing decades, social workers moved out of the hospital's physician-dominated authority structure and into one of their own. Ironically, as this practically did away with their supervision by physicians, it placed them under the supervision of fellow social workers, a development discussed in the following chapter.

Another group of social workers practicing in medical settings were the "psychiatric social workers" who from World War I on worked with psychiatrists (and psychologists) in mental hospitals and child guidance clinics. Over the years, social workers in mental hospitals have had relationships with psychiatrists similar to other hospital social workers and physicians, that is, as often supervisory as consultative. However, the unmistakably professional tasks, including "therapy," of social workers in the less-bureaucratized mental health clinics tended to make their relationship to psychiatrists in these settings more consultative than supervisory (Briar, 1971, pp. 1239–1240).

Current Problems and Prospects

As implied earlier, despite the lengthy collaboration there is unclarity on the part of physicians as to whether they should be supervising or consulting with social workers. Recently, this has become more problematical than ever as physicians, particularly psychiatrists, have had to work with social workers in new programs in unprecedented numbers and in old programs in new ways. These are exemplified, respectively, by the community mental health centers and those mental hospitals that have been administratively restructured so as to eliminate their social service departments and the pattern of professional relationships these once maintained. In both situations, as psychiatrists have typically served as administrators of not only psychiatric and medical but also social work and other professional and technical activities, they have frequently confused their administrative-supervisory and consultative-professional roles vis-à-vis the various staff involved.

Similar confusion has characterized the relationships of physician-administrators to physician-staff in nontraditional organizational settings. For example, a 1960 study of the "supervision" of physicians in two medical school-related clinics found that they readily accepted administrative supervision regarding scheduling and facilities but resisted "supervision" of their treatment of patients through routine review of their charts by the "supervising" physician. The latter was forced to "act as a consultant" giving "advice" on treatment that could be accepted or rejected by his "supervisees." All the physicians involved, as well as the researcher, conceived of both administrative direction and advice concerning patients as "supervision" (Goss, 1961). While a viable mode of operation was pragmatically arrived at in these instances, it was only after a period of strain that diverted time and energy from treating patients and training students.

In addition to such familiar problems with nonmedical professionals and fellow physicians generated by increasing practice in multiprofessional programs and organizational settings, physicians now face new ones around the supervision of and consultation with novel non-, semi-, and fully professional medical practitioners. Recognition of the critical deficit in the number of medical practitioners has during the past decade led to the development of a variety of physician surrogates, ranging from nurse practitioners to specially trained armed forces medical technicians. Analysis of the statements on such personnel issued by several professional medical bodies finds that "These various position statements generally recognize three levels of function, which can be loosely categorized as 'associate' level; 'assistant' level; and 'aide.' The distinctions are based on the particular skills and training required, the scope or specificity of functions to be performed, and the degree of independence allowed under continuing supervision. . . . All agree that the physician must retain ultimate responsibility for the performance of his subordinates. Three levels of supervision are also referred to, namely (1) over the shoulder; (2) on the premises; and (3) remote with monitoring. The question of supervision is central" (Sanazaro, 1970, p. 99). If this is not complicated enough, another discussant differentiates between "physician's assistants" as technicians who "should function under the direct supervision and authority of physicians and . . . would not make important value judgments or decisions involving the health care of patients" and "physician's associates" as professionals "making independent value judgments and providing direct health care to patients"—but goes on to discuss the latter's "supervision" by the physician, indicating that this is required by law in Colorado where such associates may "diagnose, treat, write prescriptions for, and give comprehensive care" to patients (Silver, 1971, pp. 305–307). However, the legal right of "medical assistants" to prescribe drugs recently granted them in New York State is being challenged on grounds that they are expected to work under the direct supervision of a medical doctor. Added to this array of nonprofessional "aides" and "assistants" and semiprofessional "associates" are more or less fully professionalized "nurse practitioners," trained nurses who have undergone additional medical training. It can be anticipated that a number of these various kinds of practitioners will, after further training and experience, move to higher levels of professionalism. Yet, according to medical authorities and the statutes they have helped draft, all of them must be "supervised" by physicians. This underscores the need for physicians to turn to the lengthy experience of their profession in developing appropriate collaborative relationships among practitioners of different degrees of professionalization.

However, this requires more than simply applying the general principle that professionals should be consulted and semi- or nonprofessionals supervised. In large-scale organizational settings such as hospitals, clinics, and centers, competent practice requires that professionals, including physicians, be supervised as well as consulted. Physicians who do not accept the validity of their being supervised regarding administrative matters cannot practice as efficiently as they should, while administrators who apply supervisory norms to professional matters create obstacles to effective practice. The historic experience of medicine provides valuable insights and guidelines for the differential use of consultation and supervision in the collaboration of professional, semi-, and non-professional personnel. This "medical model" of knowledge and skill sharing, however, is based on and most suited for solo and single-profession, small-scale organized practice. For additional insights and guidelines for the kind of consultation and supervision developed within and required for multiprofessional, large-scale organized practice, one may profitably turn to the history of social work (Chapter Two).

Notes

1. It would be more elegant but less accurate to contrast professional autonomy and organizational heteronomy ("control by others"), but within an organization control is not exercised by others generally, for various purposes, but by and for the organization.

2. Hughes' "new professions" is here preferred to Barber's "emerging professions" or Carr-Saunders' and Etzioni's "semiprofessions" as best describing these by-now well-developed professions with characteristics differing from the older ones.

3. In concluding the passage earlier cited on the two sets of norms, Barber observes "Inevitable strain exists . . . in this situation, but this does not mean inevitable conflict" (1965, p. 25).

4. This is supported by the insight, applicable to all the professions, that "medical education can be conceived as facing the task of enabling students to learn how to *blend* incompatible or potentially incompatible norms into a functionally consistent whole. Indeed, the process of learning to be a physician can be conceived as largely the learning of blending seeming or actual incompatibles into consistent and stable patterns of professional behavior" (Merton, 1957, p. 72).

5. This is evident from the etymology of the terms (whose Latin meanings were evident to the university-educated physicians and lawyers of an earlier day): *consultation* coming from the verb "to counsel together," "to advise one another," and *supervision* from the verb "to oversee," literally, "to view from above."

6. Medical education at the two English schools, Cambridge and Oxford, was greatly inferior to contemporary schools on the continent until the eighteenth century.

7. The compulsory nature of this scheme and the superior status of the specified consulting physicians, who were governmental and ecclesiastic officials, would have made this more like supervision than like consultation.

8. In London around 1600 there were 20 physicians and 114 apothecaries and around 1700 about 80 physicians and 1,000 apothecaries (King, 1958, p. 223). The ratio was less extreme in other European countries, but the same general situation prevailed.

9. The national government agency in charge of the registration (a form of licensing) of British physicians. This code is technically the "Warning Notice" of the General Medical Council's *Medical Register*.

10. For the professional status of pharmacists ("dispensers") and midwives in Great Britain at the time this was adopted, see Carr-Saunders and Wilson ([1933] 1964, pp. 121–125, 132–141).

11. This has also become so institutionalized in other countries that Austria and Germany have special terms for the hospital "consultation room" (Lejeune and Bunjes, 1969, p. 149).

CHAPTER 2

The Social Work Field

Alfred J. Kutzik

The characteristic supervision of social workers by social workers in certain settings since the mid 1890s and almost everywhere they have practiced since the 1930s appears to contradict the axiom that supervision does not take place among professional peers. However, we shall see that there is no contradiction, that generally when supervision has taken place among social workers they have not been professional peers and when it has taken place among peers it has not been supervision but consultation.

Analysis of the historical data requires precision as to when social work became a profession and who its members were at various periods. The beginning of the profession of social work is generally dated from the founding of the first U.S. charity organization societies (COSs) and settlement houses in the late 1870s and 1880s respectively. Some authorities go back a decade earlier to the formation of the first state boards of charities and the organization by their leaders of the National Conference of Charities and Correction (NCCC) in 1874. In light of the fundamental contributions of these three movements or fields to the development of social work, the last part of the nineteenth century can justifiably be considered the period in which this profession began to take shape. But it is inaccurate to view the profession as having emerged as such until after the turn of the century when the first schools of social work were established and the formerly antagonistic settlement and charity fields—the latter including both the private "casework" and public welfare sectors—combined forces in basic professional activities. This turning point is evidenced by the merger of their major publications, *Charities* and *The Commons,* into a single journal in 1908 and the election of a settlement leader, Jane Addams, to the presidency of the theretofore charity- and public welfare-dominated NCCC in 1910. Nor is it accurate to view the profession as full-fledged until the 1920s, when its first exclusively professional associations were organized.

In 1915 Flexner was of the opinion that social work was not a profession for a number of reasons, including the lack of "self-organization." In this connection, the NCCC and its successor National Conference of Social Work (founded in 1916) involved both lay volunteers and paid "professionals," while only the latter were members of the American Association of Medical Social Workers (1918), the American Association of Social Workers (1921), and the American Association of Psychiatric Social Workers (1926).

Even after there was a unified, self-educating, self-regulating profession, it long consisted of relatively few social workers who were educated in schools of social work (SSWs) and affiliated with associations practicing among a great many untrained, unorganized social welfare workers. From 1900 to 1920, the proportion of social workers to welfare workers was extremely small. The thirteen schools of social work organized before World War I graduated only a few hundred in these two decades. In 1921, when there were more than 10,000 paid workers in welfare positions in the United States, 1,800 were members of the newly organized American Association of Social Workers (AASW). However, a minority of these were SSW graduates. The general lack of professional education among practitioners is why the AASW only required its members to have an educational background warranting expectation of success in social work in addition to four years of practice experience. In 1931, with the same requirements in effect, of more than 20,000 paid workers the association had 5,200 members. While still a minority, a higher percentage of these must have been SSW-educated, since there were then two dozen SSWs turning out about 500 graduates a year. By 1936 AASW membership had almost doubled to 10,000, but many, if not most, of the new members had no professional education, having expressly joined before July 1, 1933, in order to avoid the more stringent educational requirement adopted then of "the equivalent of one year in a school of social work" (Kamerman and Kahn, 1976, pp. 20–21). In 1941, when there were over 45,000 paid workers and thirty-six schools graduating over 1,000 annually, 11,300 were AASW members. And, in 1951, when there were over 91,500 welfare workers and some fifty schools graduating 2,000 annually from what had become a two-year master's program, only 12,500 were AASW members. Some of the disparity between the rapidly growing number of professionally educated social workers and the minimal increase in AASW membership was due to the fact that many SSW graduates preferred to affiliate with one of the six specialized professional social work associations that had developed over the years.[1] In 1956, 9,000 members of these other groups joined with 13,000 AASW members to form the National Association of Social Workers (NASW), together constituting perhaps a fifth of those working in social welfare. A substantial minority of those "grandfathered in" from the predecessor organizations could not have met the NASW's membership requirement of a master of social work (M.S.W.) degree from an accredited school of social work. However, nearly all of the well over 50,000 who have become members of NASW during the past twenty years have been graduates of such schools. The present NASW membership of 70,000, practically all with professional education,[2] constitutes less than a fifth of the estimated 370,000 welfare workers, about half of whom do not have a college degree (Kamerman and Kahn, 1976, pp. 20–21).

While the extent of the professionalization of social work and social welfare is generally indicated by these statistics, it is important to note that professional social workers have always been and are today far more frequently employed in the private than in the public welfare sector. The latter presently has, among its 300,000 or so staff, a few thousand professional social workers. Conversely, M.S.W.s have since 1900 increasingly dominated and since the 1950s practically monopolized the staff and administrative positions in "voluntary" social agencies. Consequently, it is on the latter, in which the profession of social work has largely developed, that this analysis is focused.

Supervision and Consultation in Social Welfare: The Nineteenth Century

Earlier writers have assumed that social work supervision originated in the early COSs as the natural form of administrative control in large organizations and that, from the first, due to the absence of other forms of education, experienced supervisors provided less experienced supervisees the equivalent of apprenticeship training (Swift, 1939, p. 433; Austin, 1960, p. 579). An influential expression of this universally accepted view introduces the article on supervision in the 1965 *Encyclopedia of Social Work:*

> Historically, supervision developed as a way of training staff, paid or volunteer, to do the job at hand. . . . Both supervision and casework, in the modern sense, developed in the charity organization societies that were established in many United States cities during the last twenty years of the nineteenth century. . . . Numerous volunteer workers were needed to carry out this work [of friendly visiting], particularly during periods of economic distress. These volunteer visitors had to be instructed in charity organization principles and methods; their efforts required guidance and coordination; their interest in the work also had to be encouraged and sustained. To meet these needs—administrative and educational—supervision was developed.
>
> During the earliest years, most persons in the charity organization movement were all working and

learning together, but by 1890 a more expert group had gradually developed, the paid staff who were, in actuality or effect, supervisors of the work of volunteer visitors and of less experienced paid workers [Burns, 1965, pp. 785–786].

This mixture of myth and misinterpretation has been uncritically accepted even by critics of social work supervision, who thereby concede that their objections to its combination with education and to other questionable features were opposed to the normal practice of social work from its very inception (for example, Miller, 1971, p. 1494; Perlmutter, 1972, pp. 8–9; Toren, 1972, p. 67). The most formidable rationalization of this erroneous position appears in Kadushin's otherwise impeccable *Supervision in Social Work* (1976), which is replete with historical data that do not support his conclusion that "Thus, starting with the development of the Charity Organization movement in the 1880s, supervision gradually emerged as a necessary aspect of Charity Organization work. The agent-supervisor organized, directed, and coordinated the work of visitors and paid agents and held them accountable for their performance; he advised, educated, and trained visitors and paid agents in performance of their work and inspired them in their discouragements and disappointments. The three major components of current supervision['administrative, educational, and supportive'] were thus identifiable among the tasks assumed by the early agent-supervisor" (Kadushin, 1976, p. 13).

Records of this period do show that supervision was characteristic of the early COSs. However, they also show that during the COSs' first two decades (1877 to about 1895) there was no supervision of volunteer friendly visitors, but only of paid agents by volunteers and that such supervision was entirely administrative, without educational or "supportive" components. Although nowhere recognized in the literature, the records show that consultation among volunteer administrators and visitors was also characteristic of the nineteenth-century COS.

Before examining the actual working relationships of paid agents and volunteers, it must be noted that supervision of the volunteer friendly visitor was predicated on COS principles, the most fundamental of which was that the very example of the wise and industrious visitor was the means of uplifting the ignorant and indolent from degraded pauperism to self-respecting poverty.

Since helping those visited was assumed to derive from demonstration of the visitor's exemplary character, theoretically nothing needed to be or could be done to improve such help. Agents could increase the amount of help that the visitor gave, that is, the number or length of visits, by assisting him with preliminaries and follow-up to the visit. Any idea that these employees, whose inferior socioeconomic status was considered prima facie evidence of inferior strength and wisdom, could supervise the moral and social superiors who employed them was unthinkable. And they were in fact, as well as in name, the paid agents of the dues-paying, therefore wage-paying, organizationally active members of the COS, including those serving as friendly visitors.

Accordingly, until the late 1890s COS agents did not direct, much less instruct, friendly visitors in charity organization principles and methods. It was the latter and other volunteers in administrative positions who directed their agents' activities. The nature of certain of these activities and the status of the early COS agents[3] are indicated by the fact that an alternate title of the agent was "secretary" and one of the major responsibilities of the district agent or secretary—the position held by most of the paid staff before 1895—was doing the clerical chores of the district committee, an administrative body composed of COS members and other laypeople that directed the organization's service in different sections of the city. The agents' other major area of responsibility was assisting the friendly visitors in preparing for and following up on cases, mainly by means of in-the-field investigation. This investigatory role of the agent has been mistaken for that of a caseworker rather than caseworker's assistant or case aide, which it actually was. The true nature of the agent's technical, when not menial, dependent role, as opposed to the more autonomous protoprofessional role of the visitor, is evident from the fact that the agent acted as secretary or investigator only when and in the manner directed by visitors or the district committee. The dual role of the agent as secretary-case aide and supervisee is brought out by data from the 1880s that have been elsewhere interpreted as evidence of her roles as social worker and supervisor:[4] "The agent . . . giving all his time, naturally becomes the center of district work, receiving both from visitors and [the district] committee information and advice to be transmitted one to the other" (Smith, 1885, p. 70); "[The agent needs to be] careful to represent the committee faithfully to the visitors and the visitors faithfully to the committee" (Smith, 1887, p. 161).

That at "certain hours" the agent served as a "connecting link" (Fields, 1885, p. 18) between the district committee and friendly visitors, transmitting advice from the former to the latter and transmitting information and requests for advice from the latter to the former, did indeed put her "in the center of district work." But only her location, not her role, was central. As these statements to the NCCC by the general agent of the Boston COS make clear, the agent was expected to convey her employers' messages without adding information and advice of her own ("to represent the committee faithfully"). This messenger role was no more than a particularization of the agent's general clerical and case aide responsibilities.

The strictly administrative supervision of these low-level employees by their organizational and "professional" superiors, particularly the chairmen of the district committees, can be surmised. In fact, it must be, since there is no discussion in the COS literature of this normal mode of operation, which everyone concerned understood. However, the supervisee status of the agent and the noneducational nature of her supervision is occasionally noted in the records when, due to the unavailability of volunteers, she moved out of her normal ancillary role into that of friendly visitor. In 1892, for example, one of the district committees of the New York COS reported: "No friendly visitors have been secured to lessen the burden of the agents, and the committee have felt themselves bound to a greater care and supervision of the cases in order to supplement more fully, by advice and counsel, the efforts of the agents" (*Charity Organization Society of the City of New York, Tenth Annual Report for the Year 1891*, 1892, p. 37).

Another district committee, which did have enough volunteer visitors, reported that a number of vagrants, who obviously could not be served through friendly visiting, had been "treated" by the district agent, noting: "While the labor and responsibility of treating these homeless cases falls largely upon the agent, the committee has exercised a general supervision over them" (*Charity Organization Society Report,* 1892, p. 37).

Despite phraseology denoting that the cases, not the agents, were being supervised, supervision of the latter was in fact taking place: Organizational subordinates were being directed by organizational superiors.

The early COS's agent-supervisees just described are a far cry from the mythical agent-supervisors others have written about. But our findings do more than revise the accepted view of the supervisory role of paid agents during this period; they refute its corollary of the educational nature of the earliest social work supervision. Since at this time paid agents did not supervise volunteer visitors, the former could not have "instructed [the latter] in charity organization principles and methods" (Burns, 1965, p. 786) or otherwise "educated and trained" them (Kadushin, 1976, p. 13). Irrespective of whether the agents were supervisees or supervisors, the general assumption that the educational component of supervision took the form of apprenticeship training "from the earliest days of the charity organization societies" (Miller, 1971, p. 1494) is untenable, given the different service-occupational roles of agents and volunteers. There could have been no apprenticeship training, since "apprentice" supervisees could not emulate "master" supervisors, who had a different set of job responsibilities and skills.

While our findings revise the accepted conception of supervision in the early COS, they do corroborate its existence and prevalence, because the typical clerical and technical case aide roles of the agents and the more "professional" caseworker and administrator roles of volunteers in conjunction with their different positions in the COS hierarchy conform to the occupational and structural requirements of supervision. Even the atypical supervision of the few agents who served as visitors by the generally more knowledgeable and invariably more highly placed district committee members meets these requirements. On the other hand, the view that—somehow in addition to their supposed supervision by paid agents—volunteer friendly visitors were supervised by their district committees (Kadushin, 1976, p. 5) must be questioned on the same grounds. Visitors and district committee members did indeed collaborate in sharing knowledge and skills when discussing the former's cases. However, the relationship of these two kinds of COS member-volunteers of similar occupational and organizational status evinces the characteristics of consultation.

The COS principles that did not permit the supervision of volunteer visitors by paid agents also prevented their supervision by other volunteers, including members of the district committees. More decisive than this ideological barrier was the structural one. Just as it was impossible for paid agents to supervise their organizational superiors, so it was impossible for volunteer committee members to supervise their organizational peers. However, these social welfare practitioners of equal status could and did consult with one another. That the "advice" of the district committee given in response to the "reports" of the friendly visitors in their district was a form of consultation is evident from certain crucial facts in addition to the structural ones already referred to. One such fact was that, while visitors were expected to report to the district committee, they could and did initiate contacts with the committee for "advice and assistance." And, definitely distinguishing such consultation from supervision, visitors were not bound to and did not always follow the committee's advice. This early social welfare consultation differed from later social work consultation in that it was not part of a still-to-be-developed profession whose norms and values are shared by participants. But it did approximate this structural requirement of consultation, since most experienced visitors and district committee members shared the ideology of the charity organization movement. This is evidenced by the strictures of COS leaders against inexperienced visitors, who tended toward relief giving rather than toward character building by advice and example (Almy, 1895).

It has been calculated that "by 1890 there were 78 charity organization societies with 174 paid workers and 2,017 volunteer friendly visitors" (in Kadushin, 1976, p. 5). This ratio of one paid worker to a dozen or so volunteer visitors has been mistaken as evidence of the supervision by the former of the latter. Actually, it is evidence of the predominance of consultation over supervision, for less than 200 paid workers were being supervised, while over 2,000 volunteer visitors and at least the same number of volunteer district committee members were involved in consultation with one another.

It must be concluded that there was no educational component in supervision before the mid 1890s. However, consultative conferences of the district committees with their friendly visitors were early seen to have educational possibilities. These were obviously more effective in educating committee members than they were friendly visitors, for meetings of visitors arranged for administrative purposes were soon being used for the visitor's education (Smith, 1887, p. 160). By the early 1890s, such meetings in the better-developed societies, such as the one in Baltimore, had formal presentations followed by discussions on such topics as "How to Help Out-of-Work Families" and "The Treatment of Drunkards' Families." Less typically, the Boston society established an in-service training program for new agents in 1891 and shortly thereafter had both visitors and agents attending lectures on such topics as "Housing the Poor" and "The Sweating System of Boston." Indicative of the absence of education in the form of apprenticeship training in their ongoing supervision by volunteer visitors, the new agents participating in this in-service training program were " 'apprenticed' to more experienced workers" (Kadushin, 1976, p. 9).

Supervision of paid agents by volunteer personnel and consultation among the latter was the characteristic mode of administration of the COS until the exceptionally severe depression of 1893–1897 necessitated the hiring of unprecedented numbers of agents as well as the recruitment of many additional volunteers. The impact on COS staffing policy of the single year 1893 has been described as follows: "Where possible, charity organization societies employed many extra workers and utilized volunteer visitors. The administrative work of the Associated Charities of Boston more than doubled during the year. In New York, the local society increased its work force about 50 percent" (Watson, 1922, p. 250).

Most of the newly hired agents and the newly recruited volunteers served as friendly visitors who, due to the emergency situation, were not supervised by the overburdened district committees but by the district agents. As might be expected from their different statuses and expectations, such supervision generally succeeded with the new employees but not with the new volunteers (Watson, 1922, pp. 263–264). It is from this traumatic depression period—which not only revolutionized staffing practices but also forced the COS to revise its ideology and program from a fixation on friendly visiting based on character and social position to counseling and relief giving based on knowledge and skill—that the supervision of paid practitioners by paid practitioners dates. Concomitantly, it is from this point on that volunteer personnel recede in importance, along with the consultation by means of which they collaborated. While volunteer visitors rapidly decreased in number and significance, volunteer administrators long continued to play major roles in the district committees and city-wide boards of directors. Once the depression was over, the COS returned to what superficially seemed to be its normal mode of administration with friendly visitors reporting to the district committees. There was new administrative content within the old administrative form, since most visitors were now paid agents (Charity Organization Society, 1892). Although still generally called "advice," what had been consultation with volunteer visitors by their peers on the district committee was now supervision of paid visitors by their organizational superiors. Further, what had been a relatively simple kind of supervision when the agents' routine clerical, investigatory, and messenger activities were set up and monitored by the district committee and/or volunteer visitors now became extremely complicated: As many as fifteen committee members "advised" the paid visitor on the conduct of her various cases, at the same time that she was also being supervised by the district agent. This intolerable situation is evidently a major reason why the drive developed at this time for staffing the organization entirely with paid personnel whose organizational position and job responsibility, including that of supervisor and supervisee, would be based on competence rather than socioeconomic status. The COS's difficulties with inexperienced personnel during the depression, together with developing professionalization among the more experienced, led to the establishment of formal educational programs for charity workers, both paid and volunteer, in the late 1890s. The need for these programs underscores the absence of a significant educational component in the still prevailing supervision of paid agents by volunteers and their increasing supervision by other paid agents.

Discussion of supervision and consultation in the charity

field during the nineteenth century would not be complete without some attention to their development in the Association for the Improvement of the Condition of the Poor (AICP), a charity organization that rivaled the COS in size and importance and served as a model for it in many respects.

Founded in New York City in 1843, AICPs were subsequently organized in over two dozen cities. Like the COS, the AICP divided itself into "districts" served by volunteer "visitors," with paid district "secretaries" under the administrative control of district "advisory committees." The AICP visitor resembled his COS counterpart in providing the families he visited with moral advice but, in line with AICP principles, he also dispensed relief in kind (food, clothes, and fuel) and, to a lesser extent, cash relief. As their title indicates, the district secretaries performed clerical chores and investigations, much like COS agents, but unlike COS agents they were from the first "expected to supervise volunteer visitors" (Becker, 1961, p. 385). Concerted efforts to do so in the first four decades of the AICP's existence failed, despite leadership in this regard by Robert M. Hartley, the organization's influential founder, originally a volunteer and later a general secretary (Becker, 1961, pp. 388–393). This failure led to the replacement of volunteer by paid visitors in his own New York AICP shortly after Hartley's resignation in 1876. But the ideological commitment to the sociological impossibility of paid staff supervising their employers and organizational superiors continued in other cities, largely as a responsibility of the general secretary, with whom volunteer visitors were at least willing to establish a working relationship. In 1900, the previous two decades of AICP experience with such supervision in Boston, Chicago, and New York, where volunteer visitors had apparently been reintroduced during the depression, were characterized by the authoritative Edward Devine as follows: "The volunteer visitors were found difficult to control; many lacked judgment; most of them were extravagant and often neglected to forward their monthly reports." He took note of the typical complaint of the general agent of the Boston organization that "the visitors gave him more trouble than the applicants" (Devine, 1900, p. 180). While obviously unsupervisable, AICP volunteer visitors had always been able to participate in consultation with their peers on the district advisory committees, whose advice they felt free to disregard. As in the COS, it was not until the late 1890s, when most visitors were paid workers, that personnel in this position were successfully involved in supervision, which, from all evidence, had no educational or training component.

By contrast, throughout the 1800s supervision was the mode of administration in public welfare. It ranged from the occasional assignment of tasks to a single town clerk by the local overseers of the poor to classical bureaucratic supervision by upper levels of lower levels of the numerous staff of the public institutions for the poor, sick, disabled, and criminal that proliferated after 1820. Such bureaucracy also characterized the sizable private welfare institutions, particularly for children, developing at this time. Although far more personnel in these fields were involved in supervision than in the charity field, this had no influence on the development of supervision in social work, which is essentially a product of the charity-family service-casework experience.

Although of no influence on the subsequent development of social work supervision, the administrative pattern of settlements during this period is pertinent to this analysis, for the early settlements (1888 to around 1910) were characterized by consultation almost as strongly as public welfare was by supervision. Reversing the pattern in the charity field, consultation was the rule among settlement staff, and it was they who supervised the relatively few volunteers. This different pattern of administration was largely due to the different organizational structure of settlements and charity societies.

The settlements had no administrative bodies comparable to district committees or boards of managers, and the self-directing, self-supporting settlement staff were the socioeconomic peers and organizational superiors of settlement volunteers. The founding "residents," as full-time staff who lived in the settlement houses were called, were typically of such high socioeconomic status that they were singled out by Thorstein Veblen in 1899 as members of the leisure class (Veblen, [1899] 1953). They were, in fact, well-to-do people who had given up a life of leisure for one of social service and social reform, and consisted mainly of educated women with little other opportunity to make use of their education, of social gospel-oriented clergymen dissatisfied with the traditional ministry, and of idealistic college students. Financially and administratively in control of the agencies they had created, full-time resident staff set and implemented policies, including that of permitting nonresident, part-time volunteers to participate in settlement work, on condition that they did so under resident staff supervision. Such supervision was generally successful, since not only were the supervisors more experienced and knowledgeable than the supervisees but they were also their socioeconomic peers and organizational superiors. On the other hand, there was no supervision of regular staff. The closest thing to it was an initial training period "under experienced guidance" for new residents, which prepared them for "positions of responsibility" (Woods and Kennedy, 1922, pp. 422–423). Since the objective of this practice was educational rather than administrative, this must be considered instruction rather than supervision. Once positions of responsibility were attained, this loose supervision of new residents ended, and they were free to confer or not with any staff member. The absence of supervision among full-time staff was rationalized by the settlement ideology of the equal inherent worth of all individuals and the equal demonstrated worth of all residents who committed themselves to live among and serve the settlement's "neighbors." This absence of supervision is more attributable, however, to their actual socioeconomic equality and equal "professional" status due to the minimal differentiation in competence among them in this newly established field. The single most important factor, however, was the equal organizational status of all residents in the nonbureaucratic structure of the small-scale, relatively unspecialized settlements of the 1880s and 1890s, which required them to relate to one another nonhierarchically.

While supplemented by sporadic individual conferences, the primary means by which the necessarily consultative mode of settlement administration operated was the now commonplace but then novel mechanism of regular staff meetings. "In the earliest [settlements], a weekly meeting of residents decided details of cooperative housekeeping and outlined the program of neighborhood work" (Woods and Kennedy, 1922, p. 433). These meetings sometimes had an educational aspect, but the mainstay of staff as well as volunteer training was formal in-service courses. The extent of such courses for volunteers (for example, in the early 1890s Philadelphia's College Settlement had a seventeen-session course) indicates that the supervision of volunteers by staff in the early settlements had little if any educational component.

Supervision and Consultation in Social Work: 1900–1920

Supervision of paid staff by paid staff first became the dominant mode of administration in the charity field in the late 1890s after two decades of the COS and three generations of the AICP, in which consultation had prevailed among the far more numerous district committee members and volunteer visitors. As the latter were replaced by paid visitors during and after the depression of 1894–1897, supervision quickly eclipsed consultation. Predictably, the charity organization societies attempted to maintain their customary practice of having paid visitors "advised" by the district committees as the volunteer visitors had been. But the difficulties encountered by committees in getting the many new, unsocialized agents to adhere to charity organization principles soon led to the development of training programs for them in the form of work under the "direction" of experienced staff. For example, by 1896 the Boston COS reported: "[N]ow we have a well-organized system for training agents by having them work under direction, both in the [District] Conferences and in the Central office, before they are placed in positions of responsibility . . . a system of preliminary training" (quoted in Kadushin, 1976, p. 10).

Like the similar training of new settlement workers "under experienced guidance" preliminary to their assuming "positions of responsibility," this process was supervisory in form but educational in content. However, given the COS's structure and mode of operation, it must have had substantial administrative-supervisory content as well. This relatively brief induction of new agents, unlike the analogous process in the settlements, led to their actual supervision. For some, this was the customary loose, episodic supervision by the district committees, but for others it was intensive, regular supervision by the district secretary, who often had been the training "supervisor." Some agents were supervised in both ways concurrently. In view of this chaotic administrative situation—which still included significant numbers of volunteer visitors consulting with district committees—it is not surprising that the district secretary soon assumed most and then all supervision of paid agents.

The change in the district secretary's pre-1900 role of supervisee to her post-1900 role of supervisor has been aptly described: "When a family requested help [of the COS] the initial study was done by an agent who then reported the findings at a weekly district committee conference. The committee discussed the case and decided its disposition. The fact that cases were brought directly to the district committee for determination of action meant that, initially, the paid agent . . . had relatively little managerial autonomy. . . . Gradually, however, district committees became policy- and general administration-oriented. Responsibility for decision making on individual cases was gradually given to the paid agent-supervisor" (Kadushin, 1976, pp. 5–6). This was not so gradual, for a national study of charity organization societies between 1911 and 1920 found that practically all paid agents were either supervising or being supervised by other paid agents.

While many small societies had no supervision, the larger ones had a well-institutionalized system of supervision of the paid visitors in each district by the district secretary (Watson, 1922, pp. 476–479). This was so central a responsibility of the latter that he or she[5] was now alternately called the "district superintendent." District secretaries derived most of the information they required to carry out their supervisory roles from reading case records and reports prepared by their supervisees, which they discussed with them at "regular personal conferences." The content of such discussions has been described as follows: "The supervisory task until the 1920s was defined in the literal sense of 'overseeing,' watching the work of another with responsibility for its quality. The supervisor was responsible for the arrangement of the workload, checking on the worker's performance in terms of administrative rules and procedures, and making or confirming decisions in handling the case" (Austin, 1960, p. 579). Elsewhere, Austin makes the implied absence of educational content in this entirely administrative process even clearer: "Supervision had its beginnings as an administrative function. . . . At first the emphasis . . . was broadly conceived in management terms. The supervisor was responsible for the arrangement of workload, and so on" (Austin, 1957, p. 569). The absence of educational content in supervision before 1920 is supported by the prevalence of in-service programs in the COS of this period. These included "regular meetings of [paid] visitors for the technical discussion of case and district work" (Watson, 1922, pp. 479–480), a continuation of the educational meetings of volunteer visitors of the 1890s. District secretaries instructed "new workers" concerning agency procedures, programs, and policies. District and general secretaries were now responsible for conducting courses for new workers "in which background is presented for technical training in the district and the relation of casework to community programs is made clear." They arranged "seminars and study groups" for "old workers" to discuss "problems of peculiar interest to themselves" (1922, pp. 479–480). The absence of educational content in COS supervision at this time is supported by Kadushin's conclusion (which assumes it earlier had a major educational component) that by the turn of the century: "Although [new] staff still initially required training by more experienced agent-supervisors, a cadre of trained workers who remained on the job for some time was being built up. The demand for supervisory education and support became somewhat less onerous. At the same time the burden of educating workers in the supervisory context was partly relieved by other resources" (Kadushin, 1976, p. 9).

Included among these resources, in addition to the meetings, lectures, and courses discussed earlier, are the national and state conferences of charities and correction that had been in existence since the 1870s, the developing professional literature and the schools of social work established after 1900. Kadushin writes: "Primary responsibility for training a cadre of social work professionals was seen as a supplementary resource. But since the number of schools was so limited, the greatest bulk of paid agents . . . still received their training through apprenticeship programs in social agencies under the tutorship of more experienced agent-supervisors" (Kadushin, 1976, pp. 12–13). While similarly assuming that "the initial use of supervision in social work was associated with the master-apprentice period" in the two decades before 1900 and noting the existence of agency-based "apprentice training" in the two following decades (Austin, 1960, p. 581), as the previously quoted passages on the entirely administrative content of supervision prior to 1920 indicate (Austin, 1960, p. 579; 1957, p. 569), Austin does not consider this training part of supervision. In fact, it was not.

To grasp this essential point, one must first understand that, despite unanimity to the contrary in the literature, such training was not apprenticeship, which (as brought out in Chapter One in relation to medical apprentice training) is a form of supervision. The training in the COSs and AICPs of new staff by experienced staff could not have been apprenticeship training, since the supposed apprentices and masters typically had different jobs—those of friendly visitor and district secretary respectively. Such training was a form of education requiring the learning of skills and knowledge by the trainee different from those of the trainer. In the second place, this was "preliminary" training, rather than a component of ongoing supervision. Although provided "under the tutorship" of the same staff who acted as supervisors, it was a different and generally discrete process for "new workers," which ended after a relatively brief induction period.

While such training should not be considered part of supervision even where trainer and trainee were simultaneously supervisor and supervisee, after 1900 supervision with an integral educational component did begin to develop. This was largely spurred by and modeled after the field instruction of students from schools of social work, which from the very first required "practice work" by their students under the tutelage of "experienced" staff who were almost always supervisors of other staff. "During the first two decades of this century—a period in which the first schools of social work were established—tutorial teaching in agencies was rationalized and formalized. Its main goal was to help the trainee and inexperienced worker to bridge the discrepancy between theoretical knowledge and actual performance, and help him achieve intellectual and emotional integration of what he had learned at school. Thus, tutorial instruction in agencies was concomitant with classroom teaching" (Toren, 1972, pp. 67–68). Despite the use of the terms *trainee* and *inexperienced worker* in the foregoing quotation, obviously what is meant is *student* and *recent graduate of a school of social work*. But their example did, in fact, soon lead to similar instruction of nonstudent staff (Austin, 1957, p. 570). With increasing field instruction of students added to continued widespread training of novices by the same experienced staff who were typically supervisors, it is not surprising that these educational and administrative roles began to be confused and combined. Several other factors contributed to this development. One (already noted) is that the trainer and trainee frequently continued working together as supervisor and supervisee. Frequently, former students whose main or only experience with "supervision" had been field instruction filled supervisory positions in the way in which they had been "supervised." Another key factor was the development of social work theory as part of the professionalization of the charity-casework field taking place during this period (for example, see Warner, [1894] 1919; Richmond, 1917). The new professional standards established by the field department of the journal *Charities and Commons* and the Charity Organization Department of the Russell Sage Foundation called for "trained workers" whose training went beyond the earlier focus on practice knowledge and job skills to include a focus on theory and professional principles. "The initial user of supervision in social work was associated with the master-apprentice period which antedated the appearance of the trained graduates from schools of social work. Knowledge was rooted in experience and had to be transmitted to new workers largely on a precept level, as advice about the practical way of handling the case situation. . . . When casework was consciously viewed as a treatment method in which science and art have a place . . . [field] teaching moved to a conceptual approach" (Austin, 1960, pp. 579–580). In addition to the change in its content, education became a more explicit and expected part of the supervisory conference toward the end of this period replacing the earlier, incidental—when not accidental—result of supervision. However, despite the integration of an educational component into the content of their conferences, the predominance of administrative concerns until the 1920s identified the interaction between district secretaries and visitors—who constituted the bulk of paid personnel—as supervision.

District secretaries were primarily engaged in supervising paid visitors, but, for the first time in COS experience, in some places they supervised volunteer visitors in much the same way.[6] Yet in many places, in addition to supervision by the district secretary, paid visitors were still subject to the supervision of the district committee. As late as the 1920s, the function of these committees' weekly "case conference" was "after hearing the reports of the professional worker as to the results of their investigation, to aid in the diagnosis of the more difficult family problems of the district" (Watson, 1922, p. 134). Both the residual supervision of staff by volunteers and the unprecedented supervision of volunteers by staff were minor practices soon to disappear, leaving the already-dominant pattern of lower management staff supervising direct service staff as the mode of administrative interaction of these levels of personnel in the charity-casework field.

Although it has been overlooked in previous writings, consultation also developed during this period among middle- and upper-management COS staff. Prior to 1900, the general secretary was supposed to share in the supervision of district secretaries but actually did not. As the district committees increasingly gave up their supervisory role, district secretaries were practically unrelated to the organization's overall structure. To fill this administrative vacuum, the position of "case supervisor" was developed, which, like the case conference whose function it assumed, was generally responsible for monitoring the organization's "casework" and specifically for supervising the district secretaries. Despite the latter's supervisory form and content, it was essentially consultation. The consultative nature of their relationship is brought out by the expectation that the case supervisor would help the district secretaries "improve the quality of current treatment by frequent constructive criticism and suggestions" (Watson, 1922, p. 477). While this consultation took place, like the supervision of visitors by district secretaries, at "regular personal conferences" where reports prepared by the district secretaries were discussed, the primary basis of discussion was case records prepared by the supervisees. The "criticisms" and "suggestions" that resulted from these conferences were quite different from the "direction" and "instruction" characteristic of contemporary supervision. The very title *case supervisor* indicates the focus of this process on the cases rather than on the "supervisees" involved—on consultation rather than on supervision. In addition to the way the position was conceptualized and the expectations of those involved, the fact that the process of sharing knowledge and skills by case

supervisors and district secretaries was consultative is evidenced by
their similar professional and organizational statuses. The case supervisor was recruited from among the district supervisors. While he
or she was one of the more knowledgeable and capable of the district
staff, there was not the great difference in knowledge and skill
between them that there was between district secretaries and visitors.
Frequently the district secretary was equal and sometimes superior
in competence to the case supervisor. The latter, at the society's
central office, was generally considered first among equals rather
than significantly superior in either professional or organizational
status to fellow supervisors at the district offices. As both these
district and central positions were increasingly filled by SSW
graduates, the collegial, consultative nature of their relationship was
strengthened.

Consultation also characterized the working relationships
among other similarly recruited and educated central office staff of
the larger societies, which now had assistant general secretaries,
department superintendents, and their assistants. This is evidenced
by the fact that the general secretaries who were supposed to supervise them typically did not (McLean, 1927). In the absence of
supervision, the interaction of the professionalized staff at the central
office must have taken the form of individual conferences with a
colleague by a staff person in need of information or advice. Central
office staff meetings can also be inferred to have been consultative,
even when devoted to administrative matters, in that knowledge
and skill were thereby shared among professional peers at the same
level of organization.

To sum up, between 1895 and 1920, concomitant with the
emergence of the profession of social work, both consultation and
supervision developed among COS staff. Supervision was the mode
of interaction of the more professionalized with the less-professional
or nonprofessional staff; consultation was the mode among the
more professionalized. Supervision was generally combined with
elements of education, while consultation was frequently combined
with elements of supervision. These combinations of different processes and roles were not considered problematical by practitioners
or the profession of social work, for they not only met the practice
needs but matched the professional and organizational statuses of

those involved.[7] Unlike the resistance common in later decades, the educational component of supervision was typically welcomed by supervisees and supervisors, since it met the desire of the former for training and the latter for teaching while not imposing either supervision or training on senior staff, who felt they needed neither and had access to one another for consultation.

A similar situation existed in other casework fields, with the exception that the host settings of medical, psychiatric, and school social work built in consultation with professionals from other disciplines. As in the past, supervision was universal in public welfare, which had very few professionals or professionally oriented staff, while consultation was just as prevalent among the numerous professionally oriented, although rarely SSW-educated, settlement staff.

The continuation of consultation among the latter is indicated by the fact that the settlements' "head resident," a position common after 1900, although charged with supervising other resident staff, neglected to do so. Consultation still took place among residents through individual conferences concerning specific cases and staff meetings dealing with broader issues. "As settlements grew in size and complexity, it became necessary that someone assume continuous responsibility for the larger outline of administration and management. Under pressure of organization, settlements changed from a cooperative society to an institution in charge of a duly appointed executive. Many motives and some of the activities of administration in the cooperative system still (in 1920) remain. The more experienced residents still constitute the active cabinet of the head worker, and the resident body as a whole meets periodically to talk over problems of general concern. In many settlements, a variety of matters of practical procedure are referred to the whole group for vote, and the executives act in accord with the plans thus determined" (Woods and Kennedy, 1922, pp. 433–434). The implications of this passage were made explicit in the report of a study of thirty-four New York City settlements in 1927–1928, which concluded that among the responsibilities of the head workers "likely to be neglected" was "supervision of the staff" (Kennedy and Farra, 1935, pp. 498–499).

With little if any administrative supervision of full-time staff by their single organizational superior, there was none at all by their

organizational peers. On the other hand, the long-standing supervision by full-time settlement staff of part-time volunteers was now
extended to part-time paid staff. Settlement supervision of both staff
and volunteers resembled that of the charity field in the different
professional and organizational statuses of supervisors and supervisees, clearly evident from their respective full-time and part-time
positions. It also resembled it in that full-time staff, from whom
supervisors were drawn, were now generally paid. Influenced by the
widespread field instruction of students, some educational elements
were combined with settlement supervision. However, these constituted a smaller part of the content of supervisory conferences than
they did in the charity field, as evidenced by the totally task-centered
supervision and the many in-service training programs for supervisees in the settlements of this period (Woods and Kennedy, 1922,
pp. 436–437; Kutzik, 1967, pp. 10–12). As in the COS and other
casework settings, and for similar reasons, settlement supervision
and the minor educational elements it incorporated was accepted,
if not welcomed, by supervisees and supervisors alike. However, the
"fit" of this period's social work supervision-and-education with the
statuses, needs, and aspirations of those involved was not to continue
very long, particularly for supervisees in the charity-family service
field.

Supervision and Consultation: 1920–1950

Already before the 1920s, there were some "undistricted"
charity organization societies and AICPs whose entire staff was
located at a single central office. Within a decade, practically all
professionally oriented charity societies evolved into centralized
agencies, called *family welfare* or *family service* societies. While
they still had friendly visitors, they no longer had district secretaries.
Some former district secretaries now became members of the expanded central office senior staff where, as case supervisors or department heads, they continued to supervise friendly visitors and
generalist caseworkers as well as staff that were not in social work,
such as homemakers and visiting nurses. Since there were far fewer
departments than there had been districts, some former district
secretaries went into fields such as medical social work, where they

could get positions commensurate with their expertise. However, a number became visitors or caseworkers and supervisees in the same agencies where they had served as district secretaries and supervisors. This was not as status lowering a demotion as might be supposed, since by this time direct-service positions were beginning to be filled by SSW graduates (Lubove, 1965, pp. 132–135). However, the intensive supervision of such heavily experienced and highly educated staff by staff of similar or lower professional status, although of higher organizational authority, now became problematical, even untenable. Such supervision of "untrained" or "semitrained" staff by "trained" or professional superiors continued to their mutual satisfaction, but that of "trained" staff by "trained" professional peers (or inferiors) was replaced by what came to be known as "social work supervision." Not without historic precedent, despite its supervisory form and partially supervisory content, this was predominantly consultation. The consultative content of such "supervision" of fully trained and professional staff was not recognized then or now, since from the first it was confused with the educational content of the supervision of untrained or semitrained, non- or semiprofessional staff.[8] This is understandable in light of a number of circumstances. One is that the same staff person generally provided consultation (with some supervisory elements) to professional peers at the same time as that staff person provided supervision (with some educational elements) to the less professionalized, and some of these consultant-supervisors also served as field instructors of SSW students whose instruction was accompanied by substantial supervision and elements of consultation. The confusion of education, supervision, and consultation due to their interpenetration in the practice and role of the "supervisor" was compounded by the fact that the same "supervisee" generally participated in two and sometimes all three processes, albeit at different times. Untrained workers at first received tutorial training as well as supervision, then supervision with some further education, followed in some instances by consultation with some supervision. Even more regularly, SSW students sequentially received field instruction with some supervision, supervision with some training when first employed, and consultation with some supervision after attaining experienced worker status. In conjunction with the absence of a tradition of consultation among casework practitioners, the foregoing factors resulted in such a tradition developing within the mold of staff supervision prevalent since the turn of the century.

Confusion of consultation with education and supervision was so thorough by the time the first book on professional social work supervision appeared that *Supervision in Social Case Work* (Robinson, 1936) was addressed without qualification to both field instructors of students and supervisors of practitioners. It recognized the nonsupervisory nature of most of what transpired between professional social work supervisors and supervisees but viewed it as education. "The word *supervision* has become a technical term in social work with a usage not defined in any dictionary. Supervisors in a social agency are responsible for 'overseeing' the job in the generally understood meaning of the word, but they have, in addition, a second function of teaching or training workers under their supervision." This second function was not considered secondary but primary: "Supervision can be defined as an educational process in which a person with a certain equipment of knowledge and skill takes responsibility for training a person with less equipment" (Robinson, 1936, pp. xi, 53). Since the persons with less equipment were identified as "students in training" and "apprentice workers," the educational definition may have seemed warranted. But Robinson and later authors with a similar approach included among those to be "educated" through "supervision" all workers, irrespective of previous education and experience, who were not themselves supervisors (Williamson, 1950, pp. 19–20; Eisenberg, 1956; Pettes, 1967).

A number of factors permitted "social work supervision" to be viewed as primarily educational rather than consultative from the 1920s on. First, the supervisory conference actually did serve as a vehicle for training many caseworkers, for then, as now, "A very sizable percentage of agency staff come to the job without prior training. There is also considerable turnover and lateral job movement from agency to agency. Consequently there is a constant need to teach people to do the job of a social worker and to do the job in a particular agency" (Kadushin, 1976, p. 125). While the need for the preliminary training of untrained nonprofessionals and mobile professionals is clear, continuing education of fully trained and professional staff with lengthy tenure at a given agency cannot be justified on this basis. In particular, SSW-educated practitioners, who constituted about 10 percent of casework supervisees in the 1920s, brought this approach into question. However, at this juncture a rationalization for continuing "educational supervision" for all caseworkers developed, based on the supposed inadequacy of all previous training, including graduate education at schools of social work, for in these decades occurred the momentous change from a social science base for casework practice to a psychological-psychiatric knowledge base and the concomitant change in this practice from the socioenvironmental approach (now considered superficial and manipulative) to the psychotherapeutic ("professional") approach. The novel psychoanalytic theory soon became part of the core curriculum of schools of social work and the intellectual equipment of subsequent graduates. This body of knowledge was a mystery to earlier graduates and to the many "semitrained" workers whose training had been based on the works of Warner and Richmond. The new SSW graduates, who increasingly filled supervisory positions, considered it their professional mission to teach the theories of Freud and Rank to their generally more-than-willing supervisees (Rabinowitz, 1953, pp. 169–170). However, such education could not continue indefinitely, nor did it make sense for those supervisees who were themselves recent SSW graduates. The inappropriateness of interminable education as well as supervision per se for experienced, fully trained staff forced supervisors to move in two directions, both of them away from education and supervision. One was to expand what Kadushin has termed the "supportive" function of social work supervision from its minor role of encouragement and sympathy to a major one of helping supervisees to resolve personal or emotional problems interfering with their practice, just as the worker "investigates and treats . . . the client" (Marcus, 1927, p. 286). This rationale for continuous "supervision" regardless of the level of competence of those being subjected to it was generally accepted, although such pseudo-therapy was limited, due to the resistance of many supervisees to being "caseworked" by their professional peers or inferiors. The other—and major—direction in which supervisors moved was toward consultation (and away from supervision and education of their peers).

Despite the fact that it is invariably expressed in the terminology of supervision, the discussion of the relationship between professional "supervisors" and "supervisees" in the social work literature since the 1930s indicates that much of what has gone on has been consultation. This view is supported and exemplified by a recent analysis, which concludes: "The traditional literature in social work supervision suggests an image of the supervisor which . . . is that of a person who establishes full and free reciprocal communication with the supervisee . . . resulting in optimization of supervisee autonomy and discretion; who has a problem-solving orientation toward the work of the agency, based on consensus and cooperation . . . rather than power-centered techniques; who values a consultative-leadership relationship in supervision rather than a subordinate-superordinate relationship" (Kadushin, 1976, p. 116). Although in this passage the norms of "social work supervision" are unmistakably described and even explicitly characterized as "consultative," Kadushin does not consider it consultation. Like most writers on the subject, he views it as a professionally desirable form of administrative-educational supervision. Kadushin presents the rationale for his position when he notes that the traditional literature tends to disregard the "managerial" aspects of the content and the "hierarchical-bureaucratic" structure of "social work supervision," which, he stresses, does not leave the supervisee "free not to follow" the supervisor's "ultimate" decisions (Kadushin, 1976, pp. 116–117). Thus Kadushin recognizes and explores the consultative features of this process (1976, pp. 117, 126–127, 196) but concludes that its supervisory ones predominate.

Vinter comes closest to agreeing with the present author that the supervisory features of such "supervision" are outweighed by its consultative ones. Although he treats his conclusion as a proposal for change rather than as an analysis of past and present practice, Vinter (1959, p. 255) contends that consensual, collegial "consultation-supervision" is an "alternative" to "the traditional pattern of close supervision . . . [and] minimize[s] the former educational focus." He counters the argument that the superordinate-subordinate positions of participants in this process preclude its being consultation, by pointing out that: "Redefinition of the supervisor's role as "consultative," inducing a more advisory and collaborative relationship with the practitioner . . . distributes power more equitably between supervisors and workers, as the latter obtain a greater share in decision making. . . . A significant downward shift of decision-making power reduces the effective authority of the supervisor and thereby alters the existing structure" (Vinter, 1959, p. 256). Among the most telling pieces of evidence that this proposed redefinition of the professional "supervisor's" role has long been taking place are the facts noted by Vinter himself that "the traditional status of the supervisor" is largely based on the non-organizational, professional characteristics of "prestige" and "expertness" and that staff are generally chosen for this position "because of their knowledge and skill" (1959, p. 254). In addition to making a similar observation, Kadushin underscores his finding as to the "unanimity with which supervisors would prefer their supervisees to see the source of the supervisors' power in their expertise" (Kadushin, 1976, p. 120). Taking into account the supervisory nature of part of what goes on in this predominantly consultative process, Vinter somewhat ambiguously terms it "consultation-supervision," rather than our clumsier but clearer "consultation with some supervision." However, that he considers it essentially consultation is evident in his caution that it is "not to be confused with consultation of the specialist" (Vinter, 1959, pp. 257–258).

Social work "consultation of the specialist" also developed during this period. As noted earlier, some medical social workers from the first had a consultative relationship with physicians. By 1930, in certain hospitals, social workers were regarded by physicians as real consultants, comrades, coworkers. Building on three decades of experience with interprofessional consultation, in the 1930s medical social workers were able to pioneer in serving "as consultants in the new public assistance administration . . . [in] fields of family welfare in new ways" (Hamilton, 1939, p. 411).

Less dramatically but more significantly for this analysis, medical social workers continued to consult one another. However, under the influence of practice in the family service field, which dominated the profession and most schools of social work, this consultation increasingly took the form of "social work supervision." The actual supervision of less professionalized by more professionalized medical social workers, some of whom served as field instructors, incorporated the educational component characteristic of contemporary casework supervision.

On the other hand, the settlement group maintained its traditional forms of peer group as well as individual consultation among full-time staff and noneducational supervision of part-time staff. The oft-noted resistance to "social work supervision" by settlements, YWCAs, YMCAs, and community centers was due to a variety of factors, ranging from greater reliance on staff not educated by SSWs to less bureaucratization, as compared to casework agencies. But it can primarily be attributed to the fact that their indigenous pattern of consultation and supervision met the needs of their staff. It was not until the 1940s and 1950s, when they employed a substantial number of M.S.W.s who had received (and some who provided) field instruction in these agencies, that "social work supervision" developed to any extent in the group service field. Incorporating—and competing with—the norms of settlement staff interaction, such "supervision" of professional practitioners by fellow professionals did not attain the importance it did in casework agencies and was generally less close and more collegial—that is, more consultative.

Consultation and Supervision: 1950 to the Present

While the increase in size and complexity of family agencies between 1920 and 1950 led to increased supervision to maintain organizational control of their large staffs, the major factor spurring the development of "social work supervision" (which, by the end of this period, had become central to casework practice) was the extraordinary professionalization of these staffs. Constituting a small minority of the staff of such agencies in 1920, by 1950 M.S.W.s made up the great majority. Of particular importance, they now filled nearly all of the practitioner positions in the major agencies in the large cities—frequently under the supervision of staff with less or no professional education.[9] What resulted was the imposition of supervision and/or field instruction ("close supervision" and "educational supervision") on many professionals by supervisors accustomed to overseeing and instructing non- or semiprofessionals. While at first welcomed by M.S.W.s, who saw it as an internlike extension of field instruction and for whom its further prolongation was rationalized as staff development, after a time it was resisted. Soon criticism of this hitherto sacrosanct area of professional practice began to appear in the literature. By 1957 it was reported that "in the last five years, questions have arisen about the continuing use of supervision with a professionally trained staff" (Austin, 1957, p. 570).

In 1958, reflecting opinion within the profession as a whole, a survey of the membership of a chapter of the National Association of Social Workers found that "most social workers believed supervision should change . . . from an [initial] phase of direction and training to one of more permissive consultation" (Cruser, 1958, p. 25). This situation led to experimentation with various forms of consultation among experienced professionals, some entirely disassociated from supervision and explicitly called *consultation,* others under the rubric of "peer" or "peer-group" supervision (Fizdale, 1958; Wax, 1963; Rowley and Faux, 1966; Hare and Frankena, 1972). However, the major form that the ensuing increase took was in the consultative content of "social work supervision." While no relevant studies were conducted during these decades, this can be attested to by professionals who worked in family and children's agencies from the 1940s to the 1970s. It is evidenced by the present predominance of consultation within "social work supervision" shown by a recent study of national scope, which found that a large majority of professional social work supervisees (75.2 percent) and supervisors (69.5 percent) "felt strongly that [it] was desirable . . . that as the supervisee gains experience the relationship can become one of consultant-consultee to be used when and as the participants decide." Indicating that this is not merely desirable but actual practice, 60 percent of supervisees and 30 percent of supervisors considered their role in such "supervision" to be that of "colleague-collaborator," and the strongest satisfactions of both groups of respondents with their "supervisory" experience were consultation related and strongest dissatisfactions supervision related (Kadushin, 1974, pp. 290–292).

Another traditional form of consultation increasingly used during this same period is the "case conference" inherited from the COS. That this rather regular nonadministrative group meeting of professional staff to share knowledge and skills regarding how to deal with specific cases is a form of consultation has been even less recognized as such than "social work supervision." For example, an authoritative 1958 professional statement treats "case conferences," "consultation," and "supervision" as three different ways of "increasing skills and providing controls to the activity of the social work practitioner" (National Association of Social Workers, 1958, p. 8).

While consultation has become the norm for experienced professional staff, supervision has remained the norm for semi- or nonprofessionals. In addition to the graduate social work students and recent M.S.W.s, who have long been supervised as well as instructed, in the past decade the corps of supervisees and trainees has been greatly augmented by undergraduate social work students and B.S.W.-degree holders as well as technicians ("case aides" and "paraprofessionals") with no professional education.

While group service agencies also have used more nonprofessional staff since the 1960s, they did not have to alter their traditional pattern of consultation among professionals and supervision by them of nonprofessionals. On the other hand, as the number of professional social workers in public welfare has significantly grown in recent years (Miller and Podell, 1970), some consultation has developed within the formerly completely administrative supervision in this classical bureaucratic setting. This has primarily taken place in the relatively few instances where professional social workers have been supervised by professional peers. However, in departments of welfare as far apart as Marin County, California, and Atlantic County, New Jersey, staff in formerly supervisory positions have for some time served as specialist-consultants to nonprofessional as well as professional caseworkers, while administrative oversight of these same practitioners has been carried out by other actual supervisors. There have been similar developments in hospital settings.

Past experience and current practice in social work supervision and consultation have been summed up in a recent NASW publication (1973, pp. 8–15) dealing with appropriate staff roles for different levels of social work personnel. The "social service aide" with high school education or less and the "social service technician" with "an associate of arts degree in a technical program of social services or its equivalent" are both described as working "under close supervision of a professional social worker." The "social worker" with "a baccalaureate degree from an undergraduate college or university with a social welfare program" works "under" or "use(s) social work supervision." While the "graduate social worker" with "a master's degree from a graduate school of social work . . . use(s) consultative or routine supervision," the "certified social worker" with a master's degree plus certification by NASW's Academy of Certified Social Workers "use(s) consultation, when appropriate." Finally, the "social work fellow" with a doctoral degree or ACSW certification and two years of experience in "an area of social work specialization" works in complete independence. The graduate social worker supervises "less advanced workers," and the certified social worker supervises graduate social workers as well as social service technicians. Both these and the "social work fellow" serve as consultants outside the agency at increasingly higher levels. This explicit recognition of the "consultative" nature of social work supervision for the graduate social worker and the propriety of nonsupervisory "consultation" for certified social workers—by implication from any agency staff member with the requisite knowledge and skill—in conjunction with the differential use of supervision for less- or nonprofessionalized staff, makes this the most sophisticated statement on the subject in the professional literature.[10]

Limitation of space prevents a comparative analysis of British experience here. It must suffice to note that British social work has had a substantially different development but a substantially similar end result, demonstrating the generality of the effects of professionalism interpenetrating with bureaucracy and the appropriateness of differential use of consultation and supervision in accordance with the degree of professionalization of the staff involved. An American observer of the contemporary British scene informs us that "In many agencies the supervisor has been given 'administrative' authority but limited to a consultant role as far as casework is concerned. He has responsibility for seeing that the work is done and for making certain policy decisions, but he must not interfere with the casework and can only give advice if the worker brings a case to him for consultation" (Pettes, 1967, p. 150). This highly functional arrangement is lamented by the observer, who has brought the gospel of American "social work supervision" as "a method of student training and staff development" to British social workers. Hopefully, the latter will have the good sense to rely on their sound professional norms and the goodwill to share their exemplary experience with confused American colleagues.

Conclusions and Implications

This two-chapter analysis of one of the oldest and one of the newest of the helping professions has shown that both professions have used supervision and consultation throughout their histories, that both have at times confused one with the other—and with the training of students and neophytes—but that, whatever the confusion and however mislabeled, the appropriate process has generally taken place for the appropriate personnel in response to their needs and in accord with their statuses and the requirements and structure of their profession and/or organization. The confusion of consultation and supervision among seventeenth- and eighteenth-century physicians and their earlier uncertainty as to how or even whether consultation should be practiced has been paralleled among social workers during the past eighty years, that is, during the formative years of both professions. However, while mistakenly treating supervision as consultation had a positive effect on the statuses of early medical practitioners, professional and nonprofessional, and supported their roles, the mistaking of social work consultation for supervision has had a most negative effect on the status and role of professional social workers.[11] Since the role of supervisee has been understood to be incompatible with that of professional, their pseudo-supervision has undermined the professional status of social work practitioners and impaired their ability to practice as professionals in collaboration with other professionals in multidisciplinary settings, particularly medical settings.[12] At this point, when a third of the membership of NASW works in physical and mental health settings and our country is about to greatly expand health social services through national health insurance, it is imperative to rectify this situation.

Recognizing the consultative essence of "social work supervision" of experienced professional social workers and explicitly identifying it as consultation would also strengthen social work practice in other host settings as well as minimize the dysfunction for social workers of misapplied supervision and inadequate consultation in social work-administered social agencies. Of course, simply relabeling "social work supervision" as "consultation" would only be a first step, since the content of the resulting "consultative conferences" would still consist of a conflicting amalgam of consultation, supervision, and instruction. The present analysis should contribute to identifying and implementing the necessary next steps, some of which have been advocated for a quarter of a century, for it supports the view that experienced, professionally educated practitioners should not be subjected to "close" administrative supervision (Babcock, 1955; Wax, 1963; Kutzik, 1972; Perlmutter, 1972) nor to interminable "educational supervision" (Aptekar, 1959; Leader, 1957; Leyendecker, 1959; Vinter, 1959) and opposes the view that both these processes are appropriate for such staff and that only their combination in the same supervisory relationship is unsound (Austin, 1961; Scherz, 1958; Devis, 1965; Hanlan, 1972). Consequently, it opposes the position that the solution to the problems of social work supervision is to have separate administrative and educational supervisors and supports the counterposition that, whether separately or in combination, neophyte and inexperienced professionals should receive time-limited "close" supervision and instruction, while experienced professionals should have this replaced by "routine" supervision and consultation (Fizdale, 1958; Vinter, 1959; Kadushin, 1976). It need hardly be pointed out that this approximates the medical model of time-limited postgraduate training-supervision followed by full professional status characterized by consultative relationships. In addition to identifying consultation as such when it takes the form of "social work supervision," the analysis suggests that case conferences and staff meetings devoted to exploring program and policy issues should be considered forms of consultation. It also indicates the need for supplementing these structured forms of social work consultation with medical model consultation at the initiative of the consultee. This could range from consulting with designated agency staff to conferring with anyone in or out of the agency with the requisite expertise. At the same time, this analysis suggests that medical practitioners could benefit from adding to their repertoire of professional skills the social work models of consultation and supervision so well suited to organizational settings with personnel of different levels of training and competence.

While of particular urgency for medicine and social work, other professions, which must collaborate with them as well as deal with related problems, can also benefit from their historic experience in the differential use of consultation and supervision, always— but now more than ever—an essential component of professional practice.

Notes

1. American Association of Group Workers, American Association of Medical Social Workers, American Association of Psychiatric Social Workers, Association for the Study of Community Organization, National Consortium of School Social Workers, and Social Work Research Group.

2. In addition to the several thousand still-practicing members without M.S.W.s who joined NASW when it was formed, there are now several hundred members with Bachelor of Social Welfare (B.S.W.) degrees. This rapidly increasing group was made eligible for membership in 1972.

3. This discussion does not apply to the higher status "general agent" or "general secretary," in modern terms, executive director, although he also neither supervised nor trained the socially and organizationally superior officers and board members whom he served in a generally similar way.

4. Data directly showing the subordinate supervisee role of the agent are supported by the fact that during the nineteenth century practically all district agents were women and many friendly visitors were men.

5. Men were now frequently filling this and other paid positions.

6. This apparent contradiction of our previous analysis can be explained as being due to the new "professional" and organizational superiority and more equal socioeconomic status of staff vis-à-vis volunteers after 1900 (Kutzik, 1972, pp. 95–96). In a few places, volunteer visitors were "supervised" by a "visitation committee of volunteers" or even by individual volunteers. But these peer relationships were varieties of consultation emulating the now-stylish "professional" supervision.

7. The frequently expressed view in the social work literature that the teacher-student relationship, including the tutorial one generally combined with social work supervision, is nonhierarchical (Hanlan, 1972, pp. 43, 44; Toren, 1972, p. 69) is not accepted here. While the horizontal social

distance between teacher and student, particularly, tutor and pupil, may be less than that between supervisor and supervisee, the vertical status differential between them is as great, if not greater. Teachers and students occupy different positions in the authority structure of educational institutions. That this superordinate-subordinate relationship is also structured into the tutorial teaching-learning situation, including field instruction of social work students and "educational supervision" of social work staff, is evidenced by the one-way grading and evaluating power of the field instructor and "educational supervisor." Such a view of the superordinate positions of both instructor and supervisor and the subordinate positions of both student and supervisee supports the present conclusion that these roles can be and were at this time successfully combined.

8. In addition to differences in structure and operation, the content of consultation differs from that of education in that the former focuses on helping the consultee understand how to deal with specific cases and problems, while the latter focuses on helping the student learn general principles applicable to categories of cases and problems. The consultative nature of "educational supervision" is apparent in some of the more perceptive discussions of the process: "the individual conference . . . affords the professional person the opportunity for the exploration of ideas which will illuminate his handling of a case" (Austin, 1957, p. 571); "teaches the worker what he needs to know to give specific service to specific clients" (Kadushin, 1976, p. 126).

9. By 1950, schools of social work had two-year curricula; earlier, many had granted master's degrees after one year of study. In the 1950s, a substantial number of supervisors had had no formal social work education.

10. Indicating the need for additional clarification is the erroneous position that the "social work fellow," as an independent professional, is often a consultant but never a consultee. In medicine and other professions, the most competent practitioner-consultants themselves require consultation at certain times. In fact, not consulting when necessary is evidence of professional incompetence.

11. Receiving supervision has been functional for nonprofessional social welfare personnel confirming their status and supporting their vocational and organizational roles.

12. Typically, this has hindered the collaboration of individual social workers with physicians and psychiatrists. The extent to which this is a problem of the profession is dramatized by formal intervention of NASW in the current situation at a Maryland hospital, where social work supervision for experienced professionals has been abolished by psychiatrist-administrators unaware of its consultative function, resulting in deterioration of social service to patients.

CHAPTER 3

The Role of
the Organization

Wilbur A. Finch, Jr.

𝕴f human service organizations are perceived as sociotechnical systems, supervision must be viewed as occurring within an "organizational climate" or context that can either stimulate or inhibit individual job performance. Growing trends in service programs toward a differential use of labor and heightened worker specialization have emphasized the importance of the supervisory role; indeed, it is increasingly recognized that only managerial personnel will be able to orchestrate the varied forms of intervention needed to ensure efficacious responses to client problems. Human service agencies are, for example, maximizing their utilization of personnel with differential levels of education and training, and these workers are performing jobs characterized by specificity of function and purpose. This contemporary trend serves to accentuate the importance of managerial control, direction, planning, and coordination (Finch, 1976b). As the number of different kinds of specialized workers from individual agencies and/or community programs who simultaneously provide service to a particular client increases, supervisors will be held more accountable for arranging and coordinating diverse personnel activities into unified and coherent attempts to facilitate maximum client goal realization.

The growing complexity of human service organizations is partially a result of the increasing number of occupational specialties involved in providing services to clients. Such worker specialization, however, poses special problems in the provision of services, because the social skills of individual agency personnel are a critical part of the treatment process. For example, the structuring of collaborative working relationships among members of occupational specialties who purportedly perform complementary functions in relation to individual clients both increases the interdependence of these various workers and expands the number of different tasks performed (Becker and Neuhauser, 1975). Coordination and time sequencing must therefore become group efforts if the performance of tasks that will optimize client goal attainment is to be evidenced.

Human service organizations largely select their environments from ranges of alternatives, often using incremental and disorderly processes, and then selectively perceive the environments they inhabit (Starbuck, 1976). Workers' productive endeavors within an organizational setting, including their interactions with clients, can be either augmented or hindered by environmental influences. While education and life experience contribute to individual problem-solving skills, organizational climate enters as an intervening variable that either encourages or discourages certain types of worker actions or responses. Although it would seem unwise to use disabling and debilitating strategies, many agencies may in fact be characterized by the presence of such maladaptive phenomena. In public social services, for example, a new employee often quickly learns that a frequent "reward" for prompt case closure is an increase in the assignment of new cases to an already heavy workload. Thus, despite the hours of admonition supervisors devote to the necessity of closing cases, the worker is encouraged to respond in an opposite manner.

The way in which work is organized and structured has been increasingly recognized as a major determinant of the kinds and quality of services provided to clients (Finch, 1976b). Line supervisors must increasingly possess managerial skills and a knowledge of the dynamics of human behavior within an organizational context if they are to successfully guide and coordinate the provision of social services to clients. The purpose of this chapter is to examine those attributes of the work setting that are largely determined by supervisory and organizational practices and how such environmental characteristics affect or alter the behavior of employees; further, the organizational roles of the supervisor will be reconsidered in light of recent changes in the human service field.

Performance Problems

Perhaps the most striking feature of service delivery is that its provision has not been totally precluded (Udy, 1970). Contemporary problems of differentiation, integration, coordination, and dissemination of information make human service organizations inherently unstable and technologically complex; further, they serve as a source of confusion and frustration for individual employees. One is therefore not surprised to hear the question, "Why don't workers do what they are supposed to do?" While such a question can be stated in a variety of forms, it may well represent the most frequent cause for deliberation in many organizations. Kaufman (1973, p. 2) offers three possible explanations for this tendency toward noncompliance: "The subordinates don't know what their superiors want, they can't do what their superiors want, or they refuse to do what their superiors want." While examples of each explanation can probably be found within most organizations, performance problems resulting from unclear and contradictory messages received by line staff increasingly appear to explain most behavior that contradicts managerial intent. Indeed, it can be easily surmised that the clearer supervisory staff understand the nature of the organization, how it works, and the relationship of its various roles, the more capable they will be of positively adapting the structure of work both outside and within the setting to changes that occur (Brown, 1960).

At this point, several questions can be raised. Does the worker, for example, know *what* to do and *when* to do it? Is he or she *clear* in completing assignments, how these contribute to the achievement of agency purposes? The answers to questions of this kind increasingly must involve much more than a mere assessment of knowledge. An individual may "know" how to do something but may behave otherwise for a variety of reasons. The existence of performance problems—differences between what people do and what is expected of them—is often not the result of skill deficiency (Mager and Pipe, 1970). The work behaviors one observes may instead be seen as the unintentional result of the reward system within the organization.

Mager and Pipe (1970, p. 48) identify four general causes of nonperformance where skill deficiency is not a factor: (1) the desired behavior is punished; (2) nondesired actions are rewarded; (3) workers do not care whether they perform as expected; and (4) organizational obstacles prevent or discourage optimal worker responses. To achieve employee behaviors congruent with goal attainment, those conditions of the work environment that presently prevent adequate performance must be changed. Ideally, then, organizational arrangements should derive from social service goals, should remove unnecessary obstacles that can hamper or prevent effective job performance, and should provide convenient procedures supportive of expected employee actions. From such a perspective, a primary function of management is the establishment and maintenance of the conditions under which social services can be effectively provided to clients.

In the constantly changing environment of human service organizations, it is difficult to avoid some inconsistencies in the application of strategies designed to reinforce desired worker behaviors. Sometimes policies, rules, or procedures are contradictory and adherence to one requires noncompliance to another. Seemingly positive messages communicated to personnel from the environment in which they work often elicit harmful responses; for example, paraprofessionals who are encouraged to believe that they possess "professional" skills may be prevented from fully utilizing the expertise of others. Similarly, professionals who are encouraged to be overly concerned about "their" clients may acquire an overpossessiveness that deprives these service recipients of the use of other organizational resources.

Present trends in the growing use of different kinds of manpower and increasing specialization in human service organizations pose particularly difficult problems for the supervisor. As previously stated, the provision of social and mental health services to clients occurs within a social structure designed to carry out the work of the agency. Such an argument recognizes that organizations are primarily *social* entities characterized by purposeful, goal-oriented activity (Porter, Lawler, and Hackman, 1975). In addition, this position mandates partial consideration of the organization in terms of subgroups of individuals who share common interactions as well as some degree of shared values and norms. Further, because the nature of services is constantly changing, a concomitant emphasis on continual agency adaptation is advocated; different benefits, for example, should accrue from the employment of different kinds of workers, and one would therefore expect human service programs to utilize varying criteria to measure individual employee success. Finally, if one can assume that educational preparation and experience influence how various kinds of workers will define client needs and what methods are utilized for mitigation or alleviation of these difficulties, problems of unclear and debatable role boundaries must be an inevitable product of this employee heterogeneity (Finch, 1974). Role definition as an evolving and adaptative process that can organize a group of workers around a common purpose in working with clients therefore requires supervisors both to possess a knowledge of individual abilities and to utilize orchestrating skills to ensure coherent, accessible, and comprehensive service delivery (see, for example, Gilbert, 1972).

If successful service delivery must increasingly rely on the ability of line supervisors to plan, organize, and coordinate the diverse but complementary activities of different kinds of workers, one certainly cannot assume that all managers presently possess such skills; the opposite, in fact, may frequently be true. The author's previous findings substantiate this statement: "The reliance of this organization upon the assumed expertise of staff at the unit level to achieve meaningful and appropriate use of paraprofessionals has resulted in its attainment resting mainly upon individual ability rather than organizational planning. Often, desired paraprofessional behaviors are inconsistently reinforced, if even understood at all. For example, where the paraprofessional's use of personal experience in work with clients is confused with client overinvolvement, organizational rewards may be available only at the price of giving up 'natural helping skills' for behaviors which more closely resemble social work practice" (Finch, 1974, p. 117). Regardless of what a human service organization may say an individual worker's job should be, it is what the supervisor *does* that conveys the critical information that determines performance (Fine, 1967). Similarly, work-group members participate in a two-way flow of social influence that will further determine the individual and collective relationships of various occupational specialties to each other. In other words, members of the work group exercise concomitant control over what information is available to the individual by providing a role definition within the group, by offering needed explanations of the group and its larger environment, and by responses which offer the means of self-assessment.

As the number of different kinds of workers in human service organizations expands, the ways in which work is allocated, the means by which expectations are set, and the methods adopted for appraising employee efforts offer needed control measures (Dornbusch and Scott, 1975). The nature and extent of information communicated in the process of allocating work and the understanding that each group or category of workers has in relation to what is expected of them will provide the initial definitions utilized to guide work behavior, including the methods of service delivery. Thus, in some psychiatric clinics where the structure of work limits client contacts to set periods of time, office interviews, or primary consideration of individuals rather than the larger family group (or vice versa), the client's social situation unintentionally may be partially or totally excluded from the treatment process because of organizational constraints with respect to service provision.

The establishment of criteria for assessment of worker performance can further modify employee behavior by the degree to which it facilitates identification with standards and/or emphasizes means versus ends with respect to delivery issues. For example, an overemphasis upon a specified time limit to agency services, without a corresponding consideration of individual client differences, can easily result in the premature closing of some cases. Those work characteristics that supervisors consider and emphasize as focal in group or individual conferences will influence personnel behaviors. Directly related to this, of course, are the indicators used by both the supervisor and organization as a basis for judging work performance. Blau (1974b), for example, found that statistical reports influenced line workers by inducing them to concentrate their efforts on those factors that were recorded or counted for organizational review. He further found, however, that to the degree to which indicators of performance used by either the organization or the line supervisor were not adequately representative of the phenomena they claimed to measure, employee interest in maximizing "scores" could encourage unresponsiveness to items not measured (Blau, 1974b). The "selective emphases" of criteria become an impediment to the flow of all information needed by the worker in order to perform effectively.

Appraisal of worker performance always entails the evaluation of both actions and the actor (Dornbusch and Scott, 1975). Not only does it reflect the differences in status between the supervisor and supervisee, for example, but the assessment of performance activities occurs in relation to a particular individual. The standards used and held constant by supervisors, the extent to which consideration is given to such factors as extenuating circumstances, experience, and time constraints will of course all influence appraisals of individual effectiveness. In most organizations, an effort is made to achieve essentially neutral criteria for evaluation, but it must be recognized that the disregard of some standards or the overemphasis of others can easily diminish the effectiveness of performance indicators as incentives for worker behavior. Further, it is difficult to avoid the covert comparison of one worker's performance with that of others.

Concomitant with the characterization of human service organizations by their increasing use of persons with different kinds of education has been emphasis on their increasing specialization (Meyer, 1969). The dilemma that increased division of labor poses for the supervisor is not resolved easily. Specialization is essential to an adequate command and utilization of knowledge, but it also can and does have the adverse consequences of encouraging rivalry, blocking the sharing of accurate information, and heightening parochial points of view (Finch, 1974, p. 169). The more specialized an agency becomes, the greater its mandate will be for coordination to ensure realization of more general and pervasive social service goals. At the opposite extreme, the less specialized an organization chooses to become and therefore the more general the knowledge and skills it expects individual employees to possess, the greater will be its chances for error or nonrealization of goals and purposes. Perhaps the growing information problems experienced by human service organizations in relation to specialization are an indication of the fact that one cannot, by simply bringing together more facts pertaining to the results of specialized activity, expect to achieve coordination. In a study of the use of paraprofessionals in public welfare, the author found that: "All things being equal, a more complete use of paraprofessional skill and expertise can be achieved through the use of more discretionary assignments. However, the greater the discretion in paraprofessional assignments, the more important communication and information sharing become. Such sharing between paraprofessional and social worker can be critical in determining the success of social services to clients. Unless an organization is willing to work for adequate feedback mechanisms, disruption can easily occur" (Finch, 1976a, p. 56). Thus, growing specialization and an expanded use of occupational specialties within social service and mental health organizations will increase communication and coordination costs in order to ensure that service provision is characterized by logic, coherence, and efficacy. A tradition of collaboration in human services exists, but it may prove less successful than formerly as the interdependence of workers increases. Specialization means that workers with different skills must perform complementary functions, because whenever program success depends on the selection of a particular combination of service personnel on the basis of feedback from the client, information and coordination demands become more intense. The organization and structure of work must therefore encourage continuous communication and teamwork among workers having contact with the same clients.

Human service organizations have traditionally defined

specialization in terms of program areas (such as protective services and homemaker services) to the exclusion of technological considerations. Thus, for example, some tasks performed by a protective services worker with natural parents need not dramatically change when a decision is made to temporarily place the child in foster care (although a new dimension of knowledge must be added). At the present time, however, many public welfare agencies would respond to such a decision by transferring the total case to another specialty. This method of operating assumes that the placement worker receiving the case possesses the skills required for continued work with the natural parents, has adequate knowledge of foster care, and even perhaps is able to treat the child directly.

Traditional definitions of specialization implicitly assume a broad range of worker skills with respect to the ability to respond to client needs within individual program assignments—a practice that ignores the many different levels of capability possessed by manpower now available to human service organizations. Viable compensatory alternatives are available, although they have not been fully considered by many agencies. Regardless of the particular mix of different kinds of workers selected by an organization, however, both benefits and costs must be considered. The greater the variety of workers involved in service provision, the greater the need to achieve a division of labor that will maximize the use of individual employee skills. Similarly, as more workers become involved in a particular case, costs rise with respect to the information and communication processes required for organizational success. Finally, the more success is judged in terms of client satisfaction, the greater becomes the mandate for coordination of services and worker skills. Such considerations recognize that collaborative and continuous communication among agency personnel is likely to occur only when these employees are in close physical proximity, especially where the actions of a worker must be adapted to the activities of one or several other team members to maximize client goal attainment.

Communication

The power of the manager in an organizational setting is often a function of the information vantage point of his or her position within the agency hierarchy. The ways in which supervisors utilize the data they receive, however, can either limit or enhance their functioning. For example, Long (1962, pp. 147–148) identifies three types or categories of managers in terms of informational concerns. The "upwardly mobile" managers are guided primarily by the folklore of the agency and by organizational definitions of success. In this case, beliefs relating to "how to make it" tend to dominate individual thought and action. Another adaptation can be found in more "ideologically motivated" supervisors, who adopt a professional stance and allow their use of knowledge to be guided by extraorganizational concerns. Finally, a third position can be found in managers whose primary concerns are with the "unit work group" as a source of personal support and satisfaction.

On the basis of these three categories, one might speculate that "upwardly mobile" supervisors will be less successful in confronting agency administration with the needs of supervisees, while ideologically motivated individuals will demonstrate minimal concern with respect to building organizational commitments. Unit-oriented supervisors will strive to maximize unit autonomy but are likely to avoid interdependencies with other work sections or units. An examination of the paramount information concerns of supervisors suggests that variance is evidenced in the degree to which organizational or professional criteria of success are stressed. At one extreme, organizational definitions of optimal attainment dominate individual concerns, as in the "upwardly mobile" individual. At the other end of the spectrum, the "ideologically motivated" person emphasizes professional definitions of goal realization. The third category of supervisor, who seeks support and satisfaction from the immediate work group, would rank low on both dimensions. One question, of course, remains to be answered from a typology of this kind: Under what circumstances can an individual maintain a stance that allows strong acceptance of both professional and organizational definitions of success? In other words, when are organizational and professional idealized criteria mutually compatible?

The job of the middle-level agency employee is one of continuous interpretation of management expectations to line staff and vice versa. The successful supervisor must often maintain a balance between these hierarchical extremes. An identification with management and the goals of the organization is necessary to successfully guide work-group activity in ways that are consistent with the agency's function and purpose. Concomitantly, the ability to successfully influence and guide a unit of workers is predicated by an identification with the interests of the line staff and their feelings regarding willingness to honor expectations being transmitted from above.

Recent studies of the sources of satisfaction and dissatisfaction among supervisors and supervisees suggest that practitioners may face particular problems in fulfilling managerial roles as they move into supervision. For example, Kadushin (1974) found that dominant concerns were supervisory dissatisfaction with administrative detail, the loss of client contacts, and the need to get workers to follow policies that evoked dissent. In addition, the greatest variance from supervisee ideals was found in the supervisor's ability to represent worker interests with administration, as well as in the ability to structure conferences in order to maximize learning. Such findings certainly suggest that the idealized administrative functions of communication expert, work-group catalyst, and line staff representative to higher-level agency personnel may frequently be less than optimally fulfilled. At the same time, such dimensions of middle-management functioning have been found to be important determinants of effective administrative performance (Olmstead and Christensen, 1973).

Work is by definition a purposeful behavior that seeks to accomplish a particular end result. Since organizational effectiveness is determined by both agency definitions and the ability to ensure that data reach the appropriate decision makers, the flow of information through supervisory positions grows increasingly important as human service organizations become more complex and interrelated (Olmstead, 1973). A major task of middle management then becomes the upward and downward communication of germane information, including material on purposes of individual activities and how they relate to the overall mission of the organization. Such verbal interactions must be continuous reciprocal processes based on recognition of the fact that the active participation of both the recipient and the emitter is vital for achievement of intent.

The immediate climate created by the supervisor is a major determinant of what information will and will not be disseminated to other agency personnel. For example, the selective withholding of information can increase the dependency of workers upon the supervisor. Where interaction is restricted between staff seeing the same client, for example, work may often be based on untested assumptions that may undermine service goals. There is certainly a reluctance on the part of most employees to transmit unfavorable evidence that might be used in evaluating their job performance. At the same time, however, the development and maintenance of cohesive group relations can reduce individual fears and allow a shift in focus to the common tasks that provide the rationale for interaction (Olmstead and Christensen, 1973).

As the recipients of communications, supervisors play a reactive rather than a passive role. Every compliment, suggestion, or criticism reflects an evaluation of the supervisee's work and holds the potential of influencing or changing work behavior. It has been demonstrated that workers tend to place greater importance on messages than do the supervisors who receive them—a fact that may discourage the flow of information upward through the organization. Similarly, Porter (1974, p. 234) has aptly labeled the tendency of supervisees to search for hidden meaning in messages received from higher levels as "the iceberg effect." Both of these statements demonstrate the powerful influence that supervisors may have over the types and quality of communication their subordinates receive; more importantly, such ideas unequivocally mandate a continuous need to clarify the understanding that workers have of their relationship to others in accomplishing common organizational objectives. Indeed, the need to prepare subordinates for occasional confrontations with unpleasant reality situations and pressures supplies the agency with the disturbing stimuli that lead people to seek creative new solutions.

In any human service organization, the actual "need to know" will be considerably smaller than the line staff's "wish to know" (Olmstead, 1973). The wish to know can in fact often appear excessive, especially during periods of organizational turmoil or change, in which feelings of distrust are readily felt and evidenced. At the same time, management requests for information without careful consideration of the understanding required by staff for its provision can often produce questionable results. Policy and procedural directives appear to secure a more consistent response when staff clearly understand how their performance of related tasks contributes to an improved agency program (Finch, 1974). For the line supervisor, awareness of this fact can lead to acceptance of the continual need to facilitate worker understanding by providing adequate information. Providing workers with the opportunity to question agency programs or procedures, for example, can often provide the means for developing a rationale for the agency's approach that is more compatible with individual or group beliefs. Research has demonstrated that effective communication increases understanding and acceptance of rules, helps to clarify problems, and often provides the basis for common understanding (see, for example, Becker and Neuhauser, 1975). In addition, daily communication between superior and subordinate about work processes and problems and the resulting effective coordination can increase the quality of client services.

One cannot discuss the social composition of organizations without recognizing the determinant role played by groups. Porter, Lawler, and Hackman (1975, p. 74) identify two major types of groups: "(1) those specified and created by the organization and (2) those that occur naturally in the process of individuals having the opportunity to interact with each other." To function successfully, human service organizations require recognition, consideration, and use of both formal and informal groups. In joining an agency, individual workers accept an authority relationship that March and Simon (1958) describe as characterized by agreement within some limits to accept the premises and instructions of the organization as a basic guide to work behavior. While acceptance of authority by the individual provides the organization with a powerful means of influence, it concomitantly predisposes the employee, through identification with a small work group and through attraction, to a process of mutual adjustment with and influence from coworkers. If organizational tasks performed by formal and informal groups can be achieved only through interdependent activity, shared goals develop. It is, in fact, the individuals comprising the organization who generate the will to cooperate with other members of the group. For example, an important source of supervisory influence derives from the shared norms and collective enforcement of compliance generated within the work unit itself (Blau, 1974a). For the new employee, unit members often provide critical initial definitions that allow the novice to exercise discretion in ways that both make sense to him or her and fit the folkways of the organization (Long, 1962). Recognizing and using the vitality and motivational force of the social group allows the supervisor to adopt a leadership style emphasizing guidance rather than command. Understanding the ideas members hold about their relationships provides an opportunity for the manager to become a symbol of the central idea that guides group behavior (Latham, 1970). More importantly, supervision can then shift from what sometimes appears a preoccupation with instruction on what to do to more critical issues relating to how the work-group members can be helped to achieve what they already intend to accomplish (Berkeley, 1971).

Effective supervision in human service organizations requires the ability to influence and guide workers in accordance with agency needs and objectives. It is therefore not surprising that the dominant sources of influence discussed in the literature relate to the knowledge and skill possessed by administrative personnel, to the acceptance of management's right to exercise power by subordinates, and to workers' personal liking for and identification with their superiors (see, for example, Olmstead and Christensen, 1973). It is being increasingly recognized that the power used by an organization to control its members derives from either specific positions or from personal qualities and is probably most successful when it represents a combination of both (Etzioni, 1965).

Finally, two kinds of information emerge as critical to communication processes. One is the type that each employee will need on his or her job assignment to make accurate and timely decisions in guiding work behaviors in ways that are congruent with agency goals. The second is the information each worker wants others (including management) in the organization to receive. Unless each type of information can flow freely, it seems unlikely that human service organizations will be able (1) to establish the complex process of negotiation that allows rules and regulations to be adapted to individual needs or (2) to tolerate the bargaining that must occur in order to reconcile the differences that inevitably exist between different kinds of agency personnel. These processes of negotiation and reconciliation of differences are vital to organizational viability and goal attainment, and paying attention to them through the process of effective communication must therefore be deemed paramount and imperative.

The Supervisor as Organizer

A human service organization may, of course, be characterized as a physical entity, but a more complete definition would add that it is an interactional process that occurs among its membership, and, further, that it is a network of interdependent relationships, influenced by the function and structure of services (Hanlan, 1972). Vinter (1959) has noted that all agencies must create the means for ensuring that cooperative actions are oriented toward desired ends. Previously, when social and mental health organizations had a more homogeneous staff, individuals frequently shared common definitions of agency purposes and goals, often as a result of professional education characterized by an emphasis on a limited number of experiences and themes. For example, when most or all members of a group have similar past experiences, such as prior education, the result can be a rapid and intense group effort to achieve a common goal. Such phenomena can often be observed at professional meetings but appear less characteristic of human service agencies today. As service organizations have become more heterogeneous in social, cultural, and educational background and in values of staff, the interactional processes of bargaining, negotiation, and influence have emerged as more characteristic means of arriving at common definitions of the problems to be solved and goals to be achieved in service delivery. Consideration of this fact points to the merits offered by the process of team building as a model for or means of conceptualizing important supervisory functions. Three interrelated stages of socialization, developing affective relations, and building group solidarity emerge with respect to team building (Brager and Specht, 1973). The connectedness versus the separation of the stages must be stressed, however, as they often, in actuality, occur simultaneously and assume a circular pattern, which may be thought of as a process being repeated to incorporate changes that occur within an organization.

Organizational selection is a common means of ensuring a somewhat finite number of qualities that characterize new organizational participants, while socialization, when successful, causes further modification or adaptation of individual traits to facilitate successful performance of assigned job roles (Etzioni, 1965). During the initial phase of employment, new personnel must acquire the values, expectations, and requisite behavior patterns of the organization and their immediate work groups. Such information essentially socializes new employees with respect to considerations such as basic goals, preferred means, worker responsibilities in fulfilling particular assigned roles, behavior patterns required for effective job performance, and principles or beliefs that maintain the organization's identity and integrity. The success of this phase appears to depend on two factors: (1) the motivation of the worker seeking to join the agency and (2) the degree to which the organization is capable of controlling the socialization process. Ideally, a kind of homogeneity of thinking can evolve that will form the basis of future working relationships; further, these similarities can even hopefully be evolved among members who come with highly diverse backgrounds. As Brager (1967, p. 62) has noted, "like-minded persons are more receptive to determined and concentrated effort." Both formal and informal processes therefore can be enhanced when congruence is achieved between subgroup and organizational goals.

A sorting-out process is, of course, likely to occur during this stage. Some individuals may object to basic goals of the organization, while others may leave because they dislike and/or are incompatible with other participants. It will be the individuals who make up the work group, however, who essentially generate or inhibit an impulse to cooperate as the socialization process seeks to provide a common basis for group activity. A common purpose does not automatically exist in groups; it must be defined, articulated, and incorporated into the understanding each individual has of his relationship to others. The possibility of coordinated team functioning, however, is not based on the traits of individuals, but rather on the patterning of relationships that evolve among people. Such patterning allows the concentration of influence in the supervisory role but recognizes that the work group contains an independent character that requires guidance.

During the initial phase, the new employee's identification with the work group acquires form primarily from the content of his or her interactions with colleagues. Working with people who have diverse backgrounds can stimulate persons to learn more about different attitudes and specialties, and supervision can play a crucial role in this process by facilitating and stimulating both member interaction and other variables related to organizational climate that will ultimately affect performance. Managers must therefore recognize their own importance and that of significant others in the work group as vital forces in the development of a comprehensive explanation of the organization's action system. Supervisory personnel must also realize that encouraging workers to behave differently often requires the ability both to convince the worker of the appropriateness of altered courses of action and to sell the idea to those persons with whom he or she interrelates or turns to for advice.

The ability of workers to develop affective relations with others represents the fostering of social bonds and group cohesiveness (Brager and Specht, 1973). It is in such development, then, that a sense of belonging to the group and identification with its common purpose is sought. As previously mentioned, if organization is at least partially considered as an idea that people define as their relationship with others in achieving a common purpose, then this socialization phase allows the building of interrelationships believed to be desirable to accomplish end results. Who will lead and who will follow in particular service delivery issues or cases is continually negotiated or renegotiated by weighing changing client needs, service objectives, and skill resources. One would ideally hope, of course, that members of the group would fulfill different participant roles from one case situation to another; for example, at one point a worker may be in the role of major decision maker, while in another he or she may function as the provider of a particular resource, as the therapist, or as an intervener with another agency to secure a needed form of client assistance. Ideally, then, the work group can stimulate improved performance through a diversity of assignments for individuals and therefore can benefit from the different skills and knowledge its members both have and acquire as they strive toward common goals.

Organizational enhancement is concerned with accommodating task and expressive functions in relation to the agency's mission. It must therefore be recognized that each group member enters the organization with social and professional needs that can be fulfilled through on-the-job problem solving. This fact should be of paramount consequence to supervisors and should be used as a basis to stimulate the group by offering meaningful direction and feedback and to engender a climate conducive to the integration of ideas and information, the facilitation of communication for utilization of member skills in group endeavors, and the stimulation of individual self-development and job satisfaction.

Work has different meanings for different people. There is nothing intrinsic in work that confines its relevance solely in terms of instrumental rewards. Indeed, the importance of the more subtle meanings of work is becoming increasingly emphasized through consideration of work as a means for individuals of achieving self-expression, self-esteem, group endeavor, and creative activity (Neff, 1968). It should be recognized, however, that the immediate work group will influence the aforementioned variables as well as individual self-perceptions of capability and identity. Consider, for example, the situation in which a line worker is promoted to a supervisory level. Frequently, under such circumstances, a change in attitudes, beliefs, and behaviors can be observed, especially where rewards from new peers are desired by the employee and these are more likely to be offered when he engages in promanagement activities. Neff (1968, p. 141) observes that "man is ingenious in inventing need which his subsequent behavior is designed to gratify." Consolidating these ideas, then, leads us to conclude that group cohesiveness is built on a comprehensive but compatible explanation of the action system that provides members with mutually shared definitions of their roles in relation to others.

This model of supervision emphasizes communication and commitment building. Change efforts within human service organizations are often unsuccessful because socialization processes have failed to redefine common purposes or to rebuild commitments within critical work groups. For example, Hage and Aiker (1967) have noted that after change has been introduced in organizations, it often has disruptive and negative effects on social relationships among organizational members. Work roles must often be redefined and new relationships established before further progress toward goals can be expected. While the social work profession presently considers the baccalaureate degree as requisite for the entry level in professional practice, the utilization of workers with this educational preparation is often limited in many human service organizations by contradictory definitions regarding adequate qualifications held by some professional, management and supervisory staff. Psychology stresses doctoral preparation, as does psychiatry. In such situations, little change is likely to occur unless a commitment can be secured from agency members to strive for a more complete use of manpower resources.

Landau argues (1972, p. 6) that "as systems become more complex and integrated, more interlocking and interdependent, the cost of error increases." As human service organizations become more complex, the likelihood of conflict also increases. One can expect, for example, that different kinds of education will produce different definitions of problems; further, individuals and groups develop enthusiasm for their particular specialties and struggle within their respective agencies for dominance of their own particular definitions of organizational function, purpose, and goals. As a result, negotiation and bargaining must play a greater role in conflict resolution. At the same time, the increased use of organizing techniques to heighten the problem-solving skills of the organization's members must become an integral part of the mitigation or alleviation of conflictual issues and concerns.

The line supervisor in human service organizations can be expected to assume an increasingly important and critical role in management. Supervisory role sets are mandated, characterized by such functions as organizing, enabling, socializing, coordinating, and mediating; further, they suggest that the manager must become a communication facilitator in issues of problem resolution. The structuring of social and mental health services must clearly facilitate the ability of supervisory personnel to function in coordinating capacities. Perhaps it was recognition of this fact that prompted

Mary Follett to argue that coordination must begin at the bottom of the organization (as opposed to the top) and must permit an interweaving of skills wherever combined knowledge is necessary for more accurate judgment (in Metcalf and Urwick, 1940).

Summary

Human service organizations have been characterized by their growing use of staff members with different kinds and levels of education and increased specialization—trends suggesting that work within such settings will become more interrelated and complex. As a result, organizational climate emerges as an increasingly important determinant of agency success. Supervisors must fulfill organizational roles in a way that assures that social and mental health services are arranged, sequenced, and combined in a coherent fashion to maximize benefits for agency clientele. The accomplishment of these purposes requires managerial ability to recognize and modify those arrangements and attributes of the work environment that can negatively affect or alter the behavior of employees.

Communication problems in human service organizations are many and varied, but it is indeed possible to organize and structure work in ways that will encourage the flow of critical information between workers. The supervisor's ability to play a key role in and to encourage negotiation, bargaining, and the building of common purposes among work-group members offers a vital means of conflict resolution, can provide the basis for organizational change, and most importantly, can be utilized in attempts to improve service delivery.

CHAPTER 4

Supervision as Metatherapy

Gene M. Abroms

The supervision of psychotherapy is often conceived as a form of sideline coaching. The client's defensive patterns are analyzed, and new plays are sent in to circumvent them. In psychoanalytic case supervision, the therapist's "countertransference" problems—personal, often unconscious attitudes that interfere with play execution—also come under scrutiny. The problem for most supervisors is how far to go in this direction. When does the analysis of the therapist's "pathology" cease to be coaching and shade into illicit psychotherapy?

Different supervisors draw the line in different places. At various times, most feel uncomfortable enough to think of recommending personal therapy for supervisees, unless, of course, the process is already under way. But this is no simple matter. Both countertransference interpretation and advice to seek personal therapy are quite often resented, because the right to comment on the therapist's mental health is not usually spelled out in the supervisory contract. Even if it is, there is no guarantee that such messages will not be received as uninvited criticism and thus have a negative impact on both supervision and therapy.

I think this troublesome problem is, in large measure, an artifact of this particular conception of supervision. Although supervision often in practice takes the form of sideline coaching, this is hardly its essence. And the misconception leads not only to the coaching-versus-therapy dilemma but also to crippling restrictions on the fullest, creative utilization of the supervisory process. The task here is to redefine the essence of supervision and to draw out the consequences of the revised conception.

The Notion of Metatherapy

In a nutshell, supervision is a therapy of therapy; in other words, it is *meta*therapy. To understand the meaning of metatherapy, one must first understand the nature of therapy proper. The modern consensus is that it is a type of *interpersonal relationship* designed to promote beneficial changes in the thoughts, feelings, and behaviors of distressed clients. This feat is accomplished through the exercise of *personal influence* by socially sanctioned healers who primarily rely on verbal and nonverbal communications as the means of persuasion (Abroms, 1968a, 1968b; Frank, 1961; Haley, 1963; Strupp, 1972). The key words in this characterization are *interpersonal relationship* and *personal influence*. Older conceptions of therapy place the emphasis on intrapsychic processes rather than interpersonal transactions and on nondirective analysis rather than directive persuasion. But, out of practical necessity, this tidier, narrower perspective has in recent years given way to a broader, altogether messier view of the matter.

Once therapy is conceived in terms of transaction and persuasion, supervision, as metatherapy, must be formulated in similar terms. But who is the patient in metatherapy? And what is the nature and purpose of the influential transaction? The patient is clearly neither the supervisee nor the supervisee's client but rather the therapeutic relationship between them. In this sense, supervision is quite analogous to family therapy, in which the patient is no single family member but the family's relationship system. Taking the point to its logical conclusion, supervision is a relationship between a supervisor and a therapeutic relationship. Its aim is metatherapeutic: to promote beneficial changes in the therapist-client relationship. Once supervision is conceived in these terms rather than as sideline coaching, novel formats with extended possibilities begin to suggest themselves. Although there is a venerable tradition of doing therapy in the absence of key parties to it—child analysis, the classic prototype, had its origins in Freud's treatment of Little Hans indirectly, through his father (Freud, [1909] 1955)—one must be careful not to confuse convenience with necessity. In what follows, I describe three formats that make explicit recognition and take specific advantage of the metatherapeutic, transactional nature of supervision.

Supervision as Cotherapy

When supervisors and trainees see clients together on a regular basis, the arrangement may be properly described as cotherapy, even though the respective roles are rarely coequal. This is a strikingly underutilized format. It is most commonly encountered in family therapy, but it also works quite well with individuals and groups. Some teachers supervise exclusively in this mode (Whitaker and Abroms, 1974).

Under optimal circumstances, the cotherapy arrangement should be made right from the beginning of treatment. The individual or group is told that "we will be collaborating on the treatment," on the rationale that "two heads are better than one," a cliché that unfortunately is not always true. In the process, the senior therapist, the supervisor, quite naturally assumes the dominant role. As time goes on, the trainee gradually becomes more comfortable in offering his or her reactions and assumes a stronger role than formerly. The supervisor and therapist must make certain to leave time at the end of each session to compare notes and to map out and revise strategies.

Three objections are usually raised to this procedure: (1) the trainee is denied the experience of exclusive clinical responsibility,

(2) the transference is split, and (3) the investment of time is impractical. The first two points are obviously true and must be accepted for what they are. The third is open to question.

There is no doubt that in cotherapy clinical responsibility is shared, and for this reason it should not be the only mode of supervision the trainee experiences nor the only mode of therapy he or she does. This is particularly the case in some nonmedical settings where the tradition of individual clinical responsibility is already weak or poorly focused, and the cotherapy format only serves to erode it further (Sternbach, Abroms, and Rice, 1969). But, other things being equal, the approach has the virtue of its defect: Trainees learn to share responsibility. Too many therapists, once they go out into practice, work entirely alone, never admitting that they are sometimes in trouble and could use the help of a trusted colleague. Nor do they appreciate the dialectical process that must be gone through and the interpersonal skills that must be learned to achieve a harmonious collaborative relationship in work that comes so close to their deepest personal concerns.

Much the same kind of thing can be said about the split transference. Clearly the trainee ought to experience it in its unsplit form. But split transferences are hardly uncommon in the affairs of human beings. The prototype is, after all, the early relationship to parents. Ever afterward, one is constantly relating to organizations and institutions in which the parameters of joint leadership often split along maternal and paternal lines. The point is that deliberately split transferences can be made to foster the learning process, particularly when an adequate theoretical rationale, such as a family model, is utilized.

Although doing cotherapy may appear to be an excessive drain on a busy supervisor's time, it rarely requires more than a quarter hour beyond the time for conventional supervision. The individual or group can be seen together for forty-five minutes or an hour and a half respectively, and the additional fifteen minutes devoted to supervision proper with little time needed to review the basic facts of the sessions. The advantages of the arrangement more than make up for the modest additional investment in time. The virtues of learning to collaborate and to utilize the split transference have been mentioned. In addition, trainees are permitted to see experienced clinicians work; they can get direct feedback on their own work; they can directly observe the personal power issue in psychotherapy; and they can experience the floating-observer phenomenon in treatment.

Direct Observation. Experienced therapists do not often allow themselves to be observed while doing their work. Occasionally, a very responsible teacher-colleague will conduct analytic or dynamic psychotherapy behind a one-way mirror, but the process often succumbs to the artificiality of the arrangement. It is an undeniable fact that hovering observers profoundly affect the treasured intimacy of individual psychotherapy, and allowing strangers, however hidden and unobtrusive, to witness the process destroys something essential to it. The result is that the very therapists whom one would like to serve as exemplars of honest, sensitive work are the least amenable to being observed. Yet, watching and imitating is doubtless a much more efficient and telling way to learn than being advised from the "coaching bench." Trainees get to see useful "moves" and modes of continuity that experienced clinicians have picked up and refined over the years and that novices might require many more years to stumble on by themselves. But even more important, they are allowed to observe the qualities of tolerance and concern that are communicated in the well-conducted relationship and that make it a rich healing experience. Since these issues may never be effectively communicated in conventional supervision, the loss is considerable when able therapists refuse, for understandable reasons, to compromise their own work by displaying it. The beauty of the cotherapy arrangement is that it allows trainees to observe under conditions that are not too destructive of the relationship phenomena that need to be observed. The arrangement is a relatively genuine one, and although triadic relationships are rarely as intimate as dyadic ones they can nevertheless generate a significant enough sense of personal encounter to make the experience alive and meaningful.

Feedback. Hand in hand with watching and imitating, being watched and given feedback is an extremely efficient way to learn the work. Of course, supervisors must offer their comments with much the same tolerance and support that they manifest in talking with clients. They also enhance the "listenability" of their remarks by allowing supervisees equal time to question their own therapeutic behavior. The reciprocity of the arrangement should become more pronounced over time and should serve as precondition and indicator of the growing symmetry of the supervisor-therapist relationship. Properly managed, exposure is a salutary experience for therapists. In contrast to presentations at professional conferences, which demand a certain amount of dramatic display, more private exposures allow therapists, both new and old, to grapple with narcissistic trends in their own personalities, in the eventual hope of achieving a more selfless focus on the quality and evolution of the therapeutic relationship.

Power Hierarchy. Supervised therapy in which therapists neglect to mention to clients that they are being supervised is necessarily permeated with peculiar currents of feeling that have all the greater impact for going unmentioned. Much like the children of parents who decline to openly disclose the fact of hidden marital hostilities and who instead present a hollow united front, clients of hidden supervision sense that something is amiss, that there are unspoken currents and truths. Finding themselves unable to give substance to their malaise, however, they are left to question in perplexed silence.

In supervised therapy, what therapists often find difficult to acknowledge to clients is their inexperience and need of supervision. Instead, they adopt a façade of bravado, of therapeutic machismo. Although this is often a necessary and highly effective counterphobic coping strategy, a step on the road to true competence and self-confidence, authenticity dictates that the facts ought not to go completely unacknowledged. It is after all a step toward a higher competence to admit some measure of incompetence. Do we not compliment our clients for knowing when to come for help, for acknowledging their limitations to cope alone? Cotherapy supervision cuts to the heart of the matter.

By introducing senior supervisors into the therapeutic arrangement, trainees are immediately confronted with the power and competence issues. They see that in the client's view supervisors have more "clout." Under the circumstances, the trainee can form some impression of the relative contributions of age, role definition, experience, intellectual acuity, empathic warmth, and self-confidence in engendering this interpersonal authority. They may come to realize that initially some of their own authority can be borrowed from teachers. Although individual power is thereby diminished, yet in compensation there is provided some notion of the reality of auxiliary power, which can be drawn on in times of need. By acknowledging personal limitations and the greater expertise of others, individual therapists can expand, rather than diminish, their own therapeutic efficacy.

Observing Ego. Finally, the cotherapy relationship can be informative about the function of observing ego in therapy. When clients focus inappropriately strong feelings on the trainee, the supervisor can "draw the fire" by analyzing the transactional meaning of the hostility. The trainee similarly learns to intervene when the supervisor becomes the target. The metaposition of the hovering, therapeutic ego becomes, in the process, externalized and accessible to direct observation. What is learned can be utilized in other treatment arrangements: in solo individual therapy as well as group therapy led by cotherapists.

Supervision as Consultation

Cotherapy represents a radical transformation of the supervisory process. It is a learning experience, many of whose special benefits can be gained from a single case. For many reasons, therapists may choose to undertake it infrequently. A partial, less radical form of it, however, may be utilized more routinely. I am referring to supervision as a consultation process, in which supervisors make at least one "on-site" inspection. The willingness of therapists occasionally to call in senior colleagues to observe or to talk to their clients and themselves may repay them handsomely in terms of greater understanding of the shared power and responsibility issues already discussed in conjunction with cotherapy.

The supervisory consultation is best carried out early in the course of a treatment relationship. There often comes a time, just after the therapist has taken the initial history of the presenting problem and offered a tentative formulation of its basis, when the therapeutic process seems to pause to take a deep breath, as if uncertain of its resolve. Or the relationship may grind to a halt, stalemated in its intentions.

These are advantageous times for an experienced hand to

"have a look." The suggestion will usually come from the supervisor, who is having great difficulty understanding the nature of the relationship from the progress notes and tape recordings. At first a novel, hardly comfortable idea, the therapist may require some time to prepare himself or herself and the client for the intrusion. The potential impact on the client—sometimes of learning of the supervisor's very existence—will have to be honestly examined and reconciled with the therapist's self-image. The recommendation will then have to be explicitly presented to the client, hopefully in a genuinely convincing fashion. Otherwise the consultation is apt to prove disappointing, bearing overtones of espionage.

The conduct of the consultation is little different from any initial interview. The supervisor acknowledges that he or she has heard quite a lot about the client and often likes to meet clients whose therapy he or she supervises for the purpose of gaining more immediate impressions on which to base suggestions. And then the usual question, "What is your current idea of the problems that brought you into treatment?" During the course of the consultation, it is often useful to have both client and therapist give their individual assessments of the quality of their relationship. The supervisor is wise to end the interview on a hopeful and appreciative note as to the usefulness of the encounter, but without sharing specific impressions or recommendations. There is, after all, no use in committing a therapist to a course of action that he or she might find disagreeable. The supervisor should, however, indicate intent to talk matters over with the therapist, in the hopes of jointly coming up with useful ideas.

In practice, "on-site" consultations are rarely done more than twice in the course of a supervised psychotherapy. One visit early in treatment and another toward the end meet both the educational and humanistic requirements. The apparent need for more frequent consultations raises other issues: undue anxiety and dependency, poor matching of therapist and client, or improper diagnosis.

The potential benefits of such firsthand observations have in part been mentioned. The authentic declaration on the therapist's part of the need for guidance, the recognition of realistic differences in competence and power, and the sober disavowal of omnipotence are important milestones in the trainee's professional growth. But quite obviously the greatest potential value of a consultation visit lies in the recognition of discrepancies between the therapist's reported observations and the supervisor's immediate ones.

The most common discrepancy of practical import is the matter of diagnosis. In learning to do psychotherapy, a premium is placed on understanding therapeutic pauses and stalemates in terms of psychological conflict. This stance is often accompanied by a tendency to underdiagnose, to think of all clients as suffering from neurosis. But quite often therapy fails to progress because the clients have more than neurotic conflicts and cannot profit from standard psychodynamic approaches. They may have borderline or frank schizophrenic disturbances, unipolar or bipolar affective disorders, or severe personality disorders with schizoid, impulsive, or narcissistic features.

The treatment of each of these syndromes requires departures from classical technique. In some, particularly the affective disorders, psychoactive drugs are extraordinarily helpful, paving the way for more standard therapeutic approaches. In borderline and narcissistic disorders, the technical innovations of Kernberg (1968) and Kohut (1971) may be required to ensure therapeutic progress. Of course, undiagnosed organic brain syndromes can also account for therapeutic failures, but unfortunately the specific underlying conditions are often chronic and irreversible. The diagnostic facts are nevertheless important to the proper allocation of time, effort, and special techniques.

Misdiagnosis is not the only possibility. There may be destructive relationship factors that need to be noted and resolved. Some clients have strong feelings about the age, sex, religion, or color of their therapists and cannot bring themselves to discuss these matters without sensitive prompting. They are, after all, in the realm of "unanswerable criticism," and there can be reasonable concern about the potential destructiveness of mentioning them. Yet not to mention them is no less destructive. The way must be opened to examine stereotypes and if not always to correct them, at least to learn to live in tolerance of human differences. To many clients, particularly older ones being seen by young trainees, the appearance of an older, guiding hand who oversees the process, who "blesses" its outcome, is highly reassuring.

Therapists, too, may have failed to mention obvious characteristics of clients that immediately leap out at the supervisor when he or she arrives for the consultation. The significance of such omissions is rarely minor. Obvious physical deformities or other characteristics in clients may have aroused intense anxieties that cannot be easily confronted. Disfiguring scars, withered limbs, eye deformities, extreme obesity, or cacchexia may have been lost in the shuffle of case reporting, but should not remain lost to the watchful eye of helpful supervisors. A strong undercurrent of sexuality, sometimes homosexual in nature, may strike the supervisor, all the more so for its prior omission from discussion. Once troublesome instincts and sensitivities are encompassed in supervision, their destructive effects are usually quite easily attenuated.

Supervision as Group Meeting

The supervision of clients under treatment in a hospital or other controlled environment is a special case because many therapists are apt to be involved. Oftentimes, there is not only the primary therapist who does the individual psychotherapy and makes important general treatment decisions but also a host of part-time therapists who run the groups, work programs, behavioral exercises, and psychodrama that make up modern milieu treatment. Furthermore, other patients are often key collaborators in mounting such a multidimensional treatment program (Abroms and Greenfield, 1971), and their role can hardly afford to go unrecognized and unsupervised.

One approach to providing supervision to a treatment program rather than to individual treaters, that is, to an integrated system of specialized therapists, is to devise a type of meeting in which the relevant therapists and clients discuss their therapeutic work with each other and in which the supervisor tries to promote consensus in diagnosis, dynamic formulation, and treatment planning. In one such format (Abroms, 1969), a treatment team of approximately eight patients and four staff members had the weekly task of briefly presenting each patient's pertinent psychiatric history, of reviewing the past week's treatment program and its effect on problematic feelings and behavior, and of clarifying the requirements for discharge. The aim was for the staff to do less and less of the work of this conference until, at discharge time, the patients about to leave were doing most of it. For example, prior to discharge, a patient would be able to present his or her own brief psychiatric history and treatment plan, and would orchestrate the feedback of fellow patients and staff members as to achievement and further steps.

The task of supervision in such circumstances is to make certain that a proper diagnosis and formulation of intra- and inter-personal dynamics have been made and that the team members are working together, rather than at cross-purposes, in accomplishing the treatment program. Irrational group dynamics, such as Bion's basic assumptions (1959), may have to be pointed out to unimpede the team's productive work.

This is, of course, a most radical form of group supervision. Lesser degrees of it are found in continuous case seminars, in which trainees serially present their cases to fellow trainees and a supervisor, and in demonstration group and family therapies, in which trainees watch the supervisors doing treatment behind a one-way mirror, or vice versa, and subsequently discuss the treatment process.

The main advantage of such formats is the efficiency of information transfer. By watching and listening to others, one picks up ideas and concerns and vicariously rehearses. What is said to one can be generalized to guide others. The disadvantage is the lack of privacy in which more intimate, interior thoughts and feelings can be faced.

Supervision as Metatherapy

Having located the focus of supervision in the therapist-client relationship, rather than in the client's or the therapist's pathology, we have examined three special formats that permit the supervisor more direct observational access to the process than the standard format allows. I have alluded to the fact that the super-visor's task in such transactionally conceived formats is the therapy of therapy, or metatherapy. The question that must now be ad-dressed is the appropriate interpretive technique for metatherapy. It must be characterized in terms that distinguish it from therapy proper and also from educational instruction that is wholly non-therapeutic.

Like all therapies, metatherapy is a combination of both support and interpretation. For this to occur in a helpful manner, the supervisor's primitive wishes must, in large measure, be neutralized, so that attention can rise above sexual, competitive, and narcissistic strivings directed at the trainee's person, in order to focus primarily on the therapeutic relationship. It differs in the more abstract nature of this focus. While dynamic therapy, in its ideal state, addresses itself to the client's significant early and contemporary relationships as refracted through the medium of the therapeutic transference relationship, the metatherapy of dynamic supervision, in its most elaborate form, addresses itself to the therapist's relationship to the client as refracted through the medium of the supervisory metatransference relationship.

By the term *metatransference,* I am referring to the transference of therapist-client transference phenomena into the supervisory relationship. For example, a psychotherapy trainee presents his progress notes thoroughly and with unswerving purposiveness. He asks that the supervisor wait to make his remarks at the end of the presentation. The content of the notes concerns the client's recovery of a childhood memory in which he feels devastated and all alone in a large field. His mother had recently abandoned the family. Therapist and supervisor discuss the relationship of these early events to the client's current tendency to become explosive and paranoid when he feels vulnerable to others' taking control. The client quite unexpectedly, however, stops coming to therapy and forms an intense extramarital liaison. All efforts to induce him to return are unsuccessful.

The metatransference-countertransference phenomena were manifested in the mode of presenting the progress notes. *On whose terms are they to be presented?* If the supervisor cannot react until the end, which clearly irritates him, then the therapist's progress toward his own personal goal of an expert presentation becomes more important than the personal relationship between him and the supervisor, who needs to feel more spontaneously helpful. This is the metatransference-countertransference embodiment of the transference-countertransference complex between therapist and client.

The client cannot put his faith in the benign control of another because of vulnerability to loss and abandonment. By a partial surrender of control—going along with the therapist's request for history—he is led directly to the traumatic source of the mistrust; and, feeling utterly helpless and weak and in desperate need of narcissistic supplies, he bolts and hungrily latches on to a narcissistic supplier. At one level, the therapist's unswerving presentation of his progress notes, oblivious to the supervisor's needs, reflects his single-minded pursuit of early history, oblivious of the feelings stirred up in the client, which will require soothing and taming to prevent their being acted out destructively. The supervisor's reaction—of feeling left out and abandoned—mirrors the client's feelings.

At another level, the therapist's behavior, in a defended against, compensated form, expresses the client's fears of giving up control, and the supervisor's feelings express the threat of having one's authority challenged. For the metatransference to work out better than the transference relationship, the supervisor must next directly support the therapist through the loss of the client, attending to his wounded self-esteem, and discuss his very strong urge to bolt from supervision, emotionally if not physically, as he acknowledges the need for more direction from the supervisor. At that point, all ends will have been tied up, and the supervisor will have understood perfectly what motivates the therapist to present his progress notes compulsively.

To think in terms of metatransference is to think in parallel structures at different levels of abstraction, that is, to recognize the multilevel, isomorphic mirroring of interactional processes. The largest therapeutic screen on which such processes are played out is a therapeutic community in which interstaff group life typically mirrors the patients' group process, and vice versa. For example, a hospital ward was mourning the death of a patient who, apparently intoxicated, wrecked her automobile out on pass. In the community's examination of the missed signals that led to the unwise approval of her pass, the facts emerged that she had recently been jilted by one of the male patients—a physician with a serious manic-depressive disorder—in favor of another patient. Further exploration of interstaff relationships revealed that one of the residents on the patient's treatment team had at about the same time stopped seeing

one of the ward nurses and had become involved with another staff
member. These two triangular conflicts mirrored each other in a
complex matrix of subtle cueings and displacements that defy clear-
cut assignment of causal priority. They are perhaps synchronistic,
in Jung's sense of the term (Jung, [1952] 1973). Nevertheless, such
conflicts must be dealt with at their appropriate levels in the interests
of client and staff welfare.

Incidentally, the usual words for dealing with multilevel
mirroring phenomenon are the concepts of projective identification
and transpersonal defense. They allow us to speak meaningfully of
an individual in a group or family who expresses the feelings and
hopes of others, of being their symptom bearer, scapegoat, or shining
star. Interpersonal, rather than intrapsychic, defenses and coping
mechanisms are involved. The elucidation of such mirroring patterns
is a potent force for bringing them under volitional control.

The mode of metatransference interpretations is the same as
for transference phenomena. The language is transactional: what
the client is doing to make the therapist feel and act as he does,
and vice versa; how the transaction between the client and therapist
is affecting the transaction between therapist and supervisor by
stirring up similar areas of conflict. Such talk has no implication of
personal health or pathology, only of interactional congruences and
dissonances between different people with different styles of living.

Types of Therapy

The supervisory relationship is often instrumental in selecting
the type of therapy appropriate to a client and, in fact, determining
whether or not, under the circumstances, any therapy at all is appropriate. There are clearly situations in which the patient is too
dangerous or organic or difficult for a particular therapist judiciously
to undertake the treatment, or there may be other circumstances in
which the therapist is having personal difficulties that preclude a
particular case assignment or continuation. The supervisor has the
responsibility of seeing that such issues are confronted.

A less gross and more frequently encountered consideration
is the type of treatment that should be undertaken, considering the
client's needs and the therapist's experience and skills. It is simply
not true that all sensitive, well-intentioned human beings can work

with seductive or idealizing transference neuroses or treat a group that has a powerfully destructive esprit. The hierarchy of treatment complexity is typically conceived to begin with supportive therapy and to progress to dynamic psychotherapy, psychoanalytic psychotherapy, and psychoanalysis proper. Moving up the hierarchy, treatment becomes relatively less supportive and more interpretive, and as it becomes more interpretive it focuses increasingly on the transference-childhood linkage. The hierarchy supposedly defines the differential tasks of therapists on a continuum of increasing skill and experience.

But the hierarchy does not really work, because all therapeutic interaction involves a combination of support and interpretation, and the very people who are supposed to be merely supportive to clients feel the greatest need for a theoretical framework out of which to offer support and to make sense of their clients' difficulties. Confusion and meaninglessness are greater sources of personal suffering in therapy and in life than are lack of support or affection. By the same token, experienced therapists can become so involved in the transference-childhood linkage that they fail to attend to the climate of the therapeutic alliance, whose clemency is a precondition for effective theoretical understanding.

What is needed is a simple-to-complex hierarchy of therapy that recognizes different levels of understanding and experience, each of which involves a combination of support and conceptual understanding. This quest amounts to the same thing as a search for a hierarchy of mental health values in which drive expression, social connectedness, and other crucial elements of personal functioning find their rightful place. I have attempted (Abroms, unpublished manuscript, before 1977) to devise a hierarchy, based in part on Kohlberg's theory of moral development (Kohlberg, 1971) and in part on current notions of psychosocial evolution. Without being able to provide the empirical and theoretical bases for the conception here, I would urge that the following stages of mental health be considered in terms of their fruitfulness for discriminating levels of psychotherapy.

1. *Fit Survival.* The goal here is to promote physical and material well-being—intellectual alertness, physical vigor and health, appropriate territoriality, adequate nutrition and exercise, produc-

tive work, a living wage—in short, progressive physical and material achievement commensurate with biological endowment. Therapy here is psychophysically oriented, involving biological and medical interventions and learning theory principles (behavior therapy) geared to survival and material achievement.

2. *Drive Satisfaction.* "All work and no play makes Dan a dull boy." The business of survival-and-status must be tempered by hedonistic pleasure. Eating, sex, and physical and intellectual work may be enjoyed for their intrinsic egoistic satisfaction rather than as blind instrumentalities of biological need. An anti-repressive, evocative appeal to libidinal expression and the reinforcement of pleasure seeking are the appropriate modes of therapy.

3. *Social Belonging.* As Fairbairn (1954) put it, libido is object seeking, not pleasure seeking. The recognition here is that hedonistic satisfactions must be socialized in the course of human development. The pleasures must be had in the context of rewarding human relationships. Family and group concordance, from which the individual receives warmth and approval, are necessary achievements for humans as social beings. Individual, family, and group therapy geared to basic socialization issues—survival and pleasure in relationships—are the appropriate modes of treatment.

4. *Structural Order.* Human togetherness, as an end in itself, makes of life a perpetual encounter session in which intimacy and warmth turn into opiates. Relationships, once formed, must themselves be interrelated to form social structures: institutions, laws, schedules, boundaries, and portals. The lawful regulation of life into structures requiring dutiful observance becomes, at this stage, the goal of psychological health and therefore the aim of treatment. A therapy addressed to ego controls is the appropriate modality.

5. *Adaptive Flexibility.* Duty to law and order, once achieved, must be transcended if novel circumstances are to be created and adapted to. The emphasis moves from duty to rigid structures to the contractual procedures for the orderly generation of new ones. Treatment is directed to the making of utilitarian contracts and to the loyalty issues involved in honoring them. A tolerance for human differences goes hand in hand with these values.

6. *Formation of Ideals.* The relativity implied in adaptive flexibility must ultimately be framed by a set of enduring ideals. Treatment here is directed toward developing a system of universal values, that is, toward the idealization of the superego, which permits the individual to channel his or her ambitions toward the creative realization of social justice.

These six stages of mental health—of biological survival and material achievement, drive satisfaction and pleasure, social belonging and approval, structural order and duty, adaptive flexibility and loyalty, and formation of ideals and creative justice— constitute a natural hierarchy of treatment values. Each level subsumes and encompasses all prior ones in a higher integration. Each is sufficiently important to constitute worthwhile work for therapists and clients at varying levels of psychological development and skill attainment. The sequence implicitly recognizes that some therapeutic goals may be too advanced for either client or therapist. It also recognizes that some therapists may mistakenly aim too low for particular clients. At any rate, therapists whose own mental health values are no more developed than their clients' will necessarily provide a more limited form of help than if their values had attained a higher stage of evolution. Finally, in cases of uneven development, appropriate therapy may involve a retracting of stages to repair weaknesses in supporting layers. Some good pleasure seekers are poor survivors; the dutiful are frequently too ascetic for a harmoniously integrated life; and great adapters have been known to be less great at doing their duty.

In terms of this schema, supervisors have the exquisitely sensitive task of helping to focus the goals of therapy on what can be achieved given the psychosocial skills of both clients and therapists. Much has been written about the lack of clear-cut matching variables in psychotherapy: who is a good therapist for what kind of client. Although this schema is only a first step, it provides a rationale for encouraging less-trained workers to concentrate with their clients on more basic goals that fall within their own areas of competence; for example, self-assertion, job seeking, drive expression, rather than more refined, abstract goals, such as the realization of loyalty and social justice, which may lie beyond their own and their client's reach. And it provides a justification for aiming higher, in appropriate circumstances, than conventional technique might otherwise dictate. The renunciation of oedipal strivings may, after all, be hack work if the parental model is unworthy of such a sacrifice by identification. In these circumstances, the therapist can do nothing less than help the client find an ideal worthy of identification and surrender. At its best, supervision must serve the same model function for the therapist. If supervisors treat beginning therapists with warmth and respect for personal boundaries, they will come to mirror these very same values in their work with clients. And, similarly, if they treat more advanced therapists with loyalty and justice, they too will come to stand for these ideals in their professional lives.

Summary

In this chapter, supervision has been defined as metatherapy: a therapy of therapy. In consequence, the focus of supervision has shifted from an exclusive emphasis on client pathology and therapist technique to a wider concern with the therapist-client relationship. Noting the one-sided and restricted access that conventional supervision affords, I have discussed three formats that give the supervisor more direct observational access to the therapy relationship: cotherapy, consultation, and group staffing. Each of these has distinctive advantages, liabilities, and applications. But all demand an explicit recognition that the supervisor stands in a metatherapeutic relationship to the therapist-client relationship system.

The vexing problem of how much a supervisor can say about the therapist's "pathology" can be resolved with this framework. The proper interpretive focus is on what clients do to make therapists think, feel, and react as they do, and what therapists do to make clients think, feel, and react as they do—with no need to impute pathology to anyone. At a more advanced level of therapy, supervision is concerned with assisting therapists to locate the childhood prototypes of the client's current modes of relating—in other words, to establish the transference-childhood linkage. At a more advanced level of supervision, transference-countertransference phenomena in therapy are found to be reflected in the supervisor-therapist relationship. These metatransference-countertransference phenomena are discussed as multilevel mirrorings, again with no imputations of individual pathology.

A hierarchy of mental health values is offered to guide supervisors in helping therapists of varying levels of experience and psychological sophistication to focus their treatment goals with clients of varying levels of psychological development. Rather than assuming that it is a question of doing *either* supportive *or* interpretive psychotherapy, it is assumed that all therapy is a combination of support and interpretation. The treatment goals, however, fall on a hierarchy that progresses from basic survival and material achievement to progressively more refined quality-of-life values, culminating in a commitment to the universal ideal of social justice.

CHAPTER 5

Supervisors as Educators

Alex Gitterman
Irving Miller

The educational role and task of the social work supervisor has historically received both theoretical and conceptual emphasis. However, in agency practice as well as in social work education for supervisory practice, underlying pedagogical theory and skill about how to instruct others to provide services has received scant attention. This is unfortunate because a significant and often central part of the work is educational, even when the social worker is functioning primarily as a direct service giver, supervisor, administrator, in-service training specialist, or consultant.

Supervision for social work practice has historically been

assigned many functions and varying purposes. Emphases have tended to shift between administrative and teaching functions, that is, between asserting its essential function to be the organization's requirements, on the one hand, or to be the professional development needs of the worker, on the other hand. Supervisory practice and concepts of role and function have been modified over time as they have been influenced by the change from primarily agency-based training programs and by the changing social contexts of service. From the earliest days of charity organization societies, in which the "master" controlled the activities of the "apprentice" and passed along "practice wisdom," supervision has remained the principal method by which knowledge and skill have been transmitted by the experienced to the inexperienced, the trained to the untrained, and in professional education, from the teacher and field instructor to the student (Austin, 1960; Burns, 1965; Gitterman, 1972; Kadushin, 1976; Miller, 1971).

Although continuing attention has been paid to underlying theoretical frameworks and skills required for delivery of services, corresponding attention has not been paid to underlying theory and skills required to instruct others to deliver those services. Service delivery skills have been generally assumed to be similar or readily adaptable to the skills for teaching and helping others to deliver the services. Although social work teaching and supervisory practice have been concerned for many years with adapting educational theory (notably that of John Dewey), this effort was not pursued on its own terms but in terms of how it could be accommodated to psychoanalytical personality theory that underpinned practice.

While psychoanalytic theory did not in itself explicitly formulate an educational theory, social work supervision did adapt and utilize knowledge about and insight into the role of anxiety and unresolved libidinal and aggressive conflicts in inhibiting learning, and the mastery of learning tasks. Further, transference problems were identified and analyzed in relation to their place and use in the supervisory relationship (Austin, 1960, p. 582). These applications of psychoanalytic theory have contributed to a recurring tendency to view the supervisor-worker relationship as analogous to the worker-client relationship. This has been more apparent in casework than in group work or community organization. In this connection, there is very little literature on the subject in community organization. Group work literature is also scanty, except for the fact that about half of the textbooks written during the last thirty-five to forty years were about supervision of group work and were focused on the supervision of untrained part-time workers and volunteers (see, for example, Abrahamson, 1959; Dimock and Trecker, 1949; Lindenberg, 1939; Williamson, 1950). As casework, the most established and developed part of social work, began to be conceptualized in scientific and treatment terms, a strong individualized tutorial supervisory approach emerged corresponding to the emerging individualized case approach. Thus, overlapping goals, value preferences, and similarities have tended to obscure the important differences between psychological and educational theory for supervision and between a theory for practice and a theory for supervising that practice.

The need for attention to the differences between a theory for practice and a theory for supervision of that practice is being clarified by the growing sanction and support for the bachelor in social work (B.S.W.) as the entry-level degree and increase in the employment of B.S.W.s in front-line service jobs. This has resulted in a renewed interest in the role of educator and in individualizing staff learning in a manner rooted in pedagogical theory and skill (Richan, 1969, 1972). The renewed interest is directly connected to a growing concern about maintaining control and amplifying the influence of the M.S.W. Also related is the emergence and growth of the consultation function (Caplan, 1970; Rapoport, 1963). Consultation, although functionally distinct from supervision, often serves as a compensation for lack of suitably trained M.S.W. staff. Insofar as it consists of structured and ongoing advice giving, client problem clarification, and trying to resolve problems of professional practice, consultation becomes somewhat equivalent to supervision and similarly requires attention to educational theory and skill.

Issues in Social Work Supervision

Several issues or tensions appear and reappear in supervision, with varying intensity depending on the changing social context (Gitterman, 1972; Williamson, 1961). Included among these tensions are those between administrative and educational imperatives, between organizational accountability and professional autonomy, and, finally, between content and process. The politics of professionals and professionalism and perhaps the difficulties in enduring ambiguity seem to cause these tensions to appear in polarized forms rather than being posed as evidence of a new need to rework the balance between them in a new context. The issue of content and process is central and represents a microcosm of these persisting issues in supervisory and consultation practice. These two aspects or elements have often been polarized into a struggle between an emphasis on either one or the other. In education, these emphases represent theoretical, philosophical orientations. The "subject-centered" approach emphasizes curriculum, not students' perceived learning interests and needs. Learning is perceived as a rational, logical process (see Herbart, 1945; Locke, [1889] 1959). And the "student-centered" approach emphasizes students' perceived interests and concerns, not institutional expectations (see Froebel, 1887).

In social work, either the content to be mastered is emphasized at the expense of the practitioner's individual learning style and needs, or the practitioner's particular learning style and needs are emphasized at the expense of essential content and organizational imperatives. In the former case, neatly organized policies, procedures, structures, and abstractions are offered without reference to the somewhat less neat and less logical life context and process by which they were developed and are to be applied. In the latter case, legitimate organizational demands are sacrificed to presumed individual learning needs. Maintaining a working balance between organizational demands and differentiated staff learning needs has indeed been difficult to accomplish.

Relevant Pedagogical Concepts

Some well-established pedagogical notions (the current word is *androgogical*), some of which are particularly associated with John Dewey, are pertinent to achieving clarity about the balance between content and process, that is, the learner and the subject.

What is proposed is an organic connection between the processes of education and personal experiences (Dewey, [1938] 1947). The central task of teaching is defined as the selection and structuring of experiences that demand and induce creative problem solving. The "principle of interaction" proposes the need for the learner and the subject to interact and mutually adapt (Dewey, [1938] 1947, p. 47). In supervision, the supervisor assumes a middle ground between the extremes of authoritarian control and of total permissiveness. The central teaching task is structuring the specifics of the work demands in such a manner as to facilitate the engagement between the workers' individual learning needs and the job to be done. In effect, the supervisor is required to specify and define work situations that help bridge personal experiences and personal styles with facts, knowledge, ideas, and theories. This demands skill of supervisors and teachers or staff trainers, not only in direct practice but also in teaching methodology.

These basic concepts are further elaborated and specified by the following concepts.

The first concept is *operationalization*. Maintaining the distinction between "knowing that" (having facts and information) and "knowing how" (using facts and information) is indispensable (Ryle, 1949). Teaching about job responsibilities and expectations is not the same as teaching how to carry out job responsibilities and expectations. Knowledge or insight is not self-actualizing, and unless we pay attention to techniques for sustaining and supporting practitioners in the action situation the most eloquently formulated explanations may come to naught. Reynolds (1942, p. 83) said that "when education is oriented to the person who is to learn plus the situation to be mastered, there is something more to teaching than proving to the learner that one knows the subject." We have all observed practitioners who have more than adequate knowledge and information about professional issues, strategies, techniques, and skills who simply cannot operationalize such knowledge. Knowing "how" represents a trained capacity, a competence, and a potential source of professional influence. Hence a central objective for the social worker as teacher is to help the practitioner to specify and to apply knowledge. Essentially, this objective emphasizes turning knowledge into action.

The second concept is *generalization*. Just as social work practitioners can have an academic knowledge of practice issues, strategies, techniques, and skills without having internalized them, so too practitioners can have professional skills without having knowledge about them. "Knowing how" is not quite enough—professional competence, proficiency, and mastery require being able to comprehend the linkages and generalize about the knowledge on which actions are based. As administrators, supervisors, and consultants, unless we pay attention to helping practitioners conceptualize the patterns of practice issues, their learning may be bound to the specific situations in which the learning took place. We have all observed practitioners who effectively learn to deal with specific situations or content, without being able to either organize their learning conceptually or to transfer it appropriately to other situations or clients. Thus, an equally important objective for the social worker carrying out an educational function is helping the practitioner with the "conceptualization" of practice issues and behaviors. This objective emphasizes practitioners learning to organize practice thinking in a manner conducive to transferability and condensability. Reynolds (1942, p. 81) defines this as the stage of "relative mastery in which one can both understand and control one's activity." Similarly, Bruner (1968, p. 77) refers to this process as "the active pragmatic ideal of leaping the barrier from learning into thinking."

The third concept to be emphasized is *recreating*. Policies, procedures, structures, and practice concepts can be experienced by practitioners as fixed formulations separate from how they evolved and the problems they initially sought to resolve. In supervisory, administrative and consultative practice, we tend to provide practitioners with premature answers, insights, and solutions to their practice dilemmas. While at times helpful, this is often not enough. Practitioners require assistance in restoring the abstraction to its original state and meaning and, essentially, to rediscover it for themselves. This process of discovery and rediscovery requires breaking down a concept, experiencing its personal meaning, and reconceptualizing its implications. Bruner (1968, p. 83) identifies four benefits derived from self-discovery: "(1) the increase in intellectual potency; (2) the shift from extrinsic to intrinsic rewards; (3) the learning of

the heuristics of discovering; and (4) the aid to conserving memory."
Hence, an important task for the social worker as educator is to
structure situations that provide the opportunity to "catch the
point," to experience the "aha," to capture the pattern of relationships and the repetitions of behavior. To capture the living character
of an abstraction by personally discovering its meaning for oneself
is to indeed understand it (Dewey, 1966, pp. 11–12).

The fourth concept is *peer learning*. Cognitive skills can be
stimulated and reinforced through peer learning. Workers and/or
students will be better able to learn, to think, and to venture into
new practice or theoretical possibilities when they have been involved in an active, cooperative, educational process. Thus an important objective is to generate a group learning climate conducive
to the interactional processes of mutual problem solving and aid.
Emphasis on the usefulness of mutual problem solving and aid is
particularly relevant where staff have a common relationship to the
work to be done. Group teaching and learning must be seen as a
means to acquiring knowledge and skill and not, as is sometimes
the case, as a reified end in itself. People do not simply "learn by
doing" or by participating in group discussions; rather, the structure
and quality of these exchanges is significant. Thus, it is extremely
important to structure and to define the boundaries within which
the interaction with each other and the subject takes place.

The fifth, and last, concept is that of the *role model*. The
social work supervisor represents a critical professional role model
for workers. The supervisor's behavior will best demonstrate what
he or she hopes will be learned by the supervisee. Workers are
particularly influenced by a superior who demonstrates skill in
practice, maintains high standards, and shows excitement, curiosity,
and openness to differing perspectives and possibilities. What effective supervisors "say to do" needs to be congruent with what they
themselves "do." In any case, supervisors must maintain a distinction between how much they know and how much they tell. Finally,
what brings it all together is a faith demonstrated by action that
good professional practice and continuing professional education is
worth all the effort it takes.

The three case illustrations that follow, the first two from
individual supervisory conferences about group records and the third

from a group supervisory session, show the supervisor as educator helping workers with several practice dilemmas.

In the first illustration, the supervisor became concerned about a worker's lack of spontaneity and immobilization in the face of anticipated loss of control. Through prior conferences, the supervisor became aware that the worker's translation of concepts into actions was rather stilted and intellectualized. Consequently in preparing for this conference, he particularly considered the importance of helping the worker to "experience" relevant practice concepts and to operationalize them. The worker's records were reviewed with an eye toward understanding how the worker might have experienced client contacts. Care was taken not to mark up the margins with supervisor comments and criticisms so that the conference could more fully reflect the worker's concerns and self-defined learning needs.

The record excerpt that is pertinent to the conference and that follows is from a first group meeting for mothers. After some discussion about group purpose and expectations, one member suddenly got up and decided to leave the meeting.

> Mrs. W. announced that she had to leave. She said, "I have to go now, my ride is waiting outside, my kids will be home soon, and my husband doesn't know I'm here." I was dumbfounded by this, knowing that this wasn't true. Mrs. Y. responded, "Your house and them kids can wait. I'm not a slave to my house. . . ." Mrs. A. suggested, "It's probably time for your kids to take some responsibility." I mirrored, "Mrs. W., your ride is waiting outside and you feel you have to go." She became quite upset, wringing her hands and exclaiming— "You can't keep me here, I have other things to do. . . ." I said that if her ride was waiting outside she had to go. As she left, I felt my whole meeting left with her. I came back to the group, sat down, and was dumbfounded about what to do. I sat stunned and remarked, "I guess she had to go."

In supervisory conferences, the worker would routinely ask for the supervisor's assessment of his practice. When this was given, he often accepted it passively and at times antagonistically. In this conference, we decided to structure and recreate this episode with the worker, hoping he would operationalize his own knowledge and experiences, and conceptualize his own learning.

> Mr. A. asked for my assessment of the situation of Mrs. W. leaving the meeting. I responded that I'd like to work a little differently, and help him explore the situation himself. I suggested we begin by trying to understand Mrs. W.'s feelings. Mr. A. responded that she seemed quite anxious and upset, perhaps feeling ignored by other members and by him. He didn't know what to say to her when she informed the group of her intention to leave. This time I didn't tell him what he could have done, rather I reflected that he seemed to freeze. He replied, "Yes, she was lying to the group; she knew how long the meeting was going to last; I didn't know what to say." I commented that I could see he had trouble with this. He responded with anger, "Look, I have no right to keep this lady—don't you understand?" I suggested that we try again to go back into the experience. I dramatized, "Here we are in this group, it's the first meeting, people are working on purpose, getting connected, and there's this one lady—she's having trouble—she's not clear about what's going on—she's not sure if anyone notices her, and finally, she gets up and walks out. At that moment, what were you thinking and feeling—tell me from your shoes?" He responded that he found himself overwhelmed—kind of immobilized. I asked what was immobilizing him— what was going on inside of him. He exclaimed, "Anger! I was becoming more and more upset and angrier and angrier." I gently asked, "Angry about what?" He continued, "Well, I felt angry with myself because I had ignored her—I felt her leaving was somehow my fault— my failure; I felt angry at her for making me feel this way." He sat silently awaiting my reaction. I credited his ability to recreate what he was thinking and feeling. I suggested that we try to role play—make believe he had another chance—and asked how might he try to use his emotions—his insights at that moment. In the role play, as Mrs. W. prepares to leave, he responded, "Mrs. W.,

you're very upset right now and I'm upset also—I realize that perhaps I haven't paid enough attention to you— please don't leave—stay, let's try to talk about it." He was stunned and excited to gain understanding into his client's needs and to learn to respond with caring and spontaneity. He commented, "This is what you have been trying to get across to me—up to now it's been a vague concept—now I can use it. Now I understand how my reactions affect my practice and how I can use myself more helpfully."

Through structuring and recreating experience and through role rehearsal for a future similar occurrence, the supervisor operationalized an important concept, helping the worker to "discover" it and to be able to generalize from it. The worker's energy is harnessed for the learning-service process rather than for warding off supervisory criticisms. The worker was learning how to do and how to add up the meaning of the experience. Abstractions took on personal meaning. They became his.

In the second illustration, we see the supervisor trying to maintain an integrating balance between content and process and to develop an understanding of the dynamic interrelations between "knowing," "feeling," and "doing." Through it all, the worker's technical competence in executing his tasks remains the major criterion for assessing effectiveness. Whether or not we make such judgments, clients certainly do. They experience the worker's actions, behavior, and skill in providing service, not what the worker knows or believes. This emphasis on the primacy of skill requires that the supervisor transmit his own knowledge and insight into relevant helping actions. The supervisor has to show in his own actions what he is teaching. This requires integrating and applying a complex variety of educational, administrative, and helping skills.

R. came in at 1:00 P.M. and seemed worried. She stated that she was worried about her relatives' group. She didn't feel helpful, involved, or connected. She said loudly, "I just don't know what to do; I am at the end of my rope." (In previous conferences, I found myself either becoming overwhelmed by her despair and making psychological interpretations, prematurely reassuring her, or directly solving her concerns. I was determined to help her begin to assume greater responsibility for various practice binds.) I said, gently but firmly, "In our first few conferences, we haven't looked at your records; you have a lot of material, let's look at your concerns *more specifically*—why don't you *begin reading the record*." She hesitated, stating that parts were left out and the recording wasn't really accurate about what happened, she forgets to record important things. I said, firmly but gently again, that she had recorded a lot of material—*we should look at what was in there before we learned about what wasn't,* and again asked her to begin reading. She paused, looked at me, and I encouraged her to begin. She shook her head in agreement and began to read clearly. She read the contracting at the beginning of the group and said that she wondered, is it OK? *I asked her what she thought.* She responded that her efforts were very specific, but she did talk too much. She thought some more and continued that she did get what she wanted and the people seemed to dig into their concerns right at the beginning. I added that *I thought that her being very specific about many of their concerns certainly helped them make a beginning.*

The supervisor's effort to eschew previous psychologizing about the worker's problem or offer immediate reassurances is shown by the demand for focus, by the clarification of boundaries, and by encouragement of the worker to examine her own practice. The worker then begins to assume greater responsibility for her own learning. The supervisor's emphasis on a line-by-line examination of the record material sets the terms of their exchange and keeps the work specific, concrete, and operational. As the conference continues, the worker becomes increasingly free in directing her own inquiry:

We got to the part of the record where one relative began talking about problems with unexpected bowel movements with the patient at home. The relative asked R. a question to which she didn't know the answer. R.

offered to invite a doctor to the next group meeting. She read on, but I stopped her and said, "*I feel that you have missed the relative's concerns.* Let's go back into the experience. What were your feelings at that moment?" She began to laugh uncomfortably and spoke about the whole bowel movement business making her uncomfortable. I asked her, "What did you feel at that moment?" After a pause, she responded that at that moment she didn't really want to listen or get too closely involved with the relatives *re* giving patient digitalis. I responded that I could understand and *suggested that she might have felt* hopeless—"like what good is talking about these things going to do?" She agreed, describing her anxiety and a sense of being trapped by it. After having her *assume the role* of the relative and obtain a "feel" for the specific underlying concerns, we *role played* different ways in which she might have reached for the member's concerns. She particularly liked her idea of reflecting the member's concern to the group, asking whether anyone else had similar concerns or experiences. *I found myself being caught in her excitement* as we both threw ourselves into the role playing. R. searched the record for other places where she disconnected and suggested a doctor to "explain" the reasons behind problems; for example, bowel movements, catheter, sex. She exclaimed, "Wow, I see how I ran away—that was really scary, but I do sense how I will do it differently next time." This felt good to me. I realized that my previous conference in which I *lectured or solved questions must have been experienced by R. as real aggressivity, an assault, rather than what I had intended, a giving of my expertise* [Gitterman, 1972, p. 37].

In this record, the supervisor helps the worker reenact the situation that she evaded, rather than discussing it abstractly. The reconstruction of experience provides the opportunity for both supervisor and worker to struggle to integrate the logical and psychological, the substance and the feeling. At the same time, the difficulties in the worker's practice became partialized into more manageable segments and then generalized into more meaningful patterns. Finally, the supervisor acts like and is the kind of professional person he is trying to help the worker become.

In the third illustration, the supervisor is concerned about the mechanistic quality of the staffs' interventions. In attempting to introduce and socialize untrained staff to professional norms and discipline, the supervisor begins to observe an attenuation or constriction of natural creativity and understanding. In response, the supervisor structures a group session to focus on the "art" in social work practice.

> After several presentations, I asked them what "skills" meant to them. Shirley responded that it was what you did, the offering of concrete assistance. Rose identified awareness. I inquired into the relationship between self-insight and skills. Rose and Mark responded that self-awareness had to be turned into actions. Debby elaborated the theme further, identifying the worker's professional disciplined use of self—the capacity to control self—to separate self from the client and the helping process. Gabe described the ability to transfer a conceptual skill to new situations. I requested examples of their efforts to help. Mark identified his empathy for an ADC client. When the client shared how her baby died, Mark responded, "I know you must feel terrible." Even though his affect was totally bland, Diane credited Mark for his "verbalizing the client's feeling." Rose also supported his empathy, suggesting he demonstrate an "interest and concern." Since they continued to offer conceptual labels, I asked them to *role play* the situation. Mark repeated his interaction with a student volunteer. I asked the group members to experience being the client in the situation as Mark responded—"I know that you must feel terrible." This time they "heard" his blandness; a painful silence followed. I asked Mark to go back *into the experience,* "What did he feel when the client shared her tragedy?" He exclaimed, "I felt outraged, horrified—as if the whole roof caved in on her." In reaching for the others' reactions, they identified the difference between Mark's affectual inner response and his detached professional response.

They lit up. Jennifer was struck by how the professional effort was experienced as "empty words," while his inner reaction [was experienced as] a sensitive human response. This led into a discussion of their desire to "say the right thing," stifling their creativity and humaneness. Numerous examples were offered, differentiating the "book" and the "person" skills. Diane identified the difficulties in learning to be a good practitioner: "To be in, but outside of the process; to be involved, but to be detached; to be spontaneous, but to be disciplined." Bill suggested that it felt "schizy," trying to feel a client's pain, but remaining distant. I asked if others experienced this "schizy" feeling. Numerous examples were offered. They were helping each other very nicely to identify the "art-science" dimensions. I reached for Phil, who seemed to be working on something. He responded, "You have been helping us to learn the conceptual skills—to know what to do, when to do it, and how to do it. This is the first step—now we have to learn to connect these skills with our own personalities." I responded, "Yes, with your own unique personal styles—with the artist in each of you." Carl exclaimed, "This is the crux of the challenge, integrating me with the skills—it sounds impossible." Paul added, "I'm beginning to realize that I have to own these skills—not just learn them—they have to become part of each of us." Carl analogized their learning experience to an "uncut diamond . . . it possesses natural qualities. These natural qualities are its preciousness, but it needs to be shaped, the edges smoothened and polished." They became intrigued by this analogy and applied it further.

What the supervisor might have been thinking about and what the authors would like to impute to the supervisor goes something like this: Theory is to help classify and organize knowledge. Inexperienced practitioners tend to "learn" theory by adopting simple, linear, cause-effect relationships. But human experience and social reality are characterized by reciprocal and mutual interdependence of events. Thus we have to help workers appreciate the complex interdependence of time, people, and situations. Also, while present human behavior is influenced by the past, it is not wholly determined by it nor is it only a futile imitation of the past.

What the supervisor actually did in the last illustration was to help the staff group operationalize an abstraction and discover its fuller meaning by structuring and recreating an essential practice task. In capturing the art-science dimension of professional practice, the untrained staff learned a lesson readily applicable to a variety of situations. The supervisor's application of educational concepts to group process facilitated problem solving and mutual aid. (For elaboration of the purposes and uses of group supervision, see Abels, 1970; Getzel, Goldberg, and Salmon, 1971; Kaslow, 1972.) Group process, however, has to be a means to meeting substantive service needs and requirements. The social worker as educator focuses the interactional process on the acquisition of substantive knowledge and skills. This requires engagement in a structured activity rather than being caught up only in the process itself. We cannot afford to permit the contemporary tendency to emphasize self-defined need for self-expression and self-actualization to transcend the content to be mastered or the tasks at hand that need accomplishment. The process of education must not be removed from the substance of education. Group or individual conferences that emphasize such preoccupations may result in feelings of participant satisfaction and understandably so, as it is usually more interesting to discuss one's own feelings than what exists "out there." Real learning takes place when the interaction or process is essentially a structured and goal-directed activity in pursuit of substance and competence.

CHAPTER 6

Training of
Lay Helpers

Willard C. Richan

In the past decade, professions have passed through a crisis of demystification. Consumers have been questioning the product they have received, whether from schoolteachers or psychiatrists, with unprecedented vigor. The lofty positions of lawyers and physicians have been eroded by the post-Watergate cynicism and by Medicaid scandals. The drastic increase in medical malpractice suits has affected physicians' willingness to intervene medically and led some to consider giving up the field entirely. And more and more the public has been turning to a variety of lay helpers[1] (paraprofessionals) and self-help techniques (Bott, 1971; Collins and Pancoast, 1976; Hertz, 1972).

The movement to lay helpers has been greatly accelerated by the critical shortage of professional helpers (U.S. Task Force on

Social Work Education and Manpower, 1965; Levine, 1966) and, especially in the late 1960s, a tendency to glamorize indigenous paraprofessionals in some fields (Hallowitz, 1969; Specht, 1972). More recently, cost-conscious government agencies have sought to lower the credentialing requirements for positions that traditionally have been professional (Wiseman and Silverman, 1974). While some of the factors that have contributed to the expanded use of lay helpers have been transitory, the movement itself is not (Gartner, Nixon, and Riessman, 1973). The helping professions will weather the transition successfully to the extent that they give up the notion that all intervention in serious human problems requires the laying on of professionally credentialed hands and look instead to the important business of helping the lay helpers do an effective job.

Professional Intervention in Human Affairs

It is the business of the human services to intervene in ongoing social systems. They thus must disrupt systems in order to enhance their functioning. So the potential helping function carries with it certain risks. The object, then, is to maximize the potential for helping and minimize the risks of harming the people in need of help. Traditionally, the professions have had certain well-defined ways of serving these two functions.

The essence of professionalism is special expertise, based on abstract principles selectively applied to concrete problems (Goode, 1965). Because the laity does not share this special expertise, the professional community seeks a monopoly over the given practice in order to protect the public against the unqualified. The vulnerability of clientele, who are expected to cooperate in the professional relationship and who lack the special knowledge required to evaluate the quality of practice, requires that professionals be bound by professional discipline. Because of the potential for exploitation of the clientele and more generally the public, who also lack the special knowledge with which to evaluate, the professional monopoly is expected to be governed by a service, as opposed to a commercial, orientation. The abstract nature of the basic knowledge and the need to develop special skills and a disciplined approach to clientele require an extended period of professional education, a major part of which takes place in a university setting (Wilensky and Lebeaux, 1958).

All of the foregoing observations on professionalism are based on an ideal conception. In reality, every one of these principles has been violated to a greater or lesser degree by all professions. Through licensure, physicians achieved a monopoly throughout the United States well before they had anything approaching special expertise based on abstract principles as a standard in most medical colleges (Flexner, 1910). Long after lawyers had achieved a monopoly, many were being trained by "reading law" in the offices of practicing attorneys. Social work and psychology, on the other hand, have striven to achieve academic standards of professionalism in the absence of a monopoly. The difference between fee-charging practices in many professions and commercial profit-making activity in business is slight, both as to spirit and consequences for the practitioner.

But the ideal image provides a standard against which to measure professional practices. More to the point in this discussion, it helps illuminate the differences between professional socialization and the training of lay helpers.

The Lay Helper

In considering the lay helper, it is important to get away from thinking of this person as simply a watered-down professional helper (Richan, 1972; Pearl and Riessman, 1965). Especially in the current mood of skepticism about professionals, the lay helper can perform a vital function in reaching and relating to populations that otherwise would remain inaccessible.

As a general principle, the lay helper does not need a high degree of skill in handling abstract concepts. In fact, major emphasis on such skill in the socializing process can be dysfunctional, because it may create a social distance barrier between lay helper and helpee,[2] or at the very least, providing a frustrating learning experience for many lay helpers.

Expectations for professional and lay helpers differ in terms of orientation to their work and their clients. Lay helpers are less in a position to control the helping relationship or exploit the client than are professionals. This being so, there does not need to be the same degree of internalized discipline in the lay helper's approach to the helping process, and he or she can thus be more spontaneous and personal in giving help.

Yet clearly there are serious risks involved in intervention in other people's lives by persons without professional training. Inadvertently, through ignorance or unrecognized feelings, the lay-person may do great harm in the guise of helping. One manifestation of the current reaction against professionals is an array of self-help books and programs that encourage persons of various ages and conditions to express themselves more freely, to abandon old behavioral inhibitions, and get in touch with their true feelings and that are based on theories and approaches of dubious quality or on no theory other than the intuition of the helper. The fact that the established professions have not been able to demonstrate the effectiveness of their own approaches to any great degree makes these new approaches more plausible.

The human service professions should seek to introduce order and rationality into this situation. The traditional means of doing this—namely, monopolization of direct helping roles—is no longer feasible nor desirable. Instead, professionals have a vitally important role in developing the capacity of lay helpers through training and providing supervisory and consultative support to their ongoing efforts.

Since professionalism rests on special expertise that is not shared by the laity, there is a strong temptation to try to "make over" helpers in the professional image. But this can lead to the eradication of natural gifts in the lay helper that do not happen to conform to the professional model. The primary function of the enabler[3] is to bring out and capitalize on those assets that the lay helper already possesses. This takes a high degree of flexibility on the part of the professional, especially when the lay helper's social class and cultural background lead to a personal style that runs counter to traditional professional notions of "normal" (that is, middle-class) behavior. For example, the person who is loud or expresses anger easily or engages in a lot of physical contact with consumers may be more "real," and therefore more trustworthy, in the eyes of clients than the more restrained professional. The helper who seems too nosey, protective, exuberant, or sentimental may likewise convey a sense of warmth that those in need of succor find lacking in professionals. The risk that such spontaneous and personal tendencies will be harmful to clients is lessened by the fact that, unlike professionals, the lay helpers have less power in the relationship; the clients approach them more as equals than as subordinates. Obviously, there are exceptions to this general rule, and special care must be taken to protect highly vulnerable clients, such as young children or the mentally retarded (Richan, 1961).

The adult lay helper will already have a well-developed repertoire of responses and styles of interaction that work reasonably well most of the time. But the helping role makes special demands that require the development of new skills and understanding. In particular, two major limitations need to be overcome: the tendency for responses to be geared primarily to meeting the helper's own personal needs and the tendency to rely on a few favorite ways of responding. Therefore, *training and supervision need to be directed to increasing the helper's ability to empathize and to broadening his or her response repertoire.*

Individuals vary in their capacity to empathize. The selection process should ensure that lay helpers rate relatively high on this dimension to start with (Brager, 1965; Grosser, Henry and Kelly, 1969). The task of the professional is to build on this natural tendency by sensitizing the helper to the impact of events on the client. Role playing is an excellent technique for helping the worker put him- or herself in the place of the client. It can be used either in a group or in one-to-one contact. The role-playing situation can be introduced naturally and without elaborate advance preparation. For example, "You say that Charlie kept switching the subject to his wife, when you were trying to show him about filling out the food stamp application. OK, let's pretend you're Charlie and I'm you. Show me what he was doing."

After going through this process for a while, the roles can be reversed, with the professional or other workers assuming the role of Charlie. In such exercises, helpers need ample opportunity to discuss what they thought was taking place. The discussion should be kept at the level at which the lay helper is going to apply it, not generalized to too high a level of abstraction. While role-playing

exercises of this kind also give the enabler an opportunity to demonstrate the helping role, care should be taken not to present a
professionalized model that is not appropriate. There is a natural
tendency of lay helpers to try to imitate professional behavior
(Richan, 1972).

There are several reasons why lay helpers tend to rely on a
few well-chosen ways of operating. The response-for-all-occasions
problem in part grows out of a tendency to stereotype, to see different situations as the same. In part it is a result of simple inertia—
it is easier to use the familiar than to learn something new. And in
part it comes from insecurity about one's ability to handle the
situation.

Stereotyping of situations can best be dealt with by getting
workers to question their original perceptions and assumptions. The
trainer or supervisor can aid this process by injecting his or her own
questions into the discussion, as long as an inquisitorial or "examination" atmosphere is avoided. It is better that the new insights come
from the lay helper's own experience than be supplied by the professional, even if the results at the time seem limited or mistaken.
The intent is not simply to create a different perspective on the
situation at hand but, more important, to enhance the general
versatility and openness of worker perceptions.

There are a number of techniques for getting helpers to
break out of fixed modes of handling situations. Brainstorming is
an excellent device for helping groups to expand the response
repertoire. A member of the group presents a problem to which a
solution is needed. The group then runs out as many solutions as it
can think of. No attempt is made in this rapid-fire process to weigh
the merits of any one answer. The more spontaneous and "far out"
the range of ideas, the better. This approach helps a group avoid
the common tendency to write off certain approaches without really
considering them. Not only does this technique open up new possibilities for dealing with the problem under consideration, but it
also helps group members begin to think about solutions in a
different way.

Once the group has exhausted the list of possible solutions,
either the whole group or the problem presenter then narrows down
the list by eliminating those ideas that are patently impossible.

Eventually, the one or two most viable solutions remain. The group then repeats the brainstorming process, this time listing different strategies for achieving the solution. Again, the problem presenter, with the help of the group, eliminates strategies that are not feasible. The remaining ones are then developed into a set of sequential steps.

Almost invariably, two things happen to groups that go through this kind of brainstorming process. One is that their horizons have expanded far beyond what they were at the outset. The other is that the group members have a sense of accomplishment, and the problem presenter has a new sense of optimism and confidence. This latter effect is directly related to the third factor in the problem of the narrow response repertoire, the feeling of insecurity about one's ability.

The lack of self-confidence of the lay helper is accentuated by the presence of professionals. It can create a vicious circle, in which, as the worker becomes more limited in his or her response to situations, the professional tries to compensate by introducing more ideas. Very often the upshot is a passive lay helper who either mechanically plugs in what is proposed or else ignores the advice— in either case a frustrating experience for both teacher and learner. This does not mean leaving the lay helper where one finds him or her. Confidence is gained by mastering new tasks, not by standing still.

The concept is that of an active learner, one who participates fully in the developmental process. This approach to learning is facilitated by the fact the expertise of the lay helper is on the level of experience, not at higher levels of abstraction. Whether individually or in groups, lay workers take major responsibility for setting their learning objectives as well as engaging fully in the learning process itself. The "agenda" evolves out of the problems workers encounter in the helping process. A group of peers can aid one another both in setting objectives and achieving them. It is essential that a supportive atmosphere be established in such groups so that they build confidence rather than demoralize. This may be difficult to achieve, because of the competitive atmosphere in most work situations, but it can be done.

The term active *learner* suggests someone who acquires new

material. Indeed, there should be no illusion that all wisdom resides in the learners, although together they possess much more, generally, than they are aware of. How can new content be introduced in such a way as to maximize the active participation of learners and enhance their sense of confidence? An important principle is to convert learning tasks into graded experience, so that the learner can begin with a relatively simple task, then move on progressively to more difficult ones. At each stage of the way, as the learner masters a particular task, there is a sense of achievement, so confidence is built on a foundation of actual accomplishment, not false encouragement.

One might begin by encouraging a worker to list all of the problems he or she is experiencing in the helping process. Suppose, for instance, the worker is assigned to help elderly persons obtain health care. The problems encountered in this work are put down:

- I become confused by different procedures in health care facilities.
- I get impatient with older people who cannot understand my directions.
- Hospital and clinic staff do not listen to me, do not respect me.
- I get nervous when talking to doctors and nurses.
- I get mad at clients who refuse to go to the hospital once I've made an appointment for them.

The problems fall into three basic categories: (1) handling procedures and forms, (2) working with clients, and (3) dealing with health care personnel. The worker decides to start by working on Item 1, handling procedures and forms, deferring Item 3, the most formidable, until last. The professional may disagree with this particular order of priority, but goes along with the worker's ordering.

The helper and the enabler then identify all of the tasks in the chosen category that give the helper trouble. The professional pushes for as much specificity as possible. For instance, it turns out that only certain forms are difficult, while others are not; the procedures in some health care facilities are more confusing than those in other facilities; and so on. Once the full array of tasks is identified, the worker and enabler order them in terms of degree of difficulty. For this particular worker, the problems of filling out forms are placed at the head of the list. These, then, should be the focus of their beginning work together as they concentrate on the forms that are only moderately difficult.

As the worker comes to master the easier forms, the achievement is recognized, and he or she goes on to progressively more challenging ones. The pace at which this happens is determined jointly with the professional. At points along the way, worker and enabler review progress, so that the worker is aware of where he or she has come.

When the focus shifts to more complex areas, such as those involving interpersonal relations, the learning may involve role playing. For instance, the worker might take the role of a clinic nurse, and the professional might take the role of the worker. An essential component of such learning is an opportunity for the worker to discuss his or her reactions to these situations.

It is important for the trainer to keep clear the objectives of such learning activity. The purpose is neither to aid the worker in general interpersonal relationships nor to teach him or her to behave professionally. The skill in dealing with hospital personnel is taught in order to accomplish work tasks—as a lay helper—more effectively.

The illustration used here is of a particular kind of helper and a one-to-one training or supervising relationship. But the underlying principles would apply equally to groups of workers in a variety of settings. In the case of the group, each member would develop a learning agenda, with the aid of the peers, and the learning process would involve the total group as well as the enabler.

A role that lay helpers are frequently called on to play is that of advocate—champion of an aggrieved party. And encounters with persons in authority or those with professional status can be especially threatening to lay helpers' self-confidence. Thus development of the ability to be assertive in appropriate ways may be particularly important. Needless to say, the emphasis is on *appropriate;* helpers need to know how to make their point without gratuitously putting down a person or turning every encounter into a major confrontation. Here the principle of graded steps, starting with the least difficult and working up gradually, is useful. Fensterheim and Baer (1975) offer a large number of exercises for assertiveness training in different contexts.

Such aids should be used selectively and with clear understanding of the objectives, since this material is written primarily in terms of protecting one's own interests, and some of it borders on the downright manipulative. While it is true that one needs to be able to make demands in one's own behalf in order to be able to act in another person's interest, it is essential that the worker understand the difference between these two and understand where the priorities lie in the helping role.

Generally, paraprofessionals are called upon to deal with situational problems and offer concrete services or crisis intervention aid. Rarely do they assume therapeutic roles, although how they help clients resolve tangible problems can have therapeutic benefits. Some of the capacities in which they serve are: child care workers, psychiatric aides, correctional officers, case aides in public welfare agencies, advocates regarding evictions or turning off utilities for lack of payment, and mediating neighborhood and family quarrels. If assigned to help a retardate, they might engage in tutoring, chauffeuring, or arranging residential or day care services or all three.

The Use of Information in the Enabling Process

Many kinds of specific information are needed in the helping process, so the imparting of information to the lay helper is a key function of the professional. The relevance of such knowledge to the work of the helper needs to be made clear at every step of the way. To the extent that it can be applied immediately in action, it will have the greatest meaning to the worker. Three types of information are discussed: resource information, knowledge of human functioning, and the underlying value orientations of the helping process.

Resources. Many lay helpers have exceedingly limited knowledge of relevant resources for referrals. This kind of information includes not only identification of service providers and formally stated functions but also strategic contacts in an organization and unofficial ways of getting a positive response from the service source. For example, it may be far more valuable for the person who wants access to a particular service to know how to get to the local political leader than to know the formal procedures for intake. Given the variety of human ills with which lay helpers are likely to be involved, the potential range and volume of such information is virtually unlimited.

Information regarding resources in the community is nobody's monopoly. Lay helpers may have information of which professionals are unaware, so the sharing of resource information is a mutual process between lay and professional workers.

Knowledge of Human Functioning. The hallmark of professional helpers is their sophistication about human functioning, drawn from a range of psychological and social theories. Lay helpers should not be expected to develop this kind of sophistication. However, there are vital areas of information that they need. They should become knowledgeable about signs of personal malfunctioning such as major physical ailments, serious psychological disorders, and child abuse. They need to learn the symptomatology without becoming diagnosticians regarding the underlying processes.

Secondly, greater understanding of human functioning can help to enhance workers' skill in dealing with clients and others. To the extent that such knowledge relates to their previous experience and can be applied directly to their work, it will have the most meaning to the lay helpers. This sort of knowledge can come from many sources—pamphlets and bulletins, outside resources persons, and the enabler's own store of knowledge.

Humanistic Values. The social and political attitudes of lay helpers, especially those from low-income and working-class backgrounds, sometimes shock members of human service professions, which are identified with liberal, humanistic values. Lay helpers may sound excessively moralistic, punitive, or politically conservative. In considering how and how much to get involved in trying to influence such attitudes, the professional needs to weigh the degree to which such views affect the ability of the helper to function. Conceivably, for example, an archconservative in the political arena could provide supportive help to a retardate or a homebound octogenarian. But, in many instances, the values expressed by a lay helper will indeed raise questions about his or her ability to play a constructive role.

A peer group is a useful means of dealing with workers'

values and attitudes. Through the group process, workers can be helped to reexamine their value assumptions. Much of what was said earlier regarding fixed perceptions and fixed responses in the work situation applies to the area of values and attitudes as well.

At times lay helpers are recruited from community constituencies that are explicitly hostile to the service delivery system itself. In fact, one of the purposes for using such helpers may be to establish better communication between the community and the agency (Richan, 1972). Assuming that ties with the community are one of the key assets that lay helpers bring to the situation, it may be important not to tamper too freely with their outlook, lest they become alienated from the community. Hopefully the human service professionals in the system can reexamine their own assumptions and learn from the lay helpers and their constituency.

One principle of professional helping is important enough to warrant special attention: confidentiality. It is both central to professionalism and often poorly understood by laypersons. In their open, spontaneous, and personal involvement with clients, lay helpers are likely to use personal information about clients for their own ends or simply engage in idle gossip unless trained not to. They may be under considerable pressure from friends and neighbors to share information. The fact that clients sometimes do not object to such sharing can be confusing for the worker. The message should be clear and unequivocal: The client's privacy must be protected; any exceptions to that rule—such as the use of information as part of the service function—should be just as clearly specified. And the lay helper needs to know the consequences of violating the rule. What if the worker wants to withhold information that the agency wants? Here judgment must be exercised; the risks entailed in gaps in information must be balanced against the risk of consumers' loss of trust in the helper.

Thus far we have considered general principles that apply to both modes of enabling, training and supervision. We now consider the distinctive characteristics of each mode separately.

Training Lay Helpers

The term *training* is used here to refer to a planned process, outside of ongoing work activities, aimed at enhancing work skills.

The phrase "outside of ongoing work activities" is important because of the tendency for work demands to usurp the on-site training process. In order to keep training content relevant to the work experience, the format should consist of relatively short-term sequences arranged on an as-needed basis and focused on specific work-related problems.

Especially when there is considerable work pressure, workers may consider training as an intrusion that takes them away from more vital tasks. It is therefore desirable that trainees commit themselves to a given period of training beforehand. The use of a *learning contract* is one way to clarify the commitment of both trainee and trainer. Obviously, this requires a spirit of mutuality and full participation of the trainees in defining goals. The contract also gives the parties a set of criteria against which to gauge progress in the course of training.

The value of the peer group of learners has been stressed. Lay workers have a particular need for this sort of group milieu because they lack support from a professional community. The informal and participatory enabling process that has been spelled out thus far can accelerate the development of group solidarity. When group members are relative strangers to one another, this process may be enhanced by the use of a range of techniques. The simplest is to subdivide a larger group into small subunits, even down to two and three persons per subunit. The initial awkwardness of a group can often be dispelled by the introduction of a small amount of structure, enough to channel people's energy without restricting communication. To cite a minor problem, the tension aroused for group members when they are asked to introduce themselves to the rest of the group is not a major crisis, but often part of the purpose is lost, since members may be so preoccupied with what they themselves are going to say that they fail to listen to one another. A simple device for getting around this is to pair members off and have the two members of each pair engage in informal discussion with one another; each member of the pair then introduces the partner to the rest of the group.

There is a wide range of simple exercises that may facilitate group development as well as the learning process itself. Napier and Gershenfeld (1973) and Pfeiffer and Jones (1974), for instance, describe many such interactional experiences. Trainers are some-

times reluctant to "play games" with trainees, but experience with
adult groups of many kinds suggests that such exercises are generally
quite acceptable and need not be viewed as excessively artificial.
It is important that the trainer be prepared to adapt this kind of
learning experience to the particular purposes of the occasion and
not mechanically plug in material that is out of context. Examples
of such exercises include presentation of anecdotal case material,
with trainees asked to speculate as to what happened next; mock
encounters with professionals, in which body movement is the only
kind of communication allowed; exercises in observation of the
behavior of others; and simulated decision-making situations in
which pennies are allocated to various purposes or members of the
group. Such activities can provide rich stimuli for group interaction
around learning objectives. The possibilities are limited only by the
imagination of trainer and trainees. Because some of these exercises
are one or two steps removed from the actual work situation, it is
vital that trainees understand their intent.

Supervising Lay Helpers

Like training, supervision has elements of staff development.
Unlike training, it involves a control function. And, instead of being
a distinct and separate set of activities, it is an inherent and ongoing
part of the work situation. The developmental side of supervision
can be looked on as creation of conditions in which the lay helper
can learn. It involves the total work experience and the total work
environment.

In assessing developmental needs and resources, the supervisor considers all of those forces that influence the working behavior
of the lay helper: the official expectations of the human service
system; the unofficial norms and expectations of various internal
subsystems, including peers; the resources available inside and outside of the human service system; the past accumulation of experiences on which the lay helper draws; and the supports and expectations in the community.

By conceptualizing the lay helper's needs and resources in
terms of all relevant influences, the supervisor can get away from
trying to be the sole influence on the helper. Together they can

work out plans for enlisting various elements in the environment, such as special experts and peer workers, in the developmental task.

The control function in supervision of lay helpers differs from that for professional helpers. By definition, professionalization involves the internalization of values and constraints, so that the professional helper operates in a disciplined manner that is not dependent on external elements. Lay helpers derive their sense of responsibility to helpees from a variety of sources—personal humanitarian commitment, agency rules and expectations, peer pressure, and community influences. The way in which this sense of responsibility is translated into behavior is less predictable in the case of lay helpers; thus there are special risks involved in their use. It is necessary, therefore, that the human service system in which the lay helper operates make its own expectations very clear and that these be presented by the supervisor in a consistent manner.

We must recognize the limitations on the wisdom of the human service professionals and the organizations in which they function. A unilateral control relationship in which the organization is assumed to be right and strict compliance is demanded of lay helpers may not only alienate the helpers but may also restrict the vision of the organization and its professionals. One of the significant advantages that lay helpers can bring to the human services is a fresh view of the world outside. This is especially so when these helpers come from socioeconomic strata that are different from those predominating in the agency's professional staff. Thus, just as in the case of the developmental function, the control function with lay helpers calls for a high degree of openness. Behavior that deviates from the rules of a system may point to the need to reassess the rules of the system.

There is no illusion that the difference in outlook between human service organizations and their professional helpers, on the one side, and lay helpers, on the other, is a contest among equals. The organized human services have the resources, the public sanction, and the ability to concert their energies in a way that is impossible for the lay helpers. And, not incidentally, professionals have an accumulation of experience on which to draw. Lay helpers are capable of doing harm through ineptness and veniality, and it is the responsibility of the professionals, insofar as they are capable, to see to it that this does not happen. But in meeting this responsibility, professionals have to be mindful of some built-in problems in the delivery of human services.

The relationship of an organization to its lay helpers is especially vulnerable to a high degree of regimentation, because lay helpers lack internalized professional discipline. As one considers the range of human service organizations, many of which employ a predominantly nonprofessional work force, one finds they are characterized by excessive bureaucratic controls. The lay helper poses a dilemma for the organization, particularly as highly vulnerable clientele are involved. But the risks of allowing the exercise of the lay helper's own intuition are probably greatly exaggerated, while the risk of having the regimented helper place the helpee under similar constraints—to say nothing of the generally dehumanizing climate generated under such circumstances—tends to be overlooked.

Reference was made earlier to the use of contracts and of peer groups in the training process. These tools are also valuable in the supervisory relationship, for both the developmental and control functions. Perhaps more important than the potential of the contract for "legally" binding the parties to the conditions of the agreement is the sense of commitment that psychologically binds the parties to the relationship. What is referred to here as a "contract" is different from a formal document specifying the terms of employment. Instead, it is an agreement that is entered into jointly by the helper and the supervisor and may carry with it no official sanctioning power.

Summary and Conclusion

Professional helpers have special expertise, based on abstract principles selectively applied to concrete situations. They are expected to be disciplined, guided by norms of service, and able to maintain a significant degree of scientific detachment. Not only are lay helpers less in need of these attributes but to impose professional expectations on lay helpers may also lessen their ability to respond freely and spontaneously to need, thus lessening their distinctive value. However, professionals in the human services have an important role in training and supervising lay helpers in order to protect the interests of consumers of service.

The training and supervision of lay helpers need to stress applicability and direct relevance of content to the demands of the work situation. These enabling processes should draw heavily on the experience and insights of the workers themselves. This requires a high degree of flexibility in the trainer or supervisor. The lay helper needs to be actively engaged in expanding his or her range of insights and repertoire of tools and acquire strategic information. The degree to which the professional trainer or supervisor should try to influence the values and attitudes of the lay worker should be related to what is being asked of the worker.

Training is a planned process, outside of ongoing work activity, aimed at enhancing the helper's performance in specific aspects of the work role. It is most effective when it grows out of the emergent needs and concerns of the workers themselves. Supervision is a continuous activity that is an intrinsic part of the work experience. It involves both developmental and control functions.

Historically, professions have sought to establish boundaries around a sector of work and restrict such work to those bearing requisite professional credentials. The practice can be traced back to the medieval craft guilds from which the first professions sprang. With expanding demand for human services of all kinds, some professions have spawned ancillary occupational groups, over which they have maintained tight control. These secondary fields have themselves often become professions or, in the view of some writers, semiprofessions. Meanwhile, growing affluence and complexity in postindustrial societies has led to a sharply rising demand for services of all kinds, especially for human services, and the trend promises to accelerate in the future. This rising demand for services, on the one hand, and the increased availability of people to provide them, on the other, are creating a situation that could rapidly get beyond the control of the organized professional fields. Professions exist in a political environment. They maintain their monopolies at the pleasure of the wider society. There are limits on the degree to which professions can open their own ranks in response to the pressure and still maintain high educational standards. Inevitably, then, professions will have to accommodate themselves to the entry of vast numbers of laypersons into helping roles. The interests of human service organizations, taxpayers and fee payers will all press in this direction. And unions may supplant many professional bodies in many of their proprietary functions.

Insofar as human service professions recognize these trends and act in response to them, they will be able to evolve new roles that can serve to protect the public, just as professional monopolies have sought to do in the past. A field such as social work, which has long been accustomed to utilizing nonprofessionals in many roles, will be in a strategic position to make a valuable contribution to this development. The alternative is to draw ever-higher barriers around an ever-shrinking sector of work.

Notes

1. As used in this chapter, the term *helper* means one who intervenes directly to aid individuals, families, small groups, or local communities to cope with problems of personal functioning, interpersonal relations, or environmental conditions. A *lay helper* is one who has not had formal training in one of the human service professions, that is, nonprofessional or paraprofessional.

2. The terms *helpee, client,* and *consumer* are used interchangeably here.

3. The term *enabler* refers to both trainers and supervisors.

CHAPTER 7

Staff Development for Grant and Proposal Writing

Eugene C. Royster

This chapter is devoted to a discussion of a particular art in the process that has become known as *grantsmanship,* namely the art of proposal writing. The discussion is oriented to the structure of the proposal and to the processes involved in developing a proposal. Through the specifications of the structure and process, guidelines for training of staff in agencies are presented. However, there is no substitute for the actual involvement in the proposal process, and, while the points presented here may act as a guide, one learns this skill primarily by doing. The chapter also argues that proposal writing has other functions for the helping service practitioner and the agency beyond that of obtaining

funds. Proposal writing also serves to focus on the important processes of program planning and evaluation. The following pages
explicate these ideas in great detail with the intent that this chapter
may serve as an elementary handbook for those undertaking staff
training and consultation in this vital area so often neglected in
graduate and professional training programs.

All too often workers in human services areas believe that
their functions are limited to service delivery. They have, as a consequence, neglected such related activities as research, evaluation,
and planning. This is not to suggest that these latter activities have
not been or are not concerns of their training nor a part of their
professional identity (Main, 1971; Shapira, 1971). Rather, activities other than direct service delivery are often viewed as tangential
or secondary. There are, however, a number of reasons why more
members of the helping professions should become concerned with
and involved in the preparation of proposals. The following paragraphs discuss just a few functions of proposals and a few reasons
why greater interest should be accorded proposal writing.

The chief source of program, research, and evaluation
monies is the federal government, although more and more federal
funds today are being channeled into states for distribution to key
program areas. We too often assume that the content and structure
of the various programs come from some mysterious fountain of
knowledge. In reality, the policy and program people in the bureaucratic structure often provide the new ideas and the leadership in
the development of programs. There is a continuous need for interaction between the policy maker and the service deliverer. It is
particularly important that practitioners involve themselves in this
process in order to help the policy maker to ask the "right questions," which form the basis for policy discussions and on which
dollars and energy are eventually expended. The policy makers are
aware of the need for refinement of policy and of the program
options through which policy is implemented. Thus they continue
to question the efficiency and efficacy of programs. It is important,
as a consequence, that the service provider assist not only by offering
their ideas for action but also by asking (or perhaps answering)
the "right" questions. One purpose of proposals is to provide the
questions to broaden our understanding of programmatic systems.
Too often the questions and answers are left to the nonpractitioner,

to the researcher who is concerned but not "on the line." There is a necessary place for such activity, but there is an even more important arena for the involvement of the practitioner and the agency.

It seems also justified that the agency should be involved in this process, since these funds can provide for activities and services above and beyond those which the agency can now provide. The need for expanded services hardly seems to diminish. Therefore, one justification for more involvement by the human service practitioner is to provide better questions to be answered and, perhaps, better answers that more adequately reflect reality. Too often, this reality, how programs operate rather than what the "plan" says, is too far removed from decision makers and researchers.

Proposal Writing as Agency Planning

The essence of the proposal must be to inform the reader, that is, the funding agency, of the specific plans one has for the funds being sought. The proposal is a statement of plan and purpose for that program. In making these explicit for others, the proposal writers are forced to go through a number of important planning steps that will ultimately aid the agency and its personnel in its functioning and programming. Proposal writing provides an opportunity for a review of where the agency and practitioners are and of where they wish to go in the future. Writing the proposal forces the agency to look at its proposed course of action within the context of its history, charter, and functions. The requirements for the writing of a good proposal establish a guide for an overall planning scheme utilizing program and proposal as interdependent elements in the total service delivery system.

The steps in both proposal writing and using the proposal process as a planning guide include the following:

1. *Setting Goals.* Setting goals is the process of placing the agency within the context of the larger community, of establishing the purpose of the organization now and in the future. Goal setting, in this sense, includes the long-range, general statement of purpose (objectives, if you will).
2. *Developing Objectives.* Objectives, as distinct from goals, are specific, time-oriented behaviors, or products of behaviors to be

achieved. A necessary adjunct to their development is the establishment of subobjectives that help to further define the larger objectives and eventually the goals of the organization.

3. *Formulating Action Plans to Achieve the Objectives.* After the objectives have been stated clearly, in measurable terms, then the actions to be taken to achieve each objective can be specified and tied more closely to the objectives. Action plans detail the activities that must be taken to achieve those events that lead to the attainment of objectives. Note, consequently, that this logical framework should include activities (behaviors) and the events (end states) that *build* toward the objective.

4. *Implementation.* Action plans, having been specified, then need to be implemented. Implementation requires extensive planning of time, resources, and personnel. It requires the establishment of criteria against which the performance can be measured and mechanisms to regulate and remediate problems of nonperformance regarding the criteria. This will help not only to ensure that the implementation is geared toward the stated objectives and action plan but also to provide a baseline from which deviations in the approach can be documented. Such documentation is essential if at some future time the program is to be replicated in another site or repeated in the same site.

5. *Evaluation.* Finally, review and evaluation of performance are needed, in order to identify and remedy problems in terms of the established goals and objectives.

This brief summation is not meant as a guide to planning in human service agencies. Rather, it is intended to point out the steps professionals, formally and informally, take in the development and implementation of human service and mental health programs. It also shows the importance of proposal writing as a planning device for agency personnel. Through this process, the agency can, and should, assess itself, its goals, and its future programs.

Proposal Writing as Evaluation Preparation

The complement to proposal writing as a planning process is proposal writing as evaluation preparation. Unfortunately, many agency staff members are afraid of evaluation. They fear that an evaluation will cause them to lose their jobs or to lose the funds for a program. Often, they are afraid that an evaluation will not reflect the "true" purposes or accomplishment of their program and their efforts. Many of their fears are justified. When evaluations are done by "outsiders," the evaluators often do not have the requisite experience or knowledge to perform their task with sensitivity and understanding.

There is a tendency by helping professionals to deny or to forget that there is a need to know how a program works, how it is meeting its stated goals and objectives. In a very real sense, human service personnel make evaluative judgments all the time. If they are to serve their clients and meet the charter of their profession, they must be concerned with how well they and the program are meeting the needs of the persons they serve. However, the times demand a movement away from a dependence solely on subjective evaluations to more objective criteria. Accountability to funding sources and society is essential.

The practitioner should no longer duck the responsibility of the challenge of evaluation. If sensitivity to program conditions is needed, then these workers should help to provide for the definition and measurement of such sensitivity. Their involvement and contributions can be made through the proposal process. The proposal writer, in the setting of objectives, has the opportunity to build that sensitivity of philosophy, training, and experience into a statement of objectives, even into the exposition of what measures will be utilized to evaluate the impact of the agency or program.

While it is important to provide the evaluation of the overall impact of a program (that is, a summative evaluation), it is as crucial for the agency to provide a formative evaluation. (For a discussion of types of evaluation see Wholey, 1970.) In the latter, the program is evaluated at stages during its operations, and feedback is provided to improve performance and achievement. In the formative evaluation, therefore, the following questions are asked: Is the program achieving its objectives? Is the program being implemented in the manner proposed? And how can changes be made to make the program be more effective? The inclusion of such plans provides the agency with the means to monitor its programs and developments through an evaluation plan that feeds back information to use for changing the program.

This has been a brief statement of some reasons for increased agency involvement in proposal writing, which should in turn hopefully lead to greater involvement in the development of programs and research of these programs. The following sections discuss the process of proposal writing that a staff trainer or consultant might try to convey to staff members charged with the responsibility of writing grant proposals.

Structure and Content of the Proposal

The outline for the proposal should be written in accordance with general standard guidelines. However, many funding sources have their own requirements for proposals in terms of structure and content. It is therefore important that each proposal effort be cognizant of the demands and requirements of the proposed funding source; usually these are available on request. The following discussion is not meant to be exhaustive; rather, it discusses those areas that are commonly thought to be important in the preparation and submission of proposals.

Title. Although the title given to the proposal may seem to be of minor import, it is often one of those items to which too much time is devoted and to which too much concern is given in terms of trying to be complicated or fancy. The title of the proposal should reflect the focus of the project and, as such, should be short but concise, giving the reader an idea of the kind of work to be proposed. Such titles as "The Evaluation of a Rehabilitation Program for Juvenile Offenders" differ significantly from such titles as "The Development of a Program for the Rehabilitation of Juvenile Offenders." Since the title sets the tone for the reader, it should contain the notion of the attempt to be made in the program. In sum, the title should be a kind of action statement that focuses the work and the theme of the program to be proposed.

Abstract. In all proposals, it is a good idea to include, on the page following the project title, an abstract of what is in the proposal. This abstract should summarize the major focus and theme of the program and should set forth the main points that are to be made. It is extremely important that the abstract, one single-spaced page, should embody the entire statement of what is being proposed. The abstract should tell the readers what one is going to tell them. One should then proceed, in the proposal, to tell them and, in the concluding section, reiterate the essence of what has already been stated.

Introduction. The introductory section provides the first opportunity for the writer to catch the reader's attention and to explain why the project is important enough for funding support. The reader should be impressed with the fact that this program merits financing more than others being considered, against which it is competing for scarce funds. The key element to keep in mind and to get across to the staff writing the proposal is that unless they know precisely what they want to accomplish they will be unable to give the reader a sense of what the project is and why the project is important. Therefore, in this preliminary section, at least two objectives must be accomplished. The first is to introduce the project in somewhat broad terms to the reader and to highlight the need for that project. The second objective is to introduce the reader to the agency as an organizational entity and to provide the perspective within which the project, organization, the clientele of the project, and the community are found. While there is no one right way to go forward with the proposal, one approach is to summarize its basic elements. The strategy is to tell the readers in the introduction what one is going to propose. Therefore the introduction could set forth one statement of the problem, the proposed activities to be undertaken in dealing with the defined problem, and a statement of the host organization and/or agency and its place in the effort to deal with the malady, dysfunction, pathology, or troublesome situation. Subsequent sections should build on this succinct introductory statement.

It is important to remember, when writing a proposal, that the readers will have to be convinced of the significance and importance of the proposed activities. The statement of the project to be undertaken should be supported by factual documentation. It will not suffice to attest that it is an important activity. Rather, the readers must be convinced largely by the data presented of the critical nature of the problem and the pertinence of the project proposed to deal with that problem. Thus as much supportive data as possible, not merely an oversupply of figures, should be included. As an example, one can provide some documentation on the extent of the problem, perhaps something of the history and growth of the problem and its impact on the agency and the community it serves. In turn, this statement of the problem must be linked to the organization represented in the proposal. The stated purposes of the organization and its activities over the preceding few years must be related to the problem that is addressed and to the expertise that the organization represents. At this point, it is suggested that, since the reader usually does not know the agency, a description of the history, purposes, and location of the agency be provided for the reader. This could include, for example, the table of organization, the legal status of the agency, such as if it is a for-profit or nonprofit corporation, the focus of the services provided, the agency's location, and the unique characteristics of the population it serves. The aim of this particular aspect of the proposal is to provide the reader with a sense of the agency's expertise and an appreciation for the problem and its impact on the community. Again, documentation should be kept to a minimum—just enough to provide the reader with a good sense of the micro and macro setting within which this project, if funded, will take place.

Generally, at the end of each major section or subsection, it is a good idea to provide a transition paragraph that leads into the following sections or subsections. In the case of the introduction, for example, one can give a preview of what is to follow. Thus a paragraph stating that the next sections will address the problems of the objectives of the program, the program itself, and techniques for evaluation will orient the reader to the flow of the proposal.

The Problem. This section, which has variously been called a *statement of need* or *background to the problem,* is the one within which the problem identified as being in need of some type of action is explicated. The problem determines the major focus of the program being proposed and establishes the rationale for the need for action. At this stage, the most important task is to convince the reader that the proposed program is consistent with the need of the agency or the community and in turn is consonant with the objectives set forth. Thus this section should contain statements of the need for specific action and of the reason why the organization seeking funding should undertake to cope with this need.

Statement of the Proposed Program. This portion sets forth the program objectives and the proposed plan of action. The section must describe, in detail, the procedures and the processes to meet the objectives of the proposed course of action.

Program Objectives. The statement of program objectives is probably one of the most crucial areas in a proposal, because this statement provides the reader with the chance to evaluate the precision with which the writer has thought out and developed the course of action. More importantly, the objectives will structure other aspects of the program; these other elements will include such items as the appropriate procedures, including methodology; the personnel and budget that will be needed; and the evaluation design. It is therefore imperative that great care be taken to ensure the quality and logical consistency of the specified objectives. So many other aspects of a proposal flow directly from the statement of objectives that each reader will be greatly interested in what the objectives are and how well they are stated.

Objectives must be constructed in concrete terms—in terms of what one hopes to accomplish through the program. The statement of objectives should follow two major guidelines: First, they should be behaviorally oriented, and second, they must be meaningfully stated in terms that can be objectively evaluated.

Objectives must be stated in a way in which precise outcomes can be measured, so that actual accomplishments can be seen in relationship to planned accomplishments (Raia, 1974). If the objectives cannot be defined precisely, then in all likelihood a workable program that the reader will be willing to support cannot be developed. The exact way to state objectives is variable. For instance, an objective may speak to the general increase of the quality and quantity of some action. (Notice that we have not defined the terms *quality* and *quantity,* and thus in the evaluation section the reader will be looking for some type of definition.) Another way to state the objective is to indicate an increase in the quality and quantity of the outcome by some specifiable amount. For example, one may have a program that proposes to increase the amount of community activity on the part of the elderly, and one may specify the measurable behavioral goal as an increase in the amount of activity to be a 20 percent increase in the use of transportation services by the elderly. This provides a definite baseline for measurement as to whether the program has met its goals. However, the obvious danger with this approach is that it requires the agency to predict or guess a realistic amount of expected change. The procedures that follow in this section must be realistic enough to hold the promise that such objectives are reasonable and rational. Therefore, the statement of the objectives is perhaps the most difficult portion of this program section. However, it is this statement that will assist the reader and the writer to organize the variety of other important aspects of the program and the proposal into a manageable and rational totality.

Perhaps we can best summarize the purposes of the statement of the objectives thus (Holmes, 1971): To define the scope and the intent of the proposal; to show an understanding of the problems that make up the basis of the proposed study; and to show confidence in the agency's ability to solve the problems.

The rest of the proposal acquires its basic definition from the statement of objectives. In subsequent sections, the following information must be given: what the program is and how, where, and by whom it is to be implemented. If the proposal provides answers for these questions, the reader will have the information essential to make an adequate assessment of the viability of the proposed actions.

The Program Description. The subsection that offers the program description should give the reader the structure for the specific procedures to be employed to achieve the objectives. Herein the reader is told *what* will be done to accomplish the objectives (not *how* it will be done, because that is the subject of the next part). In this "what will be done" section, the innovative characteristics of the proposed program and those activities of the plan that will provide a unique opportunity for service or increased knowledge are presented.

Many therapists and other kinds of human service workers are used to responding "in the moment" and often on a feeling level. They hold to the idea of a dynamic diagnosis and formulating a treatment approach that changes as new intrapsychic and interpersonal material emerges or as the needs and reactions of a community shift. Thus, the precision necessary for crystallizing objectives to be pursued over a period of a year or more may be foreign to their professional mind set. The staff trainer or consultant engaged in helping them acquire a new skill, that of proposal writing, may well encounter a good deal of resistance to such specific explication of objectives and intervention strategies. The resistance—often in the form of an intellectual challenge that such specificity is not possible when dealing with such unpredictable entities as abusive parents, delinquent adolescents, or patients with severe personality disorders—must be dealt with and worked through—or it is unlikely that the staff can acquire the requisite command of proposal writing strategies to develop a competitive plan.

Method of Operations. In the next part of the program, the approach to be used should be described. Although the program proposed may have certain limitations, one should present the processes in as much detail as is feasible. Here the assumptions and methodology should be spelled out in order to enable those who are reviewing the plan to make an assessment of its merits and the agency's ability to carry it out. In setting forth plans, the use of graphic materials as well as of documentation materials can be helpful in presenting the argument. This subsection is the crucial element of the program description. Its focus should be on the actual procedures and their sequence in the implementation. The entire topic of program implementation is critical and is often overlooked in the writing of a proposal. However, the phases for implementation should be articulated and tied closely to the program objectives. Attempts should be made to provide the safeguards whereby the agency will attempt to ensure that the steps detailed are indeed followed out. This section, therefore, is the process road map, spelling out the important components of the program, the sequence of events, and their implementation, leading eventually to the achievement of the program objectives. In providing the sequence of events for the procedures, one is also giving a timetable that structures the project and guides the reader in understanding what one is going to do. One must make sure, therefore, that the sequencing and the timetable are realistic. It is through this schedule that one will plan to monitor and eventually to evaluate the effectiveness of each component and its sequence in the process. By this means and by the subsequent evaluation, one can provide for introducing change as well as for discovering the weak links in that process. Therefore it is clearly important to be able to describe in detail and definitively each element of the process that is necessary and that leads to an outcome. For example, if one is utilizing counseling as a process in the proposed program, that counseling should be specified in as great detail as possible. Simply to state that one is going to have counseling available for the clientele is not sufficient. The amount and the kind of counseling, who is to offer it, and their background are some of the details to be highlighted as precisely as possible, in order that evaluation of that component can be made.

Timing. Funding agencies are interested in and concerned with the schedule for a project. After all, they are allocating money for the achievement of certain objectives within a certain specified period of time. They are therefore attuned to the timing of the implementation, the planning phase, the preimplementation phase, the set-up and implementation of the elements of the program, and the measurement and evaluation of the project results. This section must put forth a time schedule that sets the proposed plan of action. It is important that a realistic schedule be devised and devised in a way that relates to the tasks to be undertaken. There are a number of ways this can be done. The first could be to set forth a series of tasks and next to each task the starting and ending dates for that activity. A second approach is to produce a pictorial display, like a Gantt chart. This is a chart in which time is displayed across one axis and the tasks are arrayed down the other axis. Within the body of the chart, there are a series of bar lines that tell the time required by the activity from the beginning to the end date. The pictorial representation provides a chance for the reader to see at a glance those elements which are being done sequentially and those which are being done in parallel. There are other approaches to representing the temporal dimension of the program, but these are two of the easier ways to do this. One should keep in mind that providing this time dimension is one way in which one communicates to the funding agency one's ability to manage and plan a task of this magnitude and to have a hope for coming out with observable results by the end of the proposed project period.

The "time-task matrix" is important not only for the understanding of one's ability to perform the work as proposed but also in the writing of the proposal itself, because it provides a framework for estimating costs. For each task, one can estimate the number of persons it will take to accomplish the task and the amount of time that it will take for these persons to accomplish it within the period of days, weeks, or months proposed. It is possible to use this matrix as a device for estimating the number of people required plus the amount of time required. One then has an objective basis for estimating the labor costs.

Although these tools are quite elementary ones, mental health workers, social workers, and psychiatrists often receive no exposure to such matrices and graphs during their formal under-graduate, graduate, and professional education. It therefore be-hooves the staff trainer to see that they gain familiarity with these tables and charts and know which ones are appropriate for pre-senting what kinds of data. The supervisor should have sufficient expertise in these matters to critique a proposal once it has been written and to suggest alternate ways of presenting data if the ones used are not adequate or preferable.

Facilities. The funding source will also be interested in knowing where the proposed program will take place, that is, what facilities are needed, are available, and will be used for the housing and implementation of the program. Generally, the funding source does not support the acquisition of sizable facilities, with the ex-ception of those which may be needed for such things as group homes or where the experimental program depends heavily on adding to the physical premises. It is not impossible for these kinds of facilities to be supported by the funds, but generally funding agencies do not underwrite projects that require a great deal of money for facilities. This means, in effect, that they would like to have the funds provided for the benefit of clients or for the acquisi-tion of knowledge, rather than for the purchase of material things. Again, it is important to be able to convince the funding source that one has the facilities available to carry out the proposed activity. A brief description of the facilities available that pertain to the project at hand will be sufficient. One should remember this section is to provide assurance that one has the plant and equipment availa-ble to accommodate the program and that the funds requested are primarily for programmatic use.

Personnel. The part devoted to personnel should provide

information on who will carry out the proposed program. Very often the success or failure of the proposal will depend on one's ability to convince the funding source that one has that good combination of project director and personnel plus supporting consultants who can provide for the conduct of the proposed program. It is important, therefore, that in listing staff one provides the reader with ample information about the educational and experimental qualifications of the staff who hold particularly key positions.

It is also helpful to the reader if the credentials and experience of key personnel can be related directly to the tasks to be undertaken in the proposed project. Thus, pointing out in the body of the text the extensive administrative experience the proposed project director has and how this will ensure the success of the project is another way of convincing the reader that one can really do the job. In the section on personnel, an accompanying set of paragraphs that summarize personnel experience and their proposed contributions to the project will alert the reader to the overall relationship of the project team's experience to the proposed plan. Resumés of the experience and credentials of each team member should be enclosed at the end of the proposal or in the section so designated by the funding agency.

Cost. Finally, the reader must be told how much it will cost to achieve the proposed objectives. The preparation of budgets requires a complete treatise for itself and therefore cannot be dealt with in detail in this chapter. The minimal advice one can give is to consult with the agency's budget officer before and during the course of the proposal's preparation. He or she will know the rates for overhead costs (lights, rent, and heat) and for any general and administrative (G & A) costs. The budget officer will also be helpful in the mechanics of budget preparation, the setting of established agency guidelines for job rates, and fringe benefits.

The major function of the proposal writer is twofold. First, to estimate the amount of effort, by level of person, required to accomplish each task. In this regard, it is important to gauge as closely as possible what funds it will take to complete the project. One should not try to buy a project by submitting a low budget, because eventually one will be required to accomplish the task within the funds requested. Besides, when the funding agency looks at the proposal it will be asking the question, "Can this job be done with the funds requested?"

By attaching salaries next to each person's name listed on the person-task matrix, one can determine the cost for each task and the amount of funds required for each person. If the budget exceeds the suggested guidelines, one will have to rethink the project, deciding what can possibly be diminished or cut or whether the objectives must be redefined.

The second major function of the writers is one that should be undertaken *before* writing begins; that is, estimating the amount of time needed to do the job and the level of effort needed, for each gross task category, to complete the project. This will provide an estimate of the person-years of effort that may be required. ("Person-year" is a term used to estimate the amount of funds necessary for the completion of the project and includes overhead, G & A, and support services. It is used as an estimating device and does not refer to the employment of just one person on the project.) For example, the funding agency may say, "This task is estimated to take four person-years of effort." The exact amount of dollars attached to a "person-year" will vary somewhat according to inflation and other factors. However, in 1977 the estimate probably ranged between $50 and $60 thousand. Thus, the proposer can estimate that the funding agency estimates the cost of the task to be between $200 and $240 thousand and can therefore feel fairly confident that proposals in this range would be competitive. For planning purposes, the "person-year" formula can be employed to estimate the total cost of the project. Refinements are provided by applying actual salaries to actual people proposed for actual tasks.

Organizing Agency Staff

The proposal is created through many elements—chiefly, a good idea, creativity, hard work, and planning. For the future of the project and for internal agency relationships, involvement and cooperation of staff is also needed. A proposal team should include professionals at all levels as well as support staff.

Good ideas are not the province of any one particular professional group or administrative stratum. The development of interest in and the ability to make proposals is enhanced by the involvement of various segments of agency personnel. All members of the proposal team, from secretaries to administrators, should be part of the planning from the earliest point of the proposal development. Ideas from all of these staff members will sharpen the focus and open the way for questioning the assumptions and practices that constitute the proposal contents.

The key to effective proposal development, however, must be planning and organization. To keep proposal writing as an ongoing alternative in the agency, such planning is a necessity. One way of establishing the planned approach is to develop a proposal team organized along the functional lines suggested by the proposed outline. Before discussing a proposed organizational structure, it is important to reiterate the principle that all members of the team should have an understanding of the purpose of the proposed project, of the agency to which the proposal will be addressed, and of their importance as members of the proposal team. With this caveat in mind, the following organizational context is suggested:

Proposal Manager. The proposal manager is a person designated as the one responsible for organizing, overseeing and directing the writing. It is best, of course, if this person is also to be the proposed project director. It is he or she who will have to implement the project and live with the suggested actions to be undertaken. This person must help define the project, assign writing tasks, and review all sections to make sure the disparate parts make a convincing whole. This person must also be responsible for or assist in the initial development of tasks and costs and of the outline for the proposal. (It may be advisable to have a general reviewer who checks on progress and the quality of the final product.)

Proposal Writers. Agency staff and consultants can be used to write sections of the proposal, provided that they have a complete understanding of the purpose of the proposal and of the section they will write. For ease of coordination and to reduce the differences in writing style, the number of writers should be kept low. This is a pragmatic decision based on the size of the proposal and the amount of time needed to produce a finished product. With each assignment, the proposal manager should provide an outline of the entire proposal and expect from the writer a detailed annotated outline in return. Realistic dates should be agreed on for the submission of first drafts. The polishing of the final drafts and the insertion of transition paragraphs are the ultimate responsibility of the proposal manager.

Capability Statements and Resumés. One person, probably the proposal secretary, should be responsible for pulling together— not necessarily writing—those materials that are referred to as "boilerplate." Boilerplate consists of sections of the proposal that rarely change much from proposal to proposal. These consist primarily of a description of the agency, past work done that is of relevance to the proposal, resumés of proposed staff and any statements required by the funding source of affirmative action procedures, and so on. Once such boilerplate has been developed, it can be filed and used again, with appropriate modifications, for other proposal efforts.

Tasks, Schedules and Costs. Developing tasks, schedules, and costs can be delegated to a writer, but since they are of such importance the proposal manager must be involved. It is his or her responsibility to enlist the assistance of appropriate agency personnel (such as the budget director) to generate the appropriate cost figures and other materials. The statement of tasks and schedule should be generated, as indicated before, early on in the development of the proposal. Accompanying charts and figures should be developed and made available to the section writers. This will aid them in the organization of their sections and ensure that deviations from the tasks to be done will be discovered or kept to a minimum.

Team Meetings. Frequent short meetings of the proposal team will provide the chance for feedback to team members, will keep morale and interest high, and will provide an opportunity to monitor the progress of proposal development. One possible staff training approach might be to have several interested staff members who are new to proposal writing attend these meetings. Here they can learn the language, the methodology, the format, the team nature of the enterprise, and the high price to be paid for procrastination that ends in near panic at deadline time. They can be given previously written proposals to critique in order to become conversant with what constitutes a proposal that is likely to be favorably considered for funding and what constitutes a proposal that is likely to be turned down. Thus, rather than writing proposals as a solitary venture, they can learn in an atmosphere in which there is some enthusiasm

generated by a team approach by professionals who are committed
to the task at hand.

Where's the Money?

Finding the funds for a project is always a problem, but
finding a source of money is not as difficult as convincing the potential funding agency to give it to the proposing agency. This
section will present some ideas about approaches to finding the
funding sources, but it is not intended as a "How to Do It" recipe.

There are two major sources of funds for program research,
development, and evaluation: the federal, state, and local governments and private foundations.

Governmental Agencies. Governmental agencies generally
have specified programs and objectives they wish to fulfill. Thus,
those agencies concerned with health, education, welfare, housing,
and mental health have agendas and statements of objectives for
each year of their funding. Much of this money will be allocated for
specific projects and activities; however, other monies will be allocated for objectives for which specific programs are sought; additional monies, admittedly much less, will be available on a discretionary basis to further the programs and knowledge in that agency's
sphere of concern. An agency seeking funding has a choice, therefore, of response modes to governmental agencies.

Therefore, one way to find funds is to respond to the explicit
request of the government agency for services. Such requests are—
and have to be, by law—made through requests for proposal
(RFPs), which are usually announced in the *Commerce Business
Daily*. These are competitive awards, usually made on a contract
basis, and include all kinds of work, such as evaluation services,
research and demonstration projects, technical assistance, and training services. As an example, an agency might advertise for someone
to develop a specialized child abuse treatment program for demonstration purposes. Generally, human service agencies are not in a
position to develop proposals that are appropriate for these kinds
of requests, not because they are unable or not equipped to deal
with the subject matter, but because they are not organized to meet
the demands of such RFPs. However, an agency, particularly a

private agency, should not overlook a partnership arrangement (subcontracting) with some other institution or organization.

Response to specific needs requests can also be motivated through grant requests. Grants traditionally have been given to nonprofit organizations and for this reason would be more appropriate for agencies. Many agencies now prepare requests for grant proposals in which they would like to receive requests for program development or research. This leaves the writer free to propose a project that can be tailored to their particular circumstances and approaches while meeting the needs of the funding agency.

Finally, obtaining the description of competitive grant procurements can be accomplished by writing to each agency and requesting a copy of their brochure. Announcements of grant procurements are made in the *Federal Register.*

Other approaches include the submission of an unsolicited proposal. In other words, the service agency writes a proposal for funding and submits it without being requested to do so by the funding source. At best this procedure has a minimal chance of success. Also, government agencies have "discretionary" funds through which they can fund noncompetitive projects. This process would be included under the heading of a "sole source" award. Such awards are generally given because the applicant has an unusual idea that meets the needs of the funding source or because the applicant possesses unusual capabilities to perform the task. Since the distribution of funds, particularly in the federal government, is supposed to be on an open and equitable basis, the award of a "sole source" contract usually must be approved by a special panel. This means a longer waiting period and more chance for something to go wrong.

Foundations. Foundations, like the agencies within the federal and state governments, are mission oriented and have particular areas of interest. In order, therefore, to have a chance to obtain funds from a foundation, the applicant must attempt to apply to those foundations whose missions most closely coincide with the applicant's orientation and proposed plans. This is not really difficult. Too often we tend to think of foundations only in terms of the "supers," ignoring the many medium-sized and small foundations who provide support to many projects. Source documents are available for discovering the wide variety of foundations. The *Foundation Directory* (prepared by M. O. Lewis for The Foundation Center in New York City) provides a list of the smaller foundations in each region, state, and city.

Once a foundation is identified, contact must be made and a determination obtained as to the possibility of funding. This can be done through submitting a proposal directly to the foundation. However, many foundations suggest that a short statement of the project be submitted first to give them a chance to review the purpose and plan of the proposed project and to decide if it meets their mission and objectives. If the ideas generate interest on the part of the foundation, they will notify the originator and invite a full proposal, even suggesting areas that should be expanded or included in the submission.

It is a good investment of time to research the possible sources of funding. Visit those state, local, or federal government agencies that are readily accessible. If the sources are too far away, contact can be made and information gathered through phone calls or writing. Requests for information about programs and possible funding can be obtained by writing to the funding source, asking for program guidelines, and even asking for past requests for proposals or for winning proposals. It is a function of these agencies to deal with such requests and to provide such information. Thus they are used to dealing with phone calls, discussing ideas, and providing information.

The same process is true of foundations, especially the smaller ones. They are geared to handling requests for their annual reports, their mission statements, and their current funding goals. The important point is to develop contact with the funding source whenever possible, to find out more about their needs, to get reactions to ideas and to anticipate that possible match that would increase the chances of success.

Rights of Human Subjects

Standards for the conduct of social research and program development have arisen through the experiences and deliberations of social scientists and practitioners. Often these standards have been codified by the several professional associations. However, in the past decade, the federal government has formalized some of these standards into regulations. Chief among these are the guidelines covering privacy and confidentiality for research subjects and research findings. Privacy refers to the right of the individual to share or withhold his attitudes, behaviors and beliefs from others. Confidentiality refers to the question of whether, and under what conditions, information about one person can be provided to another person. The codification of these concerns is found in the Privacy Act of 1974 (P.L. 93–579) and the Buckley Amendment (Sec. 438 of the General Education Provisions Act, P.L. 93–568). In addition, the Department of Health, Education and Welfare requires of the recipients of its funds an agreement on the Protection of Human Subjects.

These formal criteria are but a part of the concern we all should have for the kind of research we do and for what we are doing to and for those who are the subjects of our projects. Since this discussion is oriented to the writing of proposals and not the implementation of projects, it is important to point out that such precautions should be taken in the preparation of proposals. Certainly this means that the proposed activities should not be harmful in any way to those for whom they are intended and that the voluntary, knowledgeable participation of clients is assured. Where necessary, informed consent forms should be utilized. This discussion also suggests that one should be aware of the restrictions, both legal and ethical, on the kinds and uses of data which will be collected and reported from the project. Although it is not a complete safeguard, a formal or informal committee of peers, community persons and legal experts to review plans that protect rights of subjects is a helpful strategy.

There is another aspect to this problem which, while somewhat tangential, is too seldom considered. This relates to an ethical question of a kind of privacy of the individual. Many social programming and research efforts are temporary forays into the lives of communities. No matter how well intended, we enter into people's lives, tinker, snoop, and change, often with positive results. But then we leave, having disturbed their privacy by raising expectations, adapting behaviors, and creating "solutions" more relevant to their needs. And when we leave there often is nothing left for the community to use, nothing left that would allow what was created to be continued. We are suggesting, therefore, that some thought be given in the preparation of proposals for how significant functional elements of the project can be incorporated into the community and personal system when the funding for the project is terminated. This is not an easy task; there may not be an answer for most of us. However, the lack of an easily available response does not relieve us of this basic responsibility.

Summary

Proposal writing, the development of action or research programs, is an important, and yet often neglected, function of social service and mental health agencies. Since training of new helping professionals is not a function being performed adequately by most graduate and professional schools, it is one that must be assumed by staff trainers and consultants in agencies and institutions. Proposal writing can be fun and can be a natural outlet for the personal and professional concerns of agency personnel. In many agencies, proposal writing may involve a great effort to generate and coordinate, and the obstacles may be sufficient to depress efforts to inaugurate proposal activity. But proposal writing itself is not overly difficult. It is simply an extension of the writing of an article, letter, or memorandum. The same essential process is involved—the desire to effectively communicate concepts, ideas, and plans of action. Certainly, enough talent is available in these agencies; the experience of agency personnel provides a base for the development of new ideas that is unequalled in other organizations that traditionally have made it a goal to do such work. This gap between practice and research or between service delivery and development of new programs must be narrowed, and this can only be done by the greater involvement of the agencies themselves.

CHAPTER 8

Psychoanalytically Oriented Individual Therapy

Gerald A. Melchiode

A psychoanalytic model can be utilized in the supervision of trainees regardless of the trainees' experience and of the needs of the patient. A distinction must be made between psychoanalytic technique and psychoanalytic theory. This chapter will not deal with the supervision of psychoanalysis but will deal with the application of psychoanalytic theory to the process of supervision. The theory has much greater extension than the technique. The technique of psychoanalysis can only be applied to certain selected patients, who have symptom or character neuroses, by highly skilled therapists, while psychoanalytic theory can be employed as a framework to understand all human behavior.

Two major cornerstones of psychoanalytic theory are the concepts of a dynamic unconscious and of infantile sexuality. Granted, there are many other concepts that make up the core of what is considered psychoanalytic; but these two are essential in separating psychoanalytic theory from all other theories (Waelder, 1960). Any single human behavior is made up of many inter-relating complex components. Many of these components are outside the person's realm of awareness—not merely *left* out of awareness, but *pushed* out, because these components were once unacceptable to the person and were found to be threatening. The dynamic unconscious is composed of those repressed drives that continue to push for expression. The concept of infantile sexuality includes the process in which the child must master erotic and aggressive drives vis-à-vis the adults who raise the child. This process affects the way in which children view themselves and reality, their inner feelings, and their perceptions of others. When these issues are poorly resolved, distortions result and continue into adult life.

In the normal person, the dynamic unconscious and infantile sexuality are hidden from view. These only come to the fore in the person who is in conflict. Through appropriate supervision, the trainee can be enabled to see glimpses of the unconscious drives and of early unresolved difficulties in patients. Even if the patient is in supportive therapy, with the proper understanding the supervisee will be in a better position to help. In other words, I am not saying that the psychoanalytic understanding must be necessarily interpreted to the patient; rather, I am saying that the understanding is useful in helping the patient. For example, a patient with a psychosis talks about world destruction fantasies. For this patient, the fantasies represent his or her own unacceptable hostile feelings that he or she must deny and project on to the world. "It is not I who am overwhelmed with anger and about to explode; it is the world." Interpreting this to the patient will only threaten him or her, cause him or her to regress further and possibly may result in ego dissolution (A. Freud, [1936] 1967). However, this conceptualization will give the therapist the conviction to say, "I can understand how frightened you must be and how confusing the world must be for you now."

In order to attain a more complete understanding of our patients' lives in insight psychotherapy, certain measures must be taken by the therapist. There have been disputes among professionals concerning technique in that some experienced therapists feel that if one understands the patient, then technique follows. My thesis is that certain preliminary steps must take place before one can hope to begin understanding the patient and that these preliminary steps and the technique that follows can enhance one's knowledge of the patient. Let us say one wanted to see firsthand the moons of Jupiter. Would it be enough to say, "Look to the heavens and eventually you would see them?" Obviously not. One would need a telescope and would need to be able to set it properly. A map of the stars and planets would be necessary, as well as an ability to read it. Atmospheric conditions would have to be just right. Having met all these criteria, one would still be considered optimistic to expect to see the moons of Jupiter on the first attempt. This analogy applies to observing psychodynamic phenomena. It often takes a while to become attuned, but if the trainee perseveres and the stage is set through appropriate supervision then the patient, trainee, and supervisor will be rewarded.

This chapter will attempt to delineate those factors in supervision that increase the trainee's psychoanalytic understanding of the patient. The observations are drawn from my own experiences under supervision and in supervising, and from the analyses and psychotherapy of patients who were themselves under supervision.

The Setting for Supervision

The supervisor is an important role model, both positively and negatively. Behavior and attitudes conveyed by the supervisor are often carried over by the trainee in the treatment of the patient. Students often do as supervisors do instead of as they say, which is why the setting and the supervisor's behavior are worth considering.

Supervision should be conducted in the privacy of an office. Presenting case material in a public place, such as a restaurant, introduces both a distraction and a danger that the information presented will be overheard. The decision to supervise a trainee in some place other than an office usually arises out of what is expedient for the supervisor and not what is in the best interest of the patient and supervisee.

The setting should provide a milieu of two people hard at work together on a serious problem free of distractions and interruptions. For example, I have the same policy concerning phone calls when I am supervising as when I am seeing patients. No calls are put through to my office, except for emergencies. One supervisor, after greeting his trainee, told his secretary to hold all calls except for three specific people. He received the three calls and spent a third of the hour on the phone. Phone calls do not have any place in psychotherapy; neither do they belong in supervision. Accepting phone calls simply establishes a role model for the supervisee, who may then also extend the misuse of the phone into the psychotherapy setting.

The schedule for supervision must be mutually agreed on and adhered to whenever possible. I use the same principles in scheduling supervision that I use for therapy. Hours should be started promptly. If I am late, I offer to make up the time at the end of the session or at the next session. Hours should also end promptly. This gives the trainee an opportunity to see how the supervisor handles issues of time, which often constitute a problem to novice therapists. Sessions should not end early simply because the trainee has run out of material to present. If this happens, the supervisor should be on the alert for possible resistance. Again, this is valuable practice that the trainee can carry over into his therapy. If a student notifies me that the patient has canceled a session, I offer him the option of coming to supervision to discuss the possible causes of the cancellation, some aspects of psychotherapy, or some problems with another patient. I find that the better students take advantage of all sessions with the supervisor.

The supervisor should also be available to the student at times other than the regularly scheduled hour. This should be done without giving the student undue encouragement to contact the supervisor outside of regular hours, because the trainee is really the psychotherapist and must begin making decisions about handling the case. Few decisions are so crucial that they cannot wait to be discussed until the next supervisory session. Undue pressure on the part of the supervisor to call when problems arise infantilizes the trainee and raises questions about who is really the therapist. Often it is the supervisor's narcissism, need to control, or unmet dependency needs that foster this behavior. There is the danger that the trainee might copy the supervisor's behavior and in turn infantilize the patient.

There are often questions concerning the use of notes and tape recordings in supervision. I prefer that students review the notes beforehand and that they tell me about their patients without reading from their notes. This gives the student an opportunity to do some thinking about his or her patient and to synthesize and integrate the material. It also provides for a more spontaneous give and take between trainee and supervisor. However, there are some trainees who insist on sticking to their notes, and I do not press the point. If the trainee is more comfortable using notes, then I try to work in that manner.

Note taking during the psychotherapy session should be discouraged. This is a distraction for both patient and therapist and may enhance resistance. Patients often cue in on note taking and tell the therapist what they think he or she wants to hear based on what they think he or she is writing down. Some experienced therapists do not agree with this point and take copious notes (Greenacre, 1975). I do not take notes during supervision and hope that this may provide a model for the trainee in doing psychotherapy.

I have not found audiotapes of therapy to be helpful for supervision. The few times that I have used tapes, the supervisory sessions have been dull. Taping encourages too much passivity from both participants and also introduces an artifact into the treatment situation. This interferes with a sense of intimacy and may in fact jeopardize the therapeutic relationship.

I have also never used videotapes for psychotherapy supervision. Here the artifact is even greater and, in addition, there is the problem of the patient being identified. This does not negate the fact that videotapes are valuable aids in the teaching of interviewing and data-gathering skills.

In summary, the trainee should jot down notes after the therapy session, reflect on them, digest and synthesize them, and then bring his impressions to the supervisory session.

The supervisor should be tolerant of the supervisee's mistakes. I find it helpful in supervising to occasionally universalize the student's problem before I make a critical statement. For example, "This is a common problem that all beginning therapists make; that is, you tend to take for granted what the patient is saying without asking the patient to be specific or to give an example of what he means." The technique of universalizing the trainee's mistake is particularly useful when conducting a case conference. In this situation, the supervisor must be particularly tactful.

The supervisor should not appear overly critical. He or she should be able to put instructions in terms that are carefully chosen so that the trainee will not be embarrassed. Most beginning trainees consider themselves to be ineffective and bungling. The supervisor's patience and tolerance can do much to overcome these feelings. Trainees must be reminded that learning to do psychotherapy takes a long time. I sometimes compare it to playing a musical instrument. Given the proper training, the more experience one has, the more proficient one becomes. The trainee is bound to make mistakes as he or she learns. Hopefully, the accepting, tolerant, and patient attitude of the supervisor will be carried over by the trainee into the therapy situation. I have had students tell me that supervisors have instructed them to act in a certain way and yet the supervisor has acted in a quite contradictory manner. A psychiatric resident recounted to his supervisor the following sequence of events: he had handled a situation poorly and had given advice to the patient that she could have gotten from anyone. After a patient had missed a session, the patient's husband called to report that his wife wished to discontinue therapy. Worried, the resident asked to speak with his patient and pleaded with her to continue. It was obvious to the resident that he had handled the situation poorly. The supervisor told the resident that the patient could have gotten that kind of advice from anyone; this only served to embarrass the trainee. The supervisor recommended that a transference interpretation should have been made. The resident felt stupid and was angry with the supervisor. Would it have not been more helpful to acknowledge the difficulty in handling something like this over the phone and then to explore the resident's understanding of what had happened?

The working alliance is as essential in supervision as it is in psychotherapy. Through mutual trust and respect, the supervisor and trainee slowly develop a viable relationship. This can only be done in an atmosphere that fosters it. Those same ingredients that facilitate formation of the working alliance in supervision can foster it in psychotherapy. The way that the supervisor handles the relationship with the student is carried over in the way the student deals with the patient.

The First Supervisory Session

I try to meet with a new trainee before he or she sees the patient for the first time. We review the essential features of the initial interview and of the mental status examination. The patient also must be told something about psychotherapy, and we discuss this.

Before one can even begin to speculate about the psychodynamics, however, one must have data based on sound clinical observation. A common problem, one that I find particularly irksome, is trying to conduct a case conference or consult on a case for which very little clinical information is presented. Moreover, often the material is poorly organized. The following discussion on this problem is not psychoanalytic, but consideration of these issues is necessary before any analytic hypothesis can be drawn.

In the initial interview (Deutsch and Murphy, 1955), the therapist must first try to establish rapport. The trainee can do this by asking the patient questions to which he or she can easily respond—name, age, address, and so on. At this point, the trainee can make some appropriate comment about the patient's address or occupation. Usually by this time the patient is fairly comfortable, and the trainee can begin to explore the chief complaint and the history of the present illness. The trainee should use an open-ended approach and allow the patient to tell the story in his or her own style, interrupting only when something is not clear. Transition statements are helpful. They give the interview continuity and make the process more understandable for the patient. For example, to get at the next portion of the interview, the past personal history, one might say, "I find it useful in understanding a person's current problem to know something about their past life." Transition statements are also helpful in administering formal parts of the mental status examination (Stevenson, 1959). I have found that a good way of getting into the testing of orientation and memory is to ask patients if they have had any trouble with memory. Then I ask if they would mind if I test it. Before I ask for interpretations of proverbs, I always give an explanation about the use of proverbs in testing the patients' thinking. For example, I ask patients if they know what a proverb is. Then I add that proverbs are old sayings that people have about life and that there are no right or wrong interpretations but that their interpretations may be useful in understanding how they are thinking. Using this technique, I rarely encounter conscious resistances.

In the initial interview, I also determine the patient's goals and reinforce the patient's motivation for therapy. It is important to know what the patient's prior experience in therapy has been or what conceptions the patient has about treatment. A problem that occurs frequently is that the student assumes that he or she and the patient share the same understanding of the therapeutic process. This presumption often results in further misunderstandings and can subvert the therapy. Therefore, a brief role induction is necessary (Frank, 1964). I tell patients that the only ground rule that I have is that they be frank with me. My role is to help them to understand themselves; what they do with that self-knowledge is up to them. I am not going to give them advice or tell them what to do. I also inform patients that we can learn about them by anything that they talk about—present life, any feelings that they have, night dreams, daydreams—and that the past is important because it helps us to understand the present. I indicate that it is up to the patients to bring in material for the session and that they are responsible for attending every session.

One also has to set the fee and present a policy for missed sessions. The fact that many patients are seen through clinics that determine financial liability through interviews with receptionists often deprives the student of the opportunity of learning how to deal with this reality. Since all financial matters are handled by a third party, the trainee is often unaware of the amount that the patient owes the clinic. This results in the fact that the patient's feelings about money often go unexplored.

Policies regarding missed appointments vary from those that set a fixed time for notifying the therapist to those that make the patient financially responsible for all missed sessions no matter what the cause. Whatever policy is chosen, it is important that it be clearly stated early in therapy and that it be consistently applied. The principle underlying any policy is that the therapy must be conducted on a regular basis in order to have continuity and avoid confusion. Then, too, setting a policy puts the responsibility squarely on the shoulders of the patient.

A question that often arises in the first supervisory session is how the trainee should introduce him- or herself to the patient. The honest approach is always best. Trainees should not introduce themselves as doctors if they are not. If trainees deceive the patients, how can they hope that patients will be open and honest with them? I do not feel that students must go overboard and review their entire educational background with patients. For example, a trainee could say that he is Mr. Smith. If the patient then says "Aren't you a doctor?" the trainee might respond with, "No, I'm in training to be a psychologist."

Another question related to this is, "What shall the trainee call the patient?" The fact that this question comes up more often than the situations in which one really has to address the patient by name bespeaks some other concerns of the trainee. In actuality, one rarely has to refer to the patient by name during a therapy hour. There are only two people in the room. One occasion in which the therapist has to address the patient by name is when calling the patient on the telephone. With adult patients, I always recommend that the supervisee use the patient's last name. Many trainees prefer to call patients by their first names, and some suggest that the patients call them by their first names. This sometimes represents the trainees' attempt to reduce the distance between themselves and their patients. It can also indicate some discomfort in being in the professional therapist role. By doing this, the trainee may be denying the existence of transference and may inadvertently diminish the positive transference. What often happens is that many patients are uncomfortable using the therapist's first name, so they use the therapist's last name at the same time that the therapist is using the patient's first name. Instead of creating an illusion of equality, the patient thus is actually infantilized. I have found that employing last names for both the therapist and patient seems to be the best solution in the long run. This dilemma often leads to rich material if the therapist and patient can explore the patient's feelings about how he or she is addressed and wishes to be addressed.

The Beginning Phase of Treatment and Supervision

In the beginning phase, I help trainees to organize clinical observations and present cases in an orderly fashion. I try to get students to defend what they say. This sharpens their clinical skills. We also work toward making a clinical diagnosis. Some trainees may have a tendency to play down the importance of the diagnosis as necessary, treating it as a working hypothesis that can change during treatment. A mistake that is commonly made by beginning trainees is that of making a diagnosis on the basis of symptoms alone. A patient who has a schizophrenic illness may present obsessions, phobias, or depression. Novices might find themselves focusing on the symptoms of the phobia, thus making an incorrect diagnosis of a neurosis. I recommend that, along with considering the patient's symptomatology, the trainees also evaluate the patient's ego functions, the strength and malleability of the drives, and the reasonableness of the superego. Having done this, the trainees will have a clearer idea of the patient's diagnosis.

Another frequent error is that of taking the patient's words for granted. Sitting in with a medical student during an interview, a patient complained about "anxiety." I asked the patient to describe what it was like for him to feel anxious. He went on to talk about a loss of appetite, early morning awakening, feelings of worthlessness, and sadness. The words that the patient used to describe his "anxiety" indicated a classic picture of depression, not anxiety.

I often encourage trainees to be explicit and, in turn, to expect their patients to be specific. Some patients, especially those with hysterical components in their personalities, hide behind their vagueness. Yet these same patients expect others to understand them completely. When this kind of case material is presented in supervision, I find that we have nothing substantial to work on. In the early stages of treatment, the therapist can ask for specific examples or ask such patients to describe what has actually happened. If patients continue to be vague, I suggest that the trainees ask the patient if they are aware that they have difficulty being specific and then try to explore this with them.

An error found in the initial stage of therapy is that most beginning therapists talk too much. There seems to be a great deal of pressure on the student to produce. Many trainees feel that the only way the patient can get something out of a session is if the therapist directs the patient to some point or makes an interpretation. It is a revelation to the supervisee that patients get a great deal of relief from being able to talk about themselves in their own style to someone who is interested and willing to listen. Trainees confuse activity with talking and passivity with listening. I have told patients that in the beginning they will have to do most of the talking and that, in time, when I know something about the patient, I will have something meaningful to say. It is also a relief to the student not to feel the urgency of having to do a lot of the talking.

There is also a tendency on the part of the novice to make an interpretation as soon as it comes to mind. It is important to get students to control this tendency. I ask them to look for evidence to corroborate their hypotheses. They can use these examples in making interpretations. It is also important to hold off in making interpretations until the therapeutic alliance has crystallized.

I find that many students follow a fairly predictable course in their development as psychotherapists. In the first stage, trainees are content oriented. They often dig for clues as if they were detectives trying to solve a crime. Trainees pride themselves on bringing in a memory of some event that happened when the patient was four years old. This need to come up with information often affects the student's behavior toward the patient. The patient is viewed as someone who has to be interrogated, and the therapist comes across as the prosecuting attorney. During the next stage, the trainee is concerned with the interpersonal process; that is, what is actually going on between the therapist and patient. The trainee begins to concentrate on feelings and on the verbal and nonverbal clues to feelings. There is a tendency during this stage to help the patient talk about his or her feelings. Here, the evoking of feelings is considered by the supervisee to be mutative. During the third and final stage, the student therapist begins to integrate the data. The trainee learns to stand equidistant from the patient's current reality, the transference, and the patient's past life.

A useful point to demonstrate in supervision is that rarely do more than one or two themes come up during a single therapy hour. As a guide to these themes, it is essential to determine the patient's affect. Often, the patient's first few words or nonverbal behavior at the beginning of the session will be a clue to feelings. For example, a patient begins the hour by putting his feet on the furniture and asking the therapist, "What's new?" Then he tells a series of incidents in which the patient demonstrates how he is not going to allow himself to be pushed around. It is clear that in this session the patient was in conflict about his passivity and had to defend against it by trying to control the hour and by identifying with the therapist. Here, the supervisor can help the trainee understand the theme of passivity by calling attention to the patient's behavior at the beginning of the hour and his subsequent associations. Many times, the trainee will ask if he or she, in turn, should call the patient's attention to the nonverbal communication. This should depend on a number of factors. If the patient's behavior is destructive, I call attention to it immediately. When one patient rested his feet on the wall of my office, I asked him to take his feet off the wall and asked if he understood what he was doing. Missing a session is an example of behavior that is destructive to the progress of therapy. This should be explored with the patient whether the patient brings it up or not. Other pieces of less destructive nonverbal communication are not usually called to the attention of the patient. Focusing on every piece of nonverbal communication makes the patient feel awkward. It is as if one were watching one's feet as one walked down stairs. I encourage the trainee to note behavior and try to relate it to the content of the session. For instance, a woman patient's playing with her wedding ring while talking about her new boss might indicate underlying fantasies about him, an affair with him, or transference fantasies about the therapist. I would not jump to any conclusion unless I could corroborate the behavior over a period of time by noting if it came up in similar contexts. On the whole, I feel that nonverbal communication can give valuable clues to the unconscious derivatives and affects. It should be utilized by the trainee whenever possible, but not necessarily interpreted to the patient.

The Middle Phase of Therapy

The concept of transference cannot be fully appreciated unless the trainee is involved in doing intensive psychotherapy and has also been in analysis or insight psychotherapy him- or herself. Transference is an experiential idea that cannot be simply read about. Transference is the inappropriate, unconscious displacement of wishes, feelings, and attitudes that the patient has had about significant persons in his or her past life onto the therapist (Greenson, 1967). Derivatives of transference color every human interaction. It is a rare person who does not slow down when seeing a police car approach, even though the person is traveling well within the speed limits. This is such a universal phenomenon that it usually goes unnoticed. But there is a danger in applying the term transference outside of the therapy situation, because one does not have sufficient control of certain variables to determine whether a behavior is inappropriate or not. In order to observe the transference, the trainee-therapist must take a relatively neutral position. Neutrality does not mean that the trainee must remain silent or passive, nor does it mean that the trainee does not have feelings vis-à-vis the patient. Neutrality means that the therapist does not react to the patient or give advice or suggestions. Once the neutrality is broken, it confuses the picture, and one is hard pressed to say whether or not the phenomenon of transference has occurred. If the therapist is angry with a patient for being late for a session and verbalizes this, then the patient has a right to expect the therapist to be angry if he or she is late again. On the other hand, if the therapist has never verbalized or indicated anger, then the therapist is on much firmer ground in interpreting the patient's fear of anger on the therapist's part as a derivative of transference. To help clarify this point for the patient, the therapist can ask if he or she, the therapist, has done or said anything to indicate that he or she was angry. If the answer is no, then the therapist should consider that he or she was dealing with a transference phenomena. However, if the answer is yes and the patient says, "Sure, you raised your voice, and you were critical of me for being late last time," then this is not transference. In the last example, all is not lost. It might even be appropriate, in that case, for the therapist to apologize and then go on to examine the patient's reaction to the anger.

Another example along the same line occurs when the therapist falls asleep during the hour. One cannot assume that the patient's anger is transference. The therapist should apologize, not make any excuses, and then continue to explore the patient's feelings. I am not saying that transference elements are not involved. Perhaps the patient had a parent who would sleep instead of doing something with the patient. However, the therapist cannot brush off the patient's anger as being unwarranted. It may be based on the here-and-now reality of the therapist's inappropriate behavior.

Clues concerning the transference often emerge from the patient's questions. Trainees often have difficulty in the beginning dealing with these. A question is often met by cold responses such as "What do you think?" or "Why did you ask that question?" This often comes across to the patient as being critical. I do not recommend that the trainee ask "why" questions. I remind the supervisee that the only time they were asked "why" questions as a child was when they were doing something wrong. Instead, when the patient asks a question and the therapist feels that it is better for the patient that it not be answered, it is best to explain this. For example, a therapist is asked if he is married. He could say that in any other situation he would be glad to answer the question, but here it would be better for the patient if he did not answer the question now and instead explored some of the patient's thoughts about it. A patient once asked me what kind of a car I drove. I told her that that would be an easy question to answer, but I thought in this circumstance that we might be able to understand something about her if we knew more about what prompted this question. While coming to the session, the thought occurred to her that perhaps I drove a Jaguar. Then again, she thought that perhaps I drove an Oldsmobile. I asked her what kind of people drive Jaguars and what kind drive Oldsmobiles. She replied that very hip, liberal people drive Jaguars and that very stodgy, conservative people drive Oldsmobiles. She told me that she was considering moving out of her parents' home for the first time to share an apartment with a man that she was dating. The patient was in conflict about how to explain this to her parents. The patient wondered, too, what my reaction would be to the move. We can now see that her question about the car reflected the attitudes she might expect from me. Would I be liberal and permissive and accept the move, or would I be rigid and criticize her for what she was planning to do? What seemed on the surface to be a simple question conveyed the transference feelings.

Ekstein and Wallenstein (1963) discuss the use of transference to the supervisor as a valuable concept in doing supervision. They feel that the transference phenomena observed in the trainee can be utilized in understanding the patient. I wonder about the validity of such a statement. First of all, the supervisory session is not conducted from a neutral position. The supervisor is critical and does offer advice and suggestions; he or she carries an educational function. It would be very difficult for the supervisor to say that the trainee's feelings toward him or her are the result of transference and, secondly, that these feelings have a definite relationship to what is going on in therapy. I have seen this concept used to explain some aspect of the trainee's behavior. It seems that if the trainee has only the most positive thoughts about the supervisor, then this is mature and realistic. If, on the other hand, the trainee develops negative feelings toward the supervisor, then this is seen as a derivation transference. I think the danger here is that the supervisor has a handy rationalization to deal with the student's reaction to incompetency, unwarranted criticism, and bad advice. I am not saying that transference feelings do not crop up between trainee and supervisor—and, incidentally, the other way around, too—but that the supervisory situation is so complex that extrapolations to the case material are unsound.

Although most supervisors have no difficulty pointing out transference material, some are reluctant to deal with countertransference phenomena. Countertransference is nothing more than the therapist's transference feeling toward the patient. In other words, countertransference is the inappropriate feelings, wishes, and attitudes on the therapist's part toward the patient that are displaced from significant objects in the therapist's past. Goin and Kline (1976) discuss the neglect on the part of most supervisors that they studied in dealing with countertransference while working with residents. They reviewed videotapes of supervisory sessions and noted the occurrence of supervisors' remarks concerning countertransference. They defined countertransference very broadly as the therapist's conscious as well as unconscious reaction toward and feelings about the patient. I do not agree with this definition. Not all feelings and reactions on the part of the trainee vis-à-vis the patient are to be included in countertransference. Let us say that a patient presents with a value system diametrically opposite to the values of the therapist and that the therapist dislikes the patient. Is that countertransference? That is a problem in viewing all of the trainee's feelings as countertransference; that is, a tendency of both the supervisors and trainees to try to make genetic connections. The supervisory session is not the appropriate place for this as the situation is not structured properly to handle this phenomena (Sloane, 1957). It can only be dealt with in the trainee's therapy.

Other writers, notably Tarachow (1963), have viewed supervision as a didactic, patient-centered experience. He included countertransference as a concept to be taught in general terms but not as something to be pointed out to the resident. Sloane reported on a panel before the American Psychoanalytic Association in which there was a general agreement that supervision must be aimed at teaching and not doing therapy on the trainee. Although countertransference might be recognized by the supervisor, it would not be pointed out to the trainee as such.

The approach that would be most consistent with psychoanalytic theory would be to utilize all sources of information in supervision to understand the patient. I not only consider the patient's words, feelings, and behavior but also the words, feelings, and behavior of the trainee. I try to have the student become aware of his or her own feelings about the patient as a way of understanding the patient. This can often give a clue as to how other persons react to the patient. A trainee presented a case of a whining, clinging, dependent patient who overintellectualized and externalized his problems. It was clear in the presentation that the trainee was growing impatient and intolerant. I commented that the patient appeared to have rubbed the trainee the wrong way. Others in the patient's life must have had similar reactions to him. We also saw that the trainee's reaction might be a pitfall in this case. Notice that all this was done without using the term countertransference. Was this a countertransference phenomena? It could have been, but I was in no position to deal with it if it was—I was not the trainee's therapist. I have had trainees that have tried to turn supervision into therapy. The dynamics involved are myriad. The issue is that supervision is not an adequate setting to deal with countertransference. Focusing on countertransference tends to shift the emphasis from the patient to the trainee. This latter point is inconsistent with the overall thrust, which should be centered around the understanding of the patient. I believe that it is appropriate for the supervisor to discuss therapy with the trainee. It is necessary when the trainee is too anxious and seriously acting out. I do not take supervisees into analysis or psychotherapy. This amounts to a conflict of interest. If the student refuses to get help and the welfare of the patient is threatened, I intervene administratively.

The term *acting out* refers to translating some thought or feeling into action other than words. It is always a resistance, since it impedes the flow of therapy. Acting out has acquired a negative connotation over the years. Currently, to say that someone is acting out means that he or she is a "bad" patient. Many therapists deal with acting out by using prohibition. Acting out can also be used to explain some inappropriate behavior on the part of the therapist, and here it also carries a negative connotation. The danger with viewing acting out this way is that it ceases to be something that is to be understood and instead becomes something to be forbidden. Obviously, some acting out is so destructive and dangerous to therapy that limits must be set. The patient might refuse to come in for the session as a way of dealing with angry feelings about the therapist. Another example is the therapist who indulges in sex with the patient.

There are some forms of acting out that are not so destructive but that give trainees difficulty. For example, what does the trainee do if a patient begins to read books on psychotherapy or discuss his sessions with his wife? What does the trainee do if the patient has her first affair as soon as therapy begins? Should the trainee prohibit the acting out in these cases? I think that the trainee must first try to understand what is being acted out. With the patient who is reading, find out what the books are. What strikes his interest in these books? What is going on in the transference when the patient finds himself reading books on psychotherapy? What topics are discussed with the wife? Are these topics also brought up in therapy?

As to the person who has an affair, one patient with a very highly eroticized initial transference reaction did have an affair just as therapy began. I doubt if therapy could have continued if this had been prohibited. It acted as a safety valve for her overwhelming feelings about the therapist. Yes, this did represent a resistance; but without the affair this particular patient could not have started therapy. Eventually, the feelings concerning the affair were analyzed. In summary, all acting-out behavior except those rare examples that are acutely destructive to therapy or to the actual welfare of the patient or therapist must first be understood in the same way as any other communication.

There is some question about the use of dreams in psychotherapy. This, I think, reflects a relative decrease in the interest in dreams on the part of some circles in psychoanalysis. Altman (1969) sees the decrease as reflecting a shift of interest from id psychology to ego psychology. I see the dream as another road to the unconscious, and one that is just as important as the patient's daydreams, masturbation fantasies, acting out, and so on.

Trainees tend to make mistakes in handling dreams in two directions. They either neglect dreams or try to do too much with them. I feel that dreams should be dealt with in psychotherapy but that therapists must realize that they are limited in what they can do with dreams in one or two sessions a week. Here is another place that the patient needs some instruction. I tell the patient that dreaming is a way that we have of thinking about difficult matters while we are asleep. Our mind disguises the problem in order to enable us to sleep. There is usually something that happens the day of the dream that gives the dream its form. In doing psychoanalysis, I instruct the patient to associate to the various elements in the dream. It is impossible to do complete dream interpretation in once-a-week psychotherapy. Here I ask the patient what feelings are contained in the dream and if the feelings are familiar or like anything else going on in his or her life currently. I also ask the patient about the theme of the dream and again ask if this is similar to something happening in life now. Although the dream contains infantile elements from the past, I believe that in doing psychotherapy one can get more mileage out of a dream by seeing how its latent content relates to the present.

A borderline male patient with paranoid trends that I was treating in once-a-week psychotherapy presented the following dream: He was sitting in a dentist's chair and the dentist, an older man, was trying to push a long metal tube down his throat. Then the patient found himself kneeling before the older man. He woke up from the dream at this point. While telling me the dream, he became very anxious. The patient told me that he knew the dream was homosexual and that that frightened him. The current material consisted of his complaints about the lack of male friends and about a teacher, an older man, who was very important to the patient, but by whom the patient felt slighted. Now, the therapist has a choice of options. Does one make an interpretation of the dream from the transference, or from the current reality, or from the patient's past? It was my judgment that a transference interpretation would have only made him more anxious. An interpretation based on the past would have missed the mark. I told him that although he considered the dream to be "homosexual," I believed that the dream reflected his present concerns, namely his problem with men, in particular his difficulties with his professor, who he felt was very critical and by whom he felt humiliated. He was relieved with this interpretation. The interpretation also gave him something manageable with which to deal in his current life. Obviously, the dream had homosexual elements but this particular patient could not have dealt with those at this time. It is very important that the trainee help the patient in psychotherapy to understand the here and now. I often see it as a caricature of psychoanalysis when the trainee tries too quickly to bridge the gap to the past. The dream is often misused in this way.

Summary

Psychoanalytic theory is based on two cornerstones—the dynamic unconscious and infantile sexuality. In order to demonstrate and understand the patient's intrapsychic conflicts, certain measures must be taken. It is the thesis of this chapter that the behavior of the supervisor influences many factors that permit the trainee to approach the patient from a psychoanalytic point of view. The manner in which the supervisor handles the privacy of the supervisory session, telephone calls, appointment times, note taking, and the issue of availability is often reflected in the way the trainee handles similar issues in therapy.

Before one can arrive at a psychodynamic understanding of the patient, clinical material must be gathered and organized. The diagnosis, a working hypothesis, must not be solely based on descriptive features but on the structural theory. Recommendations are given in this chapter on how to approach the initial interview. It is essential to inform the patient what is expected from him or her and what the patient can expect from therapy.

The concepts of transference, countertransference, and acting out are reviewed, and suggestions are given on how they should be dealt with in supervision. Supervision should always be patient oriented and any data, including the trainee's feelings, should be used to understand the patient. Supervision is not therapy. If the supervisor feels, however, that the patient's welfare is at stake because of a problem on the trainee's part, therapy for the student should be recommended.

CHAPTER 9

Group Supervision of Students and Staff

Paul A. Abels

> *A cat teacher was discussing her class with some other cat teachers. "I don't know what's wrong with those two rabbits in my class,"* she complained. *"They just don't have any motivation. Yesterday, I gave a wonderful session on how to catch mice, and none of them paid any attention."*
>
> —*A Sufi Tale*

People develop patterns of behavior based on frames of reference that they believe to be true. Their perceptions of the world are influenced by these patterns, which in turn often determine the types of responses people make to the world.

In the helping professions, we too have developed patterns of practice, teaching, learning, and supervision that carry primacy for us and that are usually only altered by an extreme demand to change or by a slowly emerging awareness that there may be other ways. Although there may be many ways to skin the proverbial cat, most of us usually feel we need only one, and we generally use it repetitively. Likewise, there may be many ways to "understand" groups, and the circumscribed pattern of thinking we use to know group behavior may limit our use of group supervision as a helping tool. In this chapter, we will explore the structure of groups and of their supervision; we will examine their fusion into a change-oriented process—"group supervision"; and we will wrestle with ways to modify patterns.

Supervision is practice. It is a process we use to assist each other in learning and doing the things needed in order to function on behalf of our immediate and holistic professional assignments; creatively, effectively, and satisfactorily. Group supervision is just one aspect of that broad area of supervision, but its emphasis on the use of the group as a medium for bringing about consequential change in people's lives brings it closer to the natural way in which people change and grow. It is through relationships with others that most change occurs. *And it is with other people that our professional assignment—the achievement of a just society in which all people are treated with equality and dignity—can be achieved.*

The Group as a Medium for Learning

The concepts of the group as supportive mechanism for the individual, as mediator, and as link to society have been documented by writers in the area of small group and change research (Schwartz, 1961; Abels, 1970).

Experienced workers acting in supervisory positions can orient the novice to required tasks. Staff, involved in a supportive interaction process with other staff toward a common purpose, can help each other learn new skills, informally on the job and more formally in supervisory meetings. The growing use of group supervision, often projected as a time-saving device, has had secondary benefits in terms of group and individual productivity as well as in an increase in staff autonomy and the pressure for egalitarian processes within the agency. Reynolds (1965, p. 120) suggests that "In relation to the teacher's learning, it has been a comforting thought to many . . . that you can always trust a group to teach them [the teachers]. The statement is met with incredulity at first. The skills necessary to evoke from a group this revelation of their needs are not inconsiderable. . . . At first these skills seem unattainable. Soon, however—very soon if a leader is capable of some trust in people, even when the outcome is in doubt—a group begins to respond and make itself known. The joy of seeing that a relationship of trust actually works is second to no other joy in a teacher's life."

The structuralists maintain that there are sets of rules in all societies that govern the behavior of that society (Levinson, 1972). Like the unconscious, these rules or "deep structure" may not be known by all members. The paradoxical surface behavior of groups has led to the examination of basic group motivations. Bion, a psychiatrist working at the Tavistock Clinic, has developed a conception of groups very much akin to "deep structure" analysis. He suggests (1959) that groups develop emotionally based orientations that prevent them from working on the avowed goals of the group. These nonwork styles, which he calls "basic assumptions," are known to the group and take the form of "dependency," "fight-flight" and "pairing" behaviors. Groups develop their own methods of nonwork, but each is related to one of these three basic assumptions (Bion, 1959).

The nonwork group will behave "as if" it believed it had come together in order to fight or to be dependent, but "the basic assumptions of the basic assumption groups are usually outside of awareness" (Rioch, 1976, p. 124). The task for the worker is to demand that the group work on its contractual goals, and to rechannel into work the energy now being put into basic assumptions. In a sense, nonwork is transformed into its opposite, namely work, or at least is made subservient to work.

The Structural Dynamics and Patterns of Groups

The group structure is the pattern of interactions among the members of the group, particularly those interactions that they expect from one another in order to help the group function. While a group can be said to have a boundary, in that people are in or out, this is a minor element of structure. It is the interactions that mold the group. If the group members interact frequently and their attendance is expected and demanded, the structure will be tight.

If the interactions are directed more to some people than to others, or if some people's interactions are more valued than others, the structure may reflect a hierarchical development.

We might see these interactions in linear phases. The first phase consists of *people interacting* around a vague common goal; this is the prestructural stage. The structure then evolves from the establishing of *norms* or rules of behavior, the *feelings* members start to have about each other, which in turn establish the *status* hierarchy in the group. These tend to concretize the roles that individual members take and their group relationships, which then permits action toward the goals. Naturally, the interrelatedness of these elements goes beyond linear analysis. People, interactions, goals, norms, feeling, status, and actions become the basic tools for understanding the group; the parts cannot be understood in isolation.

A number of group behavior analysts have chosen to look at the development of the group over time. They suggest that groups may be viewed as having a developmental history—a beginning, middle, and end. They have attempted to break this "group life" into a series of *phases*. In addition to helping us view the processes that groups develop to help them accomplish their tasks, phase theory helps us understand that some of the problems the group faces are rather typical and are related to its specific developmental stage.

We will review briefly a few of these views of group life. As we outline the topical headings of each of the phases, note the similarity, regardless of the professional orientation of the author. In the area of training and education, Bennis and Shepherd (1956) suggest the following phases: (1) dependence flight, counterdependence flight, and resolution catharsis; and (2) shared responsibility, enchantment flight, disenchantment flight, and consensual validation. Mills (1964) suggests (1) encounter, (2) testing boundary, (3) negotiating indigenous normative system, (4) production, and (5) separation.

Psychologists studying the process of the group and its interaction likewise have observed similar developmental phases. The work of Bales and Strodtbeck on interaction analysis (1965) and Tuckman's work (1965) on group life are just two examples. Bales suggests (1) orientation, (2) evaluation, and (3) control. Tuckman proposes (1) forming, (2) storming, (3) norming, and (4) performing.

Social work has also had its stage theory advocates. Sarri and Galinski (1969) formulate a seven-step process: (1) origin, (2) formation, (3) intermediate, (4) revision, (5) intermediate, (6) maturation, and (7) termination. A five-phase model is proposed by Garland, Kolodny, and Kolodny (1966): (1) preaffiliation, (2) power and control, (3) intimacy, (4) differentiation, and (5) separation.

In summary, the phases of group life as seen by most observers seem to consist of the following rather loosely categorized steps.

1. Some type of *forming*. A period where the members are attempting to find out who the members are and what they want to do together. There is a concern with the self and individual needs. Security and safety are very important elements.
2. A process of working out the *goals* of the group and the norms among the members. There may be an element of conflict as the jockeying for position/status and goal priorities are set. Some attempts to set a contract for work occur.
3. A coming to terms with the realities of *this* group and its work, with an understanding of one's place in the group and the tasks that must be done. The work of the group starts to be accomplished.
4. A decision to continue or to disband, to renegotiate for new goals and new statuses as needed.

As the change agent is aware of these various phases, he or she comes to recognize that he or she may have different tasks to perform in relation to each phase-related task of the group. At the formation stage, security and recruitment may be urgent. Helping the group focus on an initial task to be accomplished, for example, can relieve some of the stress of concern for self, but certainly not all.

In supervision, the developmental structure (patterns of interaction) is influenced by the fact that usually one member of the group, the supervisor, is immediately seen as a person with a different, if not higher, status than some of the others (Kaslow, 1972). That person's interactions are seen as more important than those of others, although not necessarily as better. The status of supervisor may imply boss, teacher, evaluator, or parent, and the pattern often tends to reflect the hierarchical structures first symbolized by the family. This status-oriented structure may likewise lead to repetition of many familial problems of authority, rivalry, and competition. This historical pattern is structured into all groups and must be dealt with, but the pattern can be transformed into such alternative structures as brotherhood or community. These alternative structures offer other action options. "A certain type of structure permits certain kinds of mental operations to occur, so that certain behavior, feelings, perceptions, language, and thinking are the necessary consequences of that particular kind of structure" (Weiner, 1975, p. 118).

Systems analysis suggests that the structure of the group influences the parts creating the structure, just as the parts influence the appearance and functioning of the structure. We are dealing with the group as a system and with reciprocal feedback. In fact, the members merge into a system with a structure at the point at which the interacting parts are working toward a similar goal.

A valuable concept for our understanding of the surface structure is the fact that by modifying one part of the system we can often bring about changes in the total system. Generally, it does not matter which part we select as the entry point; change will subsequently take place in all as they move to a new equilibrium.

Thus in a supervisory group the entrance of new members or the leaving of a member will alter the nature of the exchanges (communication) and modify the bonds of feeling and/or power relationships. Improving the feelings members have about each other or themselves will alter their ability to interact with others. Modifying the status of the supervisor by his or her reducing the power role will open the way for other members of the group to function or at least will help them reassess their own relationship to power. The crucial element, however, is not change, but "goal-directed" change. What change in the action of the supervisor helps the group move closer to its goals?

The Practice of Group Supervision

It has become increasingly clear that we cannot work with people without understanding the reciprocal underlying patterns of behavior, not only a formulation of the "educational diagnosis" of each individual but also the interpersonal patterns that evolve when interactions occur, which are in essence the context of the exchange. Two patterns that may create problems for the group members are (1) the pattern of supervisory leadership and (2) the members' own patterns of values and reasoning.

Although there have been a number of studies relating leadership styles to group productivity, the classic and still most noteworthy of these was carried out by White and Lippit (1960). Three types of leader behavior tested were "authoritarian" (policy determined by the leader), "democratic" (all policies a matter of group discussion and decision, encouraged and assisted by the leader), and "laissez-faire" (complete freedom for group or individual decision, with a minimum of leader participation). Their studies produced evidence for the following generalizations:

1. *Authoritarian-led groups* produced a greater quantity of work over a short period of time, but experienced more hostility, competition, and aggression—especially scapegoating—more discontent beneath the surface, more dependence, and less originality.
2. *Democratically led groups,* slower getting into production, were more strongly motivated, became increasingly productive with time and learning, experienced more friendliness and teamwork, praised one another more frequently, and expressed greater satisfaction.
3. *Laissez-faire* groups did less and poorer work than either of the others, wasted more time in horseplay, talked more about what they should be doing, experienced more aggression than the democratic groups but less than the authoritarian, and expressed a preference for democratic leadership.

The evidence for democratic supervisory styles is clearly presented and is certainly consonant with the articulated ideals of the human services. It also comes closest to my concept of the role of supervisor as *contract synergist* (Abels, 1976).

The contract synergist model is the approach most likely to maximize worker participation in the decision-making process within the community. This approach does not see the worker as underdeveloped or subject to manipulations by experts who know the answers. It accepts the premises that people are seeking solutions to problems for which they do not have the answers and that they can be helped to learn either the technical skills, political interaction techniques, or interpersonal competence necessary to deal with these problems. The function of the contract synergist is to help these things happen. His actions are not on the individuals. Always they are with individuals. Decisions are jointly arrived at, and for the most part the relationship is a reciprocal one. There is a quest between workers and supervisor for an authenticity of relationship, a reaching out for each other in a way that the development of that sense of "community" among the staff and the administrators which permits authentic and satisfactory use of one another [can occur].

This thrust for contract, community support, and synergistic reasoning comes close to the postconventional moral reasoning concept of Lawrence Kohlberg and relates to our second pattern-related concern. Attempts to help people make their values explicit so that they can be assessed and modified are highlighted by Kohlberg's approach, called "moral development theory." He attempts to formulate exact levels of moral reasoning as well as to explicate the processes for raising the moral level of participants. He describes three major levels of thinking, broken into six stages (Kohlberg, 1969) (see also Abroms, Chapter 4):

Preconventional Level

Stage 1.   Right is obedience to power and avoidance of punishment.

Stage 2.   Right is taking responsibility for oneself in meeting one's own needs and leaving to others the responsibility for themselves. Fairness is "You do something for me; I'll do something for you."

Conventional Level

Stage 3.   Right is being good in the sense of having good motives, having concern for others, and "putting yourself in the other person's shoes."

Stage 4.   Right is maintaining the rules of a society and serving the welfare of the group or society.

Postconventional Level

Stage 5.   Right is based on recognizing the individual rights within a society with agreed-on rules, a social contract.

Stage 6.   Right is obligation to principles applying to all human-kind, principles of respect for human personality and for justice and equality.

Kohlberg's research suggests that peers, such as agency colleagues, can help raise the individual's moral reasoning levels.

We will examine the process of group supervision by comparing a number of critical incidents in the light of Kohlberg's formulations. The comparison of cases is a valuable method of inquiry and theory development; see Abels (1977). The following group conference took place in a public welfare agency utilizing homemaker aides administered by one department and caseworkers administered by another. The excerpt is from the supervisor's record.

> As I entered the office at 2:00 P.M., I was confronted by the desk clerk saying that there was an emergency. Immediately Aide A came into my office in an upset mood (which is unusual for this aide) with two other aides, saying, "Supe, here is a case where the caseworker is refusing to grant this client her full budget." (She went on to explain the case, and the budget had been figured incorrectly.) "Has the caseworker been contacted?" I asked. "No, that's why I brought the case to you. The client has tried to get the caseworker to change the budget, but the worker told her that she wouldn't do it until she had seen her." The aide was now very excited and angry and continued, saying, "You always said that 'right is right, and wrong is wrong,' and the worker is wrong, so what are you going to do?" Supervisor: "I felt pressed at this point, as Aide B and Aide C were in agreement with Aide A." "Wait a minute, Aide A, let me call the worker and get her side of it." ("I generally don't contact workers in other departments, but I felt this was an emergency.") "She is wrong, that's all," responded

Aide A. Aide B and C (nodding in approval) : "That's right."

I felt that the question was whether or not I would back the client or the worker and that for me to back the worker would be intolerable to the staff. I called the worker. The worker explained that she had tried on numerous occasions to contact the client and that there was a question about a bastardy filing on her last child. "This is no reason to punish the client," said Aide A. "You're right," I responded, "but it's obvious to me that there is something personal going on between the client and the worker that is not coming out. This is highly unusual for her." "She is still wrong," said Aide A. The others agreed.

Traditional patterns (Pattern 1) of supervision have had the supervisor "giving" to the worker. In the excerpt just given, the pattern is a switch from the supervisor giving to the aides to the aide giving the supervisor information, hoping to modify the traditional relationship (Pattern 2). The control of the stress is in the hands of the aide, rather than the supervisor. The pattern of worker-boss relationship is reversed, but it is still there, since the worker now wants to assume the boss role. The supervisor attempts to respond by offering "things," but this is not satisfying because the aides want a repetition of an earlier pattern—"Right is right."

The structure has not changed; instead the norms of behavior are reversed. Feelings are the same, the interactions are a mirror image of the traditional pattern, and inquiry is thwarted by the basic assumptions of fight-flight depicted in the following diagram.

S
A

Pattern 1.
Supervisor (S)
Controls the
Stress.

Pattern 2.
Aide (A)
Controls the
Stress.

The supervisory transaction reverts to a one-to-one pattern with an audience; the group is not expected to search for an approach to the problem. Reconstruction can occur if the framework

becomes an ongoing reciprocal transaction leading to a helical interaction, which may begin with distance between the supervisor and
the aide but soon begins to converge through synergistic transactions.

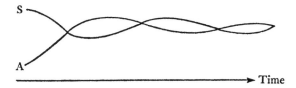

S

A

→ Time

Pattern 3. Increased Mutual Understanding and Work.

Standard supervisory approaches would see this supervisory
transaction as an experienced supervisor-teacher-administrator giving
proper instructions to a group of novices. They then would learn
and make the right interventions. If we were to analyze the group
dynamics by Bion's approach, the incident would reflect a great
deal of fight-flight, dependency, and pairing and very little work.
As long as the supervisor maintains an "answer man" response,
this symbolic one-up-manship will continue, and the group will
remain dependent. The way out is also the way in—finding a solution within the ideas and strengths of the group. Norms need to be
developed that demand that the group work on its own tasks.

Like the cat teacher, the supervisor is leading from her
cognitive structure (patterned meanings) of what is good for aides;
they, however, are not interested in mice as prey; they want higher-
ranking caseworkers, and they are better organized than are the
rabbits as a "pressure" group to pursue their own ends. The results,
however, may be the same: frustration, fight-flight, pairing, inaction,
and reasoning at preconventional levels.

The aides are operating from a low level of moral reasoning.
From their point of view, reciprocity has not been followed. They
want the supervisor to help them "get even." This supervisor has
historically operated from a low level of moral reasoning ("right
is right, wrong is wrong"; if you *do* the right thing, everything will
be fixed up), but she begins to reason at a higher level when she
recognizes that any one action directed at the caseworker will have
unintended repercussions from the system.

There is a solution, providing the group is interested in work
rather than in a fight-flight "setup." An attempt to consider alterna-

tive solutions and what the ramifications might be to client, agency, and the group's ability to function in the agency would serve as a means of mutual education. This calls for a higher level of reasoning (Kohlberg's Stages 3 and 4). What the supervisor knows about the system, the threat and the consequences of their actions for the total agency system must become what the group knows. In fact, the solution is in raising their reasoning ability and level of awareness. They are all the source for their own learning. What each knows alone is not helpful to the group, and unless they can reason on fairly similar levels each one's communications will bypass the others.

What they know together can lead to a synthesis and a synergistic solution. Mary Follett (1940, p. 3) suggested that the "first rule then, for obtaining integration is to put our cards on the table, face the real issue, uncover the conflict, bring the whole thing into the open." The objective is to develop Pattern 3 processes, to develop synergistic approaches to problem resolution.

Synergy is the noncompetitive melding of two or more often conflicting ideas into an outcome that is an advance over any of the original ideas; that is, it has a better payoff for all. It is a pattern of communication that permits this variation to take place. It provides a receptive milieu or culture in which growth can take place and in which the individual feels a response from other parts of the system that are "simpatico." Synergy is the joint search with the worker for "truth," an inquiry into how two or more people, often with differing views of what the answer might be, can find a radical, effective solution to a problem. Follett (1940) recognized this concept when she spoke of constructive conflict: Integration occurs when "a solution has been found in which both desires have found a place, that neither side has had to sacrifice anything."

In essence, we are not considering what is best for any one segment of the subsystem but what is best for all involved. As supervisor, my extrapersonal communication might be, "If, by attempting to modify the system, I can help the client and the agency (the worker and myself), then I have come up with a result that rewards everyone." Admittedly, these solutions are difficult to achieve in a complex society or system; some of the reasons they are so difficult for us are that (1) the nature of our culture infers an "I win—you lose" or zero sum game; (2) we have not learned to practice synergistic approaches; and (3) we reason at conventional levels. In synergy orientations, each party in the transaction maintains somewhat selfish thinking (what's best for me and the group). This should lead to a higher order of performance than if each looks only at what is best for himself.

New beginnings should also have within them the vision of the future, through which the group members can share their ideas of what they are here for and their hopes for the group. Any beginning can be a chance to talk out the public visions and the private hopes. Do we mean the things we say? Can the agency help accomplish the tasks to which the members are committed? It may be the time to assess what the limitations may be and to discuss that the group is part of a process of engaging the members, clarifying functions, mutual sharing, increasing awareness, and making commitments to the work. The focus is on unfolding a paradigm of supervision in which the group would like to participate. In order to do this, however, an additional agenda item must be forthcoming— *how the members will use each other and the supervisor.* In the explication of this item, the skill and sensitivity of the supervisor are put to the test. Reference to the phases of group development will remind us that during the early stages, the members are most concerned with their own needs and with their relationship with other members and the supervisor. "Will I be liked?" "Will I learn?" "Will I make it?" and "Who are the others?" will be initial encounter and formation concerns. The supervision must be sensitive to this focus and accept this situational inability to perform before these socioemotional concerns have been worked through. It is important, however, that the supervisor's part of the contract be clearly stated.

If the structural pattern of the hierarchical family is to be avoided, the supervisor needs to be aware of his self-imposed tightrope. Attempts to minimize status will create problems for some members, who will see the supervisor who does so as avoiding authority, as weak or unconcerned. They may even view it as a ploy. Levinson points out some of the dangers in this misinterpretation process. He refers to it as the *fallacy of understanding* (1972, p. 197): "The attribution of meaning to behavior is a highly arbitrary

business . . . were it possible to be correct, the content will still
be less relevant than the transformational relevance of the interpretation; that is, the patient will hear what fits the choreography
of the session." An attempt to structure sessions in a nonhierarchical
way may be seen as another authoritarian approach or, as in the
following example, a sermon. The excerpt is from a supervisory
session that took place after a two-month vacation:

> For the sake of review and for Miss Mott, who was
> new to the group, I reviewed what group supervision
> was and the purpose: I [supervisor] explained that it was
> another method of supervising. I felt that during the few
> sessions we had had in the past I had enjoyed them [the
> staff]. I realized that because of additional responsibilities
> I had not been consistent in individual conferences with
> some. There were gaps in learning of certain areas. I did
> hope that through group supervision some of these areas
> could be covered and discussed together. I, as well as they,
> would be learning.
>
> I pointed out that we must never forget that the
> purpose of our job is to help children and adoptive
> families. We discussed the fact that the responsibility for
> the meetings would be a shared one and that they would
> have an opportunity to test ideas, discuss cases. I added
> that in the previous sessions I felt that I had done too
> much talking. I hoped that in future sessions there would
> be more responsibility, preparation, and discussion on
> their part. We would be open and honest with each
> other, attempt to get into attitudes and feelings. However,
> it was meant to be constructive criticism and not directed
> at anyone personally. I then asked if maybe Miss Pond
> and Mrs. Ord had any comments to make. Mrs. Ord
> stated that she had gotten a lot from them. She felt that
> one thing she had learned from the group session was
> the beginning of a feeling of continuity in contacts and
> what to look for in supervising an adoptive home. I
> asked Miss Mott if this kind of supervision made sense
> to her. She added she liked the idea.

Although the supervisor is apparently attempting to communicate that she wants an open group, her remaining the "center"

quickly establishes the status relationships. All roads lead from and to the supervisor. The way out may have to be a transactional one, in which the supervisor states what he or she is trying to do, what he or she thinks happens when one does it, seeks staff feedback, responds, and, in a spiraling give and take, starts to evolve a new group supervision paradigm. The supervisor may attempt to restructure the situation in a way that opens the members to the deeper levels of behavior that may determine their actions in the group. He or she indeed preempts their repressed feelings by exposing them as possible obstacles, as strengths, and even as pointing the way toward other appropriate models for supervision.

Although this may appear to be a time-consuming process, such transactions, immediately successful or not, serve as common experiences to which the worker's own attempts to do something different with their clients can be compared. The questioning, doubts, fears, hostility, experimentation, patience, acceptance, and rejection all become grist for the mill. An analogy can also be made between beginning with one's own clients and the group's beginnings. In this approach, a comparison of cases and experiences becomes the scientific base for clinical and supervisory practice.

The role of the supervisor, then, in these early group meetings is to ask questions of people, to set the vision as he or she sees it, to present his or her own style, to find out what the members seek, and to present the paradoxes of trying to help, change, and teach. In addition, the supervisor becomes a major role model of higher moral reasoning. The modeling role is probably one of the most effective teaching approaches.

Group members will have their own models, their own degrees of openness and closedness to new ideas, their own levels of moral reasoning, and their own balance between certainty and ambiguity. This situation needs to be dealt with by attempts to restructure the way people look at their ways of thinking and doing. Are they satisfied with their approach? Have others tried it? Does it work for them? How often? Why are people changing their paradigms? Kuhn (1970) suggests that when the older paradigms no longer answer enough of the questions, new paradigms replace them. One needs to examine the older paradigms and to also show respect for alternative approaches. The compilation of data and comparative cases may reveal more effective paradigms on which more competent practice can be based.

Transformation. The task-centered group can use almost any experience as a means of comparison, inquiry, and growth. Nothing need be off limits to the group if it is within the breadth of the contract and promotes the work. The contract is not a limiting concept that outlines the script to be followed by the members. Too often it has been used as an excuse to impose worker goals or to limit the workers' inquiry. The basic rule of thumb seems to be that "Facts should be observed and described without allowing any theoretical preconception to decide whether some are more important than others . . . facts should be studied in relation to themselves (by what kind of concrete process did they come into being?) and in relation to the whole" (Levi-Strauss, 1973, p. 376). In other words, what does the data mean, and what is its significance in this particular context?

If the group is not interested in contractual work but is preoccupied with other "basic assumptions" such as fight-flight, the group will destroy itself no matter how relevant the material, because the work might be too threatening. The following is an excerpt from a group supervisory record. The supervisor is the narrator.

> Miss Paine said that a five-year-old, who had been in one foster home since she had been sixteen months old and was now about to be adopted, wanted to know if Miss Paine would still be her caseworker. Miss Paine said yes, even though the child was adopted by the foster parents; then the worker quickly changed the subject. Someone commented, "Well, that is one way to handle it." Miss Marlow wondered if the child might have wanted to know if the new parents were all right and where she was going. I [supervisor] wondered if Miss Paine could begin talking with the child about various people she was concerned with and review her past life. Miss Paine stated that she had done this once, but early in her contacts; maybe now it would be more meaningful. At this point, Miss Reynolds entered. She took a chair. For about ten minutes, she listened as the group became involved in conversation around children after placement who with-

draw and will have nothing to do with their workers. Miss Reynolds then asked what to do when a child does the opposite. This particular child tries to kiss you and shows affection to you instead of to the adoptive mother. She was asked how she had handled this, and responded that she tries not to get too close to such a child.

Miss Marlow asked if Miss Reynolds was rejecting the child by pushing him away. Mrs. Ord wanted to know what was wrong with a four-year-old child who wanted to kiss you. Miss Reynolds stated that she felt that the adoptive mother might be jealous of her relationship to the child and she was trying to hold back. Miss Reynolds stated that it was difficult for her to work with the adoptive mother to give the child more love and hadn't seemed to be able to get through to her. One day on the telephone, the adoptive mother told me, "The child likes you," and I didn't know what to say. One in the group commented, "Maybe you don't like the adoptive mother." Miss Reynolds shrugged her shoulders.

In this session, Miss Reynolds asks for help, but instead she is attacked. Is this a switch in the usual procedure of asking for help and getting it? Why does this occur? Why is there so much fight-flight in this supervisory meeting? Looking at the pattern here, we see that Miss Paine asks for help and is attacked by the group; the help comes from the supervisor. When Miss Reynolds asks for help, she too is attacked by the group, and, as we shall see, she is "saved" by the supervisor. We might assume that the process is repetitive and the reason for the pattern, although in the unconscious of the members, might be hypothesized to be, "Only the supervisor in this group is permitted to give help. The members' role is to criticize or attack." The record continues:

I felt at this time I should intervene, so I stated that I was aware of this case and it was a difficult one. Miss Reynolds and I were dissatisfied with the situation in the adoptive home and I hadn't been too helpful to her in our individual conferences. Perhaps I was rejecting the adoptive mother? I wondered what the group thought might be done in such a case. I could not elicit anything from the group so I added that we all had cases which might be similar to this one. They laughed.

The pattern appears similar to a family in which the siblings attack each other and compete for the love of the parent. The laughter, of course, is not a response to humor, but an acknowledgment that they will "back off," that, indeed, in the eyes of the supervisor, who knows their secrets, their performance is not any better than that of Miss Reynolds.

The Supervisor's Normative Focus. How could this situation be restructured so that the members support the work that must be done if Miss Reynolds and the group are to grow? In my estimation, the most vital learning and action task is to be able to take a holistic view, to be able to see the patterned interactions within the context of a *normative* view of supervision, normative in the sense of what working together should be like. The key questions are (Abels, 1977): What kind of an agency would we hope it to be? What consequences would we like to see for ourselves and our clients? How could we achieve our ultimate goals of a "just community"? Beyond that,

1. We can restructure roles by minimizing the status of expert, leader, parent figure, versus the beginner, novice, infant, dope.
2. We can restructure our messages: All people are worthy of respect. No one is more deserving, not even the supervisor. No one is to be a scapegoat, not even the destructive member.
3. We can restructure the situation by presenting cases that are anonymous, from "other places" or from the supervisor.
4. We can restructure the norms by clarifying the contract, the ground rules, the expectations, and reasoning ability.
5. We can restructure other persons' understanding of the situation by giving new knowledge about ourselves, others, and the situation.
6. We can restructure our ways of thinking to include viewing the consequences of our actions, not merely our goals.

The pronoun *we* is utilized in all of these procedures to emphasize the transactional nature of any effort made to bring about change. In addition, it is important to remember that "group supervision is always group supervision." For example, after the earlier dialogue, the supervisor might have asked Miss Reynolds if she felt the group had been helpful to her, or asked the group what they thought was going on, or said to the group "I always find myself giving advice or trying to save someone." By examining but not yielding to the nonwork patterns played out by the members, by maintaining the thrust of the contract, by insisting on inquiry and evidence, by raising the consciousness of the members about their patterns of reasoning and the paradoxes of perception and interpretation, the supervision can help transform the patterns into more constructive and productive ones.

Something *different* needs to be done if change to more productive patterns is to occur. The change need not come from the supervisor; members can alter the transactional procedures as well. Finally, as supervisors and workers, we may also have to work on "restructuring" the agency if service is not adequate.

Survival and Competence. Do these problematic supervisory conferences mean that these workers will not do a competent job with their clients? Not at all, providing that workers are not forced into a defensive situation. Bruner (1966, p. 129) suggests that "coping respects the requirements of problems we encounter while still respecting our integrity. Defending is a strategy whose objective is avoiding or escaping from problems for which we believe there is no solution that does not violate our integrity of functioning."

Since learning takes place constantly, we know that the members are learning something, but their learning should be related to increased competence with clients. Competency is not static; people need to continually develop their ability to help. The competent worker is one who can inquire after new knowledge about him- or herself and use that knowledge on behalf of the agency and client. Too often, as in the previous record, energies go into survival in the group.

For effective supervision, the communications must deal with expanding both the cognitive and affective consciousness of the staff. This can be done if people try to deal with why they communicate what they do and with the symbolism of the content, rather than with the quality of their communication skills. How can communication be improved? Can the unconscious be made conscious in group supervision? Perhaps not, but the structure, the patterning, can be openly examined.

The supervisor and the group can experiment with certain approaches that may help them restructure their patterns of thinking and acting. Efforts to promote more openness to ideas led to the development of "brainstorming" techniques and the Spectrum Approach (Prince, 1970). Prince believed people generally attack new ideas (following traditional fight-flight patterns). They do this by searching out the bad part of an idea and attempt to then destroy the total idea. He has evolved a process in which the members must deal with the good part of the idea and build from there. This is similar to Taoist thinking, to becoming one with the thrust of the other, rather than opposing it. If the supervisor thinks in terms of what the person is attempting to achieve and how he or she can help rather than oppose, he or she can move the group toward a synergistic solution. The ideas are now group-worked ideas, and their potential value is clear when the specific idea choice needs to be made. This procedure restructures the thinking processes in ways that alter traditional patterns. The use of analogy, metaphor, and teaching stories also permit this kind of restructuring. Our introductory "cat" story represents a traditional teaching method used by the Sufis. The story has meaning on various levels and permits the learner to tune into what he or she is ready for. Idries Shah, discussing such Sufi tales, suggests the story "may be understood at any one of many depths. There is the joke, the moral, and the little extra which brings the consciousness . . . a little further on the way to realization" (Shah, 1964, p. 63).

The use of analogies, comparisons with nature or mechanical objects, is part of a creative problem-solving process, synectics, by which traditional thinking patterns might be modified. The question, "What is the similarity between the concept of acceptance and an electric toaster?" opens new ways of thinking that do not require expertise in acceptance (Koberg and Bagnall, 1972).

A Paradigm for Our Time

Staff engaged in attempting to develop their capacities for helping are part of a vast network of interrelated acts—past, present, and future—that impact on both their clients and themselves. The more holistic the view staff can take, the more relevant the action can be on behalf of the client; that is, the more one sees and deals with the context, the more one relates to the total person. This is the model for our times—a normative, ecological approach that deals with the person as part of a system. Practice that recognizes the power inherent in this approach can lend hope to the people. But the supervisor must compose the structural complex in a way that permits staff to find a pattern of manageable proportions to deal with.

Kurt Lewin's force field analysis offers such a perspective (1952, p. 330). On a linear plane, it permits one to view all the parts of the system, including external forces. Lewin held that, first, any social situation could be perceived as being in a state of equilibrium or balance at any point in time and that the nature of that equilibrium could be assessed. Current staff functioning, for example, is held in equilibrium by a number of opposing forces that are equal in total strength. Second, certain forces are at work that promote learning and doing in a new way. These driving forces are a desire to do a good job, recognition, potentials for growth, supervision, attending classes, and an open mind. Third, certain forces are at work that retard change. The restraining forces are heavy job loads, busy supervisors, fear of the new, stereotyping, and traditional patterns of behavior. For example, Hare (1972, p. 528) points out that "Some supervisors saw peer-group supervision as an attack on their worth." This is a restraining force that would need to be worked out. Fourth (returning to Lewin), there are certain blocks that are neutral but that still influence the worker; for example, building size, budget, and laws.

Theoretically, if the current level of functioning is in balance, an alteration in either the driving or restraining forces should alter that balance. The addition of another driving force or the elimination of a restraining force should help the supervisory group move closer to the goals of improved practice. Lewin (1952) suggests specific steps in the process:

1. Unfreezing the current behavior. This may be done through confrontation, change of space (cultural island), presenting new facts.

2. Moving to a new level, preferably closer to the desired level.
3. Refreezing the behavior at the new level. Find ways of supporting those changes that have been accomplished.
4. Repeat the process.

Force field analysis can be done over a period of months in an agency analysis, or it can be done in a much smaller way in five minutes prior to meeting with a supervisee. It helps maintain a focus on the tasks to be worked. By maintaining a "point of concentration" that helps focus on the specific piece of the problem to be solved, even large problems can be partialized and dealt with. This point of concentration must be maintained by all the group members when they are engaged in problem solving. The group itself can explore the forces for and against change, and can decide which factor can provide leverage for change.

In addition to a systems analysis such as that offered by Lewin, we feel there is value in seeing change itself as an engagement process consisting of four phases: involvement, commitment, inquiry, and doing.

1. *Involvement.* The start of a change process is choice. The involvement of staff members in a change process requires them to confront their own uneasiness with their current functioning and the vision of an autonomous productive practice. Thus, motivation might then be seen as a quest for competence. An initial task of the supervisor is to help the group members search out their uneasiness and to *involve* themselves in a mutual inquiry toward competence. It is a period of emergence to awareness. A number of authors have discussed some of the techniques that they have found valuable in order to involve people in learning and change. Some have already been mentioned in this chapter; others include Thelen (1960), who suggests that the beginning of an educative experience is an "encounter" in which something happens to pique the interest of an individual, and Bion (1961), who suggests that the violation of expectations is one way of involving people in change. The key, however, seems to be the acceptance that something "different" must take place that can act as a catalyst for initial engagement. Lewin might refer to this as the "unfreezing" stage.

2. *Commitment.* The awareness involvement brings about

should, with skillful help from the supervisor and/or colleagues, lead to change-oriented work. Although the group may not yet know what needs to be transformed and into what, no uniform agreement is needed in order to accept a goal of improved practice and a commitment to work. This commitment may be a contract or perhaps a "metacontract," an understanding that the group needs each other and will work together. In some situations, the commitment is more formal, and includes assignment of roles, procedures, expectations, and evaluative procedures. A contract is not a program; it should not detail tasks and means to the extent that thoughtful experimentation and change is limited. The contract should serve merely as a grounding from which to grow.

3. *Inquiry.* There are many methods that can be used to seek new knowledge. While awareness and commitment are important traits for change, if the search for new knowledge utilizes biased (biased for the individual) means of inquiry, then no new results may be evident. A lack of sound inquiry procedures, for some supervisory groups, "merely resulted in a sharing of ignorance" (Hare and Frankena, 1972, p. 529). New methods of raising the moral reasoning level of staff must be found. The inquiry process itself must be transformed; the familiar must be made strange, and the strange familiar. A cognitive restructuring can take place that lets people see things differently. Case studies can be broadened by listing alternative solutions, tried and true maxims can be questioned by asking what would happen if the opposite were true. Comparisons with less familiar situations can be sought. For example, in looking at beginnings between worker and client, one might search out how contacts with an insurance salesperson, a conductor, teacher, a traffic policeman, or a lawyer begin. What are the similarities and differences, what insights and data from these comparative situations might we use? Similarly, comparisons need to be made from practitioner experiences.

4. *Doing.* The goal of awareness, commitment, and inquiry is the application of the newly acquired knowledge and skills to the improvement of the client situation. The consequences of these preliminary transformation processes should be enhanced client service. The doing we refer to in this section is not the doing for self-growth that the earlier steps involved, but the utilization of new

insights in the doing for others. The synergistic view recognizes that the doing for self and others is at the heart of creative, nondestructive change.

Staff can learn to risk and act, but they must feel comfortable in doing so. The comfort is related to the commitment and confidence they have in their own knowledge and skills, in the support of the group, and in the vision the agency and profession provide.

Change in the ecological pattern is a variant of the systems or structural model. It recognizes that, like practice, supervision must deal with the total person—the supervisory group is a system, a microcosm that reflects the values and patterns of interaction of the broader social structure. The system, however, is not only the group—it is also the interrelatedness of groups, their history, their present, and their dreams for the future. The basic structure of the group carries within it the possibility of a higher morality and an evolutionary potential for a just society.

The roots of the new paradigm are already here, reflected in Ivan Illich's concerns related to tools for conviviality. "The only solution to the environmental crises is the shared insight of people that they would be happier if they could work together and care for each other" (Illich, 1973, p. 53). Group supervision can offer an opportunity for a supportive community whose norms of mutual aid and client service permit only the best in practice to develop.

CHAPTER 10

Training of Marital and Family Therapists

Florence Whiteman Kaslow

The past decade has witnessed the rapid mushrooming of the discipline of family therapy in private practice, special school settings, family service agencies, mental health and child guidance clinics, psychiatric out-patient clinics, and hospital in-patient units. In a few decades, the field has progressed from its infancy, during which only a few courageous pioneers experimented with it and are even alleged to have practiced it secretly, to its occasional use as a treatment modality when all else seemed to have failed, to the present, when family therapy has grown into a major therapeutic field—an entity unto itself with a magnetic appeal for fledgling and experienced therapists alike. The awakening of the psychiatric-psy-

Appreciation is expressed to David Berg, assistant professor of psychology, Community College of Philadelphia for his help in the literature search for this chapter.

chological-social work establishment to the centrality of the family system and its impact and hold on all family members has led to an increasing demand for professionals trained in family therapy who can function as an integral part of the staff of many kinds of human service agencies. In many localities treatment-oriented agencies now are considered deficient, not fully staffed, if they do not have a family therapist. The mounting interest in and conviction of the efficiency and efficacy of family therapy has alerted professionals—practitioners and administrators, as well as educators—to the need for programs to train competent therapists. The response has been the establishment of a vast array of educational, supervisory, and training programs to meet the demand.

In this chapter, a brief history of the intertwined fields of marital and family therapy will be sketched as a backdrop against which to understand the kinds of supervision and training programs that have evolved. Current types of programs in operation will be presented, and some of the major programs will be listed. Existing ideas on standards for practice will be discussed; then different supervisory models will be described and analyzed in terms of learning objectives and techniques. Conclusions about the current state of the art and science of marital and family therapy training will be drawn, and implications for the future will be highlighted. While the existing literature is cited illustratively, this chapter is not intended to be an exhaustive recapitulation, but rather a creative synthesis enriched through experiences and observations from clinical teaching, training, consultation, and practice.

Brief History of Marital Counseling

To understand where the field of marital counseling is today, it is important to trace its rapid evolution from its inception. The post-World War I period of the 1920s and 1930s was marked by social unrest, the loosening of family ties attributable to accelerating mobility, a diminution in the authority of parents, and general family disorganization. As divorce laws were gradually liberalized and divorce per se carried less stigma, more and more Americans sought to dissolve their marriages legally as well as physically. Leaders in medicine, law, and religion attempted to help clients who were troubled by family disintegration and intrapsychic problems. Initial therapeutic interventions occurred in the one-to-one model, even though the locus of concern was frequently on interpersonal family dynamics and difficulties. Farsighted clinicians became aware of the impact of the patients' changing attitudes and actions on the patients' significant others, particularly on their mates. Sensitive therapists slowly switched from treating one person alone to working with the marital pair in tandem. When seeing two patients together, with their conflicts recreated in vivo in the therapist's presence, counselors perceived their own need for additional understanding of interpersonal transactions and dyadic interviewing. The couples' sexual inadequacies and discontents also became more obvious and were catapulted into the arena of therapeutic consideration (Kaslow, 1975). Clearly, new intervention strategies were called for; this realization led to probing discussions with other colleagues and engendered clinical experimentation.

The rapidly escalating divorce statistics generated tremendous concern and precipitated an awareness in segments of the professional community that immediate action was imperative. Thus in 1932 three marriage counseling centers were founded—in Los Angeles, New York, and Philadelphia (Mudd, 1974) by worried, farsighted therapists. Because of their endeavors, which entailed departure from orthodox analytic theory and technique, they were censored and chastised by their more traditional colleagues. Although individual psychotherapy remained the treatment approach most often utilized, during the early 1940s the more daring practitioners from psychology, social work, religion, law, and psychiatry, who had begun seeing couples and families conjointly, recognized that these new approaches constituted a distinct discipline. Therefore, they expressed their considered opinion that additional, specialized training beyond that necessary to be an individual psychotherapist was essential. They perceived a need for a separate professional organization to enable those in this young field to share their knowledge and experience and to spearhead training efforts for future marriage counselors. In 1942 the American Association of Marriage Counselors (AAMC) was born and for the past thirty-five years has been engaged in carrying out these original purposes. The organization runs clinical conferences and professional meetings, ac-

credits degree- and non degree-granting training programs, makes
audiotapes and videotapes of major conference presentations available, sets standards for practice, has promulgated a code of ethics,
and attempts to affect legislation dealing with family life. A major
thrust since the early 1960s has been the move toward legal certifica-
cation and/or licensing for practice. The name of the organization
was changed to AAMFC in the early 1970s, reflecting the fact that
many of the members had become family therapists. By the end of
1976, six state organizations had been instrumental in having licensing or certification laws enacted.

The AAMFC has continued to emphasize the importance
of training fledgling therapists and upgrading the knowledge and
skills of the more experienced clinician. Their brochure on membership standards (1976a) specifies the following stringent requirements for clinical members:

1. Recognized graduate professional education with the minimum
   of an earned master's degree from an accredited educational
   institution in an appropriate behavioral science field, mental
   health discipline, or recognized helping profession.
2. a. Two hundred hours of approved supervision of . . . mar-
      riage and family counseling, . . . to be completed in a two-
      to three-year period, of which at least 100 hours must be in
      individual supervision . . . [to] occur preferably with more
      than one supervisor and should include a continuous process
      of supervision with at least several cases.
   b. One thousand hours of clinical experience in the practice of
      marriage and family counseling under approved supervision,
      involving at least fifty . . . cases.
                              Or
   c. One hundred and fifty hours of approved supervision of the
      practice of psychotherapy, ordinarily to be completed in a
      two- to three-year period, of which at least fifty hours must
      be individual supervision, *plus* at least fifty hours of approved
      individual supervision of the practice of marriage and family
      counseling, to be completed . . . [in] not less than one nor
      more than two years.
   d. Seven hundred and fifty hours of clinical experience in the

practice of psychotherapy under approved supervision, involving at least thirty cases, *plus* at least two hundred and fifty hours of . . . marriage and family counseling under approved supervision, involving at least twenty cases.

3. Applicants may be requested to have a screening interview.
4. Demonstrated readiness for the independent practice of marriage and family counseling.
5. Upon completion of the graduate professional degree plus the required supervised clinical experience, the candidate will be expected to have mastered the important theory in the field of marriage and family counseling [therapy].

At around the same time that the name of the organization was changed to AAMFC, the category of "approved supervisor" was created, and clinical members and fellows of the organization with sufficient supervisory background could be so designated after application to and careful review by the AAMFC Committee on Supervision. This development was a logical outgrowth of the ongoing concern for training and the growing need for additional competent therapists as the reported incidence of family pathology and marital dissolution continued in a dramatic upward curve. Existing programs were not meeting this need. (A perusal later in this chapter of the professional education, degree-granting programs extant in 1970 will reveal their paucity and clarify the basis for the decision to inaugurate the approved supervisor program.)

Certainly attorneys who handle custody and divorce cases are involved with couples experiencing anguish and turmoil. Some law schools offer courses in family law, but their focus is on understanding the law and the role of the lawyer as advocate in an adversarial procedure, not on becoming a therapist. This is equally true of family court judges, who become knowledgeable about family systems, dynamics, and dysfunctioning, but whose mission is to adjudicate, not to treat. Thus any lawyer (or judge) who wishes to also be a marriage and family therapist needs supervised training, often in the kind of program AAMFC offers, as he or she is not likely to have the block of time to invest in returning to a formal graduate program.

For centuries, clergymen have been cast into the role of

confidant and counselor by many of their congregants. Yet, today, many theological seminaries still do not offer pastoral counseling courses. Thus clergymen, like lawyers and others from the three main mental health disciplines who wish to acquire skill in the specialty of couples and family therapy, often either work out individual training programs with an approved supervisor or enroll in such special postgraduate supervised training programs as that run by the Marriage Council of Philadelphia, an agency originally directed by Emily Mudd and since the 1960s under Harold Lief.

In their 1974–1975 catalogues, approximately 90 of the 115 medical schools granting M.D. degrees listed some type of courses in human sexuality and/or interpersonal relations (Mudd, 1974). Few offer marital, family, or sex therapy courses per se, as their emphasis is more theoretical than clinical. However, some, such as Temple University, Hahnemann Medical College, and the University of Wisconsin, do include practica in these areas in their residency training programs.

During the past thirty years numerous clinical psychologists and social workers have entered the marriage counseling field and by 1966 comprised 50 percent of AAMC's membership. However, the catalogues of schools of social work and departments of clinical psychology reveal that these graduate programs, like those in law, medicine, and theology, have scant offerings in treating multiperson client systems. Once psychologists and social workers acquire their degrees, they too turn to the specialized programs run at marriage counseling centers and specialty institutes or to approved supervisors. But this is getting ahead of the story, as more history bears reconstructing first.

The Evolution of Family Therapy

The first generation of family therapists who emerged in the early 1950s were self-trained. Almost simultaneously, in different locales and unknown to one another, several small groups of therapists from a variety of professional backgrounds began to experiment with seeing members of the same family conjointly. Like the early marriage counselors, they were discouraged by the slowness of results in psychotherapy with individuals and the sabotage of progress by the patient's important others and were searching for more potent and rapid ways of helping people feel and function better. They were also alarmed by the increasing statistics on rates of family disintegration and the mounting number of gloomy prophecies about the death of the family in America.

Some of the most renowned early endeavors were located on the East and West Coasts. The Palo Alto group included Virginia Satir, Don Jackson, Gregory Bateson, and Jay Haley. They drew their theoretical formulations from systems and communication theory and focused on the "here and now." In New York, Nathan Ackerman at Jewish Family Service was an acknowledged leader. Today, the Ackerman Institute stands as a living tribute to his great contribution to this field. His book, *Exploring the Base for Family Therapy,* coedited with Frances Beatman and Sanford Sherman in 1961, was one of the first seminal works to give shape and substance to the emerging profession. He followed this by authoring numerous other books and articles and by his instrumental role in launching the journal *Family Process* in 1961. In Philadelphia, Ivan Boszmorenyi-Nagy, James Framo, Geraldine Spark, David Rubinstein, and Gerald Zuk comprised part of the group at Eastern Pennsylvania Psychiatric Institute. Nearby, at Philadelphia Psychiatric Center, another group, which included Geraldine Lincoln (Grossman), Al Friedman, and Oscar Weiner was experimenting with the family system as a client unit growing out of their involvement with schizophrenogenic families. These two groups joined to form the Family Institute of Philadelphia, which has continued to expand.

Similar developments occurred in Boston, Washington, Atlanta, Chicago, and Madison. Certain luminaries moved quickly into prominence in each metropolitan area, and the names of the first generation of family therapists are well known. In addition to the aforementioned, they include Donald Bloch, Murray Bowen, Ross Speck, John Warkenten, Carl Whitaker, and Lyman Wynne. They learned of each other's work and established contact in a loose network. Periodically, they banded together to observe and critique each other's therapy, which led to collaborating in writing books. In the literature of the 1960s, the same authors reappear frequently in the edited collections.

As other therapists began to read their works and to hear

their presentations at conferences, interest was piqued. Family therapy was considered highly controversial, as it, like marriage counseling, departed from many traditionally respected dicta. But as people tried to put into practice what they were reading and hearing about, many found the work stimulating and rewarding—for them and their patients. They went to observe the key first-generation therapists doing live interviews through one-way mirrors, they borrowed videotapes of sessions of the pioneers, and they attempted to study with them directly—almost in a throwback to the apprentice-master model of the guild era. The masters became venerated and imitated. They seemed to flourish with the adulation and liked being in the limelight. There was quite a contrast between these active, dynamic interventionists, who were willing to be viewed while performing therapy, and their analytic counterparts, who were often nondirective and preferred low visibility in terms of student and colleague observation.

As demand for their tutelage and (symbolic) "laying on of hands" flourished, many family institutes were set up and established training programs so that the masters could anoint many more disciples. Several major theoretical schools have emerged: (1) the psychodynamic or psychoanalytic (see Beatman, Sherman, and Ackerman, 1961; Ferber, Mendelsohn, and Napier, 1972) or experiential, which emphasizes affect and process issues (Luthman and Kirschenbaum, 1974); (2) the structural or systems (Haley and Hoffman, 1967; Minuchin and others, 1967), which zeros in on the structure of the family as a system; and (3) the relational-existential, which is concerned with invisible loyalties and extended family networks (Nagy and Spark, 1973). Each has its staunchly loyal proponents.

Having proffered the historical development as foundation for understanding the kind of education, supervision, and training that evolved, we return to the focus on supervision and training.

Training Programs

Despite the burgeoning of numerous and varied training endeavors, the literature lacks specificity regarding training and supervisory techniques and methods. Programs do not seem to be predicated on formal theories of marital and family therapy supervision and training (Ackerman, 1973) regarding either content or process. Instead, they rely on what the teacher-trainers themselves have experienced or observed as helpful (or avoided as useless), or what they have a hunch is worth introducing. These decisions are rarely based on carefully researched comparative data. The literature reflects the discontinuity and discreteness of programs, in that new articles tend not to build on what has preceded them. Hopefully, some of this gap will be filled by the material presented in this chapter.

In what may be the first article on a family therapy training project, Satir (1963), reporting the results of a three-year training program at the Mental Research Institute, listed three program goals. In addition to having trainees acquire practice skills, this project sought to have them become proficient in consultation and in-service training in family therapy, so that they could return to their respective agencies and teach what they had learned, and to provide them with the necessary tools for conducting research in family process, diagnosis, and treatment. To Satir's list, this author would add that any training program should "turn out" professionals who also possess a sound theoretical and knowledge base and a familiarity with and commitment to the ethical precepts of the profession.

The field is still enmeshed in adolescent "growing pains," and there is a lack of unanimity as to the definition of the "identity" of the marriage and family (and one might add sex and divorce) therapist and what he or she needs to know and be able to do in order to be designated as such. Just as thirty-five years ago, when the first national organization emerged, there are still many conservatives in the helping disciplines who do not recognize this as a specialty and claim that no extra or special training and practicum are needed. Antagonism is felt from others who still argue that the only meaningful therapy is of the individual, psychoanalytic, insight-oriented variety. Perhaps because the conservators are the powerful ones in the medical and graduate schools, such courses have not been introduced at more degree-granting institutions. It is also likely that their influence has helped slow or thwart the passage of licensing laws in many states; they decry the need for dual licensing or certification and do not want others enfranchised to practice something they prefer not to be recognized.

By way of illustrating the tone and atmosphere that permeates the bastions of traditionalism and even of liberalism, as recently as 1974 Malone indicated that "there is no established clearcut theoretical model" for training child psychiatrists in family therapy and that consequently "professional identity and professional role lack clarity, and the staff and trainees . . . experience a considerable amount of strain" (p. 454). When his paper "Observations on the Role of Family Therapy in Child Psychiatry Training" (1974) was written, Malone was director of child psychiatry training at the Philadelphia Child Guidance Clinic, a facility geared to family therapy practice. Yet Malone found that the problems in training were intensified by the conflict and polarization that exist between analytically oriented child psychiatrists and family therapists and that along with the numerous advantages of family therapy, there is also the danger that its overutilization can cause a distorted view of the nature of the difficulties and the treatment of choice, just as total reliance on one-to-one interviewing can. A critical point that he posits is that "the disadvantage and danger of family therapy involves the temptation for inexperienced therapists to escape the rigors, growing pains, and vicissitudes of understanding and working with intrapsychic conflict and pain"; even though it makes possible "direct exploration of intrapsychic derivatives at the level of interpersonal process" (pp. 456–457), one can avoid dealing with intrapsychic problems by depending solely on environmental manipulation to achieve desired ends. The teacher-trainer who permits this does not help the trainees learn about "psychic development and unconscious dynamics" (1974, p. 457).

This ideological and political conflict between the professions is more lamentable, considering that in the Group for the Advancement of Psychiatry (GAP) report on *The Field of Family Therapy* (Committee on the Family, 1970) these seminal thinkers and authors stated that "family therapy combines two bodies of knowledge: personality dynamics and multiperson system dynamics" and heralded the need for integration of these "two systems levels into a comprehensive theory" (pp. 565–566). They urged that the emphasis on the transactional multiperson level of functioning should be considered an addition to, not a replacement for, the individual system level of understanding and treating behavior dynamics (pp. 565–566). Obviously their thrust toward synthesis, or at least peaceful coexistence, has not permeated the field. That Malone's experience of such strong rivalry was not unique is documented in Ackerman's finding (1973) that for residents there was little integration of family therapy training with other aspects of psychiatric training.

The reluctance of schools of medicine, theology, psychology, and social work to add courses, much less sequences or specialties, in marital and family therapy has no doubt contributed to the proliferation of the family institute, marriage council, and approved supervisor kinds of training programs under the jurisdiction of practitioner-educators. These have been the main channels developed to meet the clamor from clinicians for additional postgraduate training and from the lay population for therapists who can treat couples and families. Several will be cited to offer an overview of the spectrum of what is currently available (the list is intended to be illustrative, not all-inclusive).

AAMFC Accredited Degree Programs and Approved Training Centers. Full accreditation covers a five-year period (*Journal of Marriage and Family Counseling,* 1977, p. 95). Provisional approval ordinarily covers a two-year period and indicates that a program has met most but not all of the requirements for full recognition. (Complete addresses and contact persons are available from AAMFC, 225 Yale Avenue, Claremont, Calif. 91711.)

Accredited Graduate Programs	*Degrees Granted*
Brigham Young University (Provo, Utah) Family Counseling Program	M.A. and Ph.D.
Colgate Rochester Divinity School (Rochester, N.Y.)	D. Min. and certificate
Syracuse University (Syracuse, N.Y.) in cooperation with Onondaga Pastoral Counseling Center, Department of Child and Family Studies	M.A.

Accredited Graduate Programs	*Degrees Granted*
University of Southern California (Los Angeles), Department of Sociology	Ph.D. and certificate

Provisionally Accredited	
Loma Linda University (Loma Linda, Calif.), Marriage and Family Counseling Program	M.S. in MFC

Approved Training Centers	*Leads To*
Family Service of Milwaukee (Milwaukee)	Certificate
Institutes of Religion and Health (New York), Blanton-Peale Graduate Institute	D. Min. and certificate
Marriage Council of Philadelphia (Philadelphia), Affiliated with University of Pennsylvania	Certificate
Mental Hygiene Institute (Montreal), Marriage Counseling Service	Diploma or M.S.W. or M.Ed.
Onondaga Pastoral Counseling Center (Syracuse, N.Y.), Affiliated with Syracuse	Certificate

Provisionally Approved	*Leads To*
Indiana Counseling and Pastoral Care Center (Indianapolis)	Certificate
Westchester Institute for Training in Counseling and Psychotherapy (Rye, N.Y.)	Certificate

Degree-Granting Programs (not Connected with AAMFC)	*Degrees Granted*
Auburn University (Auburn, Ala.), School of Home Economics, Department of Family and Child Development	M.A. in Marriage and Family Counseling

Hahnemann Medical College (Philadelphia), Department of Mental Health Sciences	Masters in Family Therapy (M.F.T.)
Purdue University (West Lafayette, Ind.), Department of Child Development and Family Studies	Ph.D. in Marriage and Family Conuseling
University of Connecticut (Storrs), School of Home Economics and Family Studies	A.B., M.A. and Ph.D. in Human Development and Family Relations

Family Institute Training Programs. As of January 1977, there were some forty family institutes functioning throughout the country. The establishment of these institutes represents an outgrowth of the mainstream of activity in family therapy described earlier.

Perhaps the largest and best known is the Nathan W. Ackerman Institute in New York City. As of 1977, it is offering six summer workshops, each five days long. Topics include "Introduction to Family Therapy," "Improving Skills in Family Therapy," and "Training and Supervision." In addition, the Ackerman Institute sponsors a two-year clinical externship, which provides "an in-depth, intensive postgraduate training program in family therapy . . . to psychiatrists, psychologists, social workers, and selected, qualified, allied professionals. . . . (Ackerman Institute, 1977). The externs spend half of their time in direct treatment with families at the institute and are expected to be involved for a minimum of fifteen hours per week. Another option is a three-year program for professionals who can devote half a day per week to their training. "Participants explore their place in their own families, in their professional families, and in the families they are treating" (Ackerman Institute, 1977).

The Family Institute of Philadelphia pursues a different path. It runs a clinical training program, which is housed at a variety of local institutions—mostly psychiatric facilities. The program is offered mostly at night, with the first year consisting of an orientation course one evening per week. Three clinical years follow, during which didactic course work continues and is supplemented by supervision. Institute members serve as teachers and supervisors.

Other family institutes run training programs that are variations on the themes articulated earlier. Usually graduates of the
clinical schools become family institute members. Some institutes
also sponsor one-day seminars, workshops, and conferences. While
attendance at mass events tends to be open to the general professional public, enrollment in training schools is usually limited to
individuals who already have a graduate or professional degree in
one of the helping disciplines.

The "Approved Supervisor" Training Model. Earlier we
spoke about the designation of approved supervisors by the AAMFC
to train already proficient mental health professionals who wish to
acquire greater knowledge and skill in marriage and family counseling and who prefer personally tailored individual tutelage to entering a university- or agency-based program. The standards for supervisors are quite rigorous, and there are clear guidelines for what
must be covered (AAMFC, 1976b). Often a particular group of
concepts and techniques are encompassed in a "training block"
format. Initially the potential trainee's technical competence is
assessed by a careful screening through an application form and a
follow-up interview. Once the trainee is accepted, instructions are
given for readings—often with a bibliography—geared to the areas
in which the trainee must expand and upgrade his or her fund of
information. Questions raised during the course of the readings may
constitute material for discussion in the didactic portion of the
supervisory session. So may questions from and reactions to workshops and conferences that trainees are encouraged to attend. Careful
instructions are given for family (and sex) history taking, and existing forms may be shared with the student. Interviewing skills to be
utilized when seeing several patients simultaneously are introduced
and covered. The approved supervisor may go over kinds of questions to be asked, possible responses to be made, and what to look
for in seating arrangements and communication patterns. Over the
two-year supervisory period, the usual progression is that the trainee
shifts from being a somewhat passive learner to the role of a more
active participant.

Since the requirement is that each trainee be supervised by
two different senior clinicians during the apprenticeship period,
during the second year a transfer to another supervisor occurs, and

the supervisee receives an intensive exposure to someone else's ideas and approach. The person may, during the final months of training, return to the initial and primary supervisor. It is advisable that the trainee participate in small-group supervision as well as one-to-one precepting, to benefit from the stimulation and interchange afforded in working in the company of other trainees, who may bring very different kinds of backgrounds and treatment issues into the discussion.

The supervisor is expected to send periodic reports to the AAMFC training committee, as this is one channel of professional accountability for the private practitioner and a way of endowing the process with uniform procedures and a high level of expectation.

Additional Kinds of Programs. Some agencies, institutions, and nonspecific institutes also run family therapy training programs—usually at the postgraduate level. Illustrative of this category are the programs at the Langley Porter Neuropsychiatric Institute (San Francisco) and at the Menninger Clinic (Topeka, Kans.).

Sample Staff Training Models

Along with the recognition of the therapeutic effectiveness of family treatment has come a realization of the economic advantage—in terms of staff time and energy—of not splitting a family and the disadvantage of seeing its members separately. Its potency in preventing the pathology of older members from floating to younger members of the family has also been amply demonstrated. Therefore many agencies have hired trainers or consultants to set up and implement marriage counseling and family therapy staff training programs. By way of example, several kinds of programs conducted in different settings are summarized.

Flomenhaft and Carter (1974) describe the following program of family therapy training. Through arrangements with the Department of Public Welfare, the Institute of Teachers of Family Therapy was established as a branch of the Philadelphia Child Guidance Clinic to train and supervise staff members of community mental health centers throughout Pennsylvania. The program provided a family therapist-supervisor to each center for one day per week, over five months, to supervise a group of six to eight clinicians.

It is important to view this training in terms of a shifting gears for both the individual-oriented therapists and the agency administrators. Initially, the supervisor-trainer has to assess the level of clinical skills of each participant, along with the population and types of problems to be found in the community served by the agency. The training begins on a didactic base through lectures, discussions, readings, demonstrations, and videotapes, as well as a presentation of the particular family therapy orientation employed (structural in this case). Once training actually begins, each participant is supervised, using videotapes of his or her own sessions and through on-the-spot direct supervision with instant feedback. The supervisor also meets with agency administrative staff to keep them informed. After the program ends, the institute provides follow-up supervision through consultation for practice and teaching on a monthly basis. Flomenhaft and Carter report that the evaluative data on the program demonstrates a high "success" rate in terms of continuation of family treatment at the center.

In 1976, I served as a family therapy training consultant for the psychiatric residents at a naval hospital. This request grew out of the fact that the previous year one of the residents had been on child psychiatry rotation in the facility where I teach and had become involved as cotherapist with another student, whom I was supervising. He accompanied her to our supervisory sessions and became enamored of family therapy and with what he was learning in his semiprivate tutorials. When he returned to the hospital, he enthusiastically recommended that they all receive some training in family therapy. By the time the trainer arrived on the scene for a series of twelve weekly sessions, a receptive group was waiting. None of the need to convert described by others and alluded to earlier in this chapter was encountered. Quite the contrary—these bright, well-trained, analytically oriented naval officers were eager to expand their treatment repertoire. They read avidly, grappled with ideas that were foreign or seemed in contradiction to what they had already learned, and pushed to begin seeing families by the second week. After the first session, when they decided that it was important to begin functioning clinically right away, they realized they would need more backup supervision than the trainer could offer under the contract. Thus they persuaded senior psychiatric staff to attend, share the learning, become committed to this approach, and take on some of their supervision. The chief resident scheduled a family diagnostic intake interview for the second week, jointly led by the resident and the trainer. Since he had no prior family therapy experience, this was a courageous step and one that he handled with great aplomb. Fortunately, the distraught family had a young child with them, and the trainer moved into a somewhat maternal role by holding the baby during part of the session; this served to minimize the resident's nervousness and competitive concerns and allowed him to give free rein to his sensitive and astute therapeutic inclinations. Thus an interesting training model evolved out of the residents' willingness to quickly begin seeing families. Each week a new family was scheduled for intake during the first hour of the training session. Two of the trainees served as cotherapists for the diagnostic interview. Then the case was discussed under the trainer's leadership, and the principles and processes of family therapy were taught from what had transpired during the session. The diagnostic workup team then decided whether both or which one would carry the case if it was deemed suitable as an ongoing treatment family.

An unexpected consequence of the second session was that the men spontaneously mentioned that they were impressed with the special qualities a heterosexual cotherapy pair brought into the treatment situation and wondered if, since they did not have any female residents, they should ask several of the female social workers on staff to join the training group. They quickly achieved unanimity that they should and, as of the third session, two of the women became steady participants. Since they had rarely collaborated in the past, this changed the dynamics of staff relationships, and there was an internal push for the men to examine their own attitudes to female colleagues and female patients. Ultimately this led to their consideration of their stereotypes about male-female relationships, professional women, Navy wives, and "service" marriages. The staff as a family went through a beautiful process of getting to know one another better and differently, and several friendships were considerably deepened. Within three months, they were each carrying several families and doing so credibly well. All of the training objectives discussed earlier were subsumed in the process but were realized in very different fashion. This was truly an experiential training model, one with which all seemed quite pleased.

Sometimes one approach I as teacher and staff trainer use during longer training programs is to have the students bring their spouses in for at least one session. As many fear what might pour forth in such a session, I indicate that my spouse will also be present and therefore I am in a similar position to theirs as to revelations. We focus on how they can interpret to their spouses what family therapy is all about, the impact of this kind of training and practice on their mates and children, what anxieties are present regarding this in the families of family therapists, what concerns may have been evoked in connection with the evolving close relationship with a cotherapist of the opposite sex, and similar general concerns. Once the initial timidity and anxieties are overcome, these are extremely fruitful sessions that enhance the kind and depth of communication they can have with their spouses or lovers about their professional roles and world.

External consultant-trainers assuming a role such as that described earlier, in relation to the training of the psychiatric residents at the naval hospital, are paid either on a per-session basis or a flat fee for a certain number of sessions. However, if a consultant is provided to an agency by another agency that has as part of its mandate the offering of consultative services, the particular person doing the training may not receive any additional remuneration. In-house consultants may carry a staff training function as part of their job responsibility—in which case an external consultant may be utilized only as a very occasional supplement.

Supervision

Supervision is central to most family therapy training programs and is one of the basic processes utilized to produce competent therapists. The broad, overall goal of supervision, on one level, is the transmission of specific relevant data, the "how-to" strategies for treatment of a particular family by the novice. On a more important plane, supervision involves the imparting of a deeper understanding of concepts of family dynamics, relations, and structure to produce changes in desirable directions. If it is true that experience is the best teacher, then the supervisory relationship is the alliance that enables the trainee to tap into the vast and valuable pool of the preceptor's experience. The cornerstone in the growth of the family therapist is willingness to share clinical tribulations and positive experiences with patient families with another therapist who has passed over that same, often rough and difficult, terrain. The growth process, through supervision, should operate in both directions, with mutuality and reciprocity, providing an opportunity for an expansion of the knowledge, capabilities, and self of the trainee and the supervisor.

Supervision, in its many facets and forms, moves along a continuum. On one extreme is the concern for content and technique; on the other is a concentration on the deeper process of facilitating personal growth and creating the prototypical dyadic helping relationship in the supervisory experience, which can be translated by the trainee into therapist-patient interchanges. The trainee will initially benefit most from the content-technique orientation as he or she grapples to master the material that constitutes the conceptual base for practice and enables him or her to work with families predicated on a more solid knowledge foundation. More advanced trainees and experienced practitioners learning marriage and family therapy to add to their treatment repertoire should be exposed to the more sophisticated and complex interpretations of family history, transactions, structures, loyalties, and intergenerational legacies. They can be encouraged to read, think about, and try not only treatment of one family at a time but also such other technique variations as couples group therapy (Kadis and Markowitz, 1972), multiple family therapy (Lacquer, 1972), and network therapy (Speck and Attneave, 1972).

A student with some experience and confidence may gain a great deal from supervision conducted as a process of learning and thinking leading toward greater understanding and potency of him- or herself as person, family member, and therapist. It is with supervision as a technique that varies from "how-to-do-it," in its simplest form, to its most challenging aspect as an existential process of being and becoming that the next section of this chapter is concerned.

Learning Objectives. The mechanics of the supervisory process require an ongoing assessment of the trainee's skills and initial determination of the student's fund of knowledge and clinical and personal readiness for grappling with theory and practice. Such an assessment provides the supervisor and student a baseline from which the learning process may be set into motion. Unless this occurs, the student's progress may be seriously hampered, because supervisor and supervisee may be trying to interact on different levels, missing each other in the process. What is to be accomplished, the approximate length of time it should take, mutual expectations and responsibilities, and other important details should be explicated in a *contract* drawn up and agreed to by the parties involved. Once the supervisor becomes familiar with the student's background, experience, strengths, and knowledge gaps, work can be directed along appropriate lines to enable the trainee to meet learning and service delivery aims. Cleghorn and Levin (1973) recommend that defining of clear-cut learning objectives be an ongoing facilitative process that identifies areas of need and provides both parties with realistic expectations of progress. I find the schema suggested by Cleghorn and Levin to be a comprehensive one and build on it in the following section.

"Supervision should not become a pernicious game requiring the pursuit of objectives that cannot be defined" (Cleghorn and Levin, 1973, p. 439). Setting objectives channels the student's learning along a definitive, appropriate and profitable direction and lends itself to periodic assessment of progress. Each category of learning objectives carries with it the notion of the necessary skill to be learned and concomitantly the best type of supervision. The category of *perceptual skills* pertains to diagnostic ability and the skill "to see" the interactional nature of the family system; supervision of the perceptual skills involves direct observation of the therapy session, either live or taped. The ability of the student to formulate observations into a description of the family system—its rules, roles, and myths—comprises the category of *conceptual skills*. Perhaps the highest level of skills needed are the *executive abilities*, in which the student learns how to enter the family deeply enough to move its members in the desired direction and to produce relevant data for treatment. These skills categories are not mutually exclusive, and family therapists at all levels of expertise should achieve these objectives.

Cleghorn and Levin specify sets of learning objectives in terms of the increasing capability of the therapist; the stepwise function represents progressive mastery of each objective as the student gains experience and knowledge. Use of specified goals enables supervisor and trainee to agree on existing strengths and weaknesses so that the trainee knows precisely what must be accomplished. These objectives vary along a continuum that moves the supervisory experience from a content emphasis to a process orientation. The basic learning objectives (see Cleghorn and Levin, 1973, p. 443) are the necessary first steps and, if achieved, enable the student to deal with the family. These basic perceptual and conceptual skills objectives are to recognize and systematically describe (1) interactions and transactions; (2) the family, including assessment of current problems; (3) effect of the family group on itself; (4) the experience of being taken into the family system; and (5) one's idiosyncratic reactions to family members. The executive skills objectives are (1) to develop collaborative working relationships with the family; (2) to establish therapeutic contact; (3) to stimulate transactions; (4) to clarify communications; (5) to help family members label effects of interactions; (6) to extricate oneself from the family system; and (7) to focus on a problem. These basic skills should enable the therapist to conduct the interview, enter the family, and initiate some problem-solving strategies.

The supervisor's role entails observing therapy sessions and face-to-face contact with the trainee, hearing his or her formulations, and stimulating his or her perceptions and conceptualizations of the situation. Both deductive and inductive reasoning and formulations are to be encouraged.

Some supervisor-supervisee pairs may wish to use a checklist for the ongoing assessment, to keep track of those skills that have been learned and those still to be mastered and to enable the supervisor to continually support and build on the trainee's strengths. In the course of fulfilling the basic learning objectives, trainees will find some limitations in their ability; inherent is the notion that the beginner's progress necessarily involves certain stumbling blocks that can only be overcome with self-analyses of the trouble spot, combined with additional experience and active supervision.

Cleghorn and Levin underscore the stereotypical imitative

behavior of the novice, the lack of here-and-now quality in the identification of maladaptive behavioral consequences of the family's transactions, and the inability to process enough material during the therapy hour to label and intervene before the session ends. Such frustrating ineptness hinders the beginner's helping role and ability to filter the important dynamics of the system during the session; this often leaves the trainee vaguely aware that all did not progress sufficiently. Later, in hindsight or through supervision, he or she realizes "what he should have said or done." Presumably the supervisor and supervisee together can determine ways to cut through the mass of clinical material to arrive at the formulation of hypotheses on which subsequent interventions will be based.

Progress takes time, accumulation of experience, and a supervisor who assists the student in dealing with the acquisition of new and sometimes controversial ideas and in overcoming therapeutic limitations and frustrations in *the process* of meeting the learning objectives. In helping the student advance to diagnosis and treatment of more complex difficulties, the supervisor may specify additional objectives to reach and skills to be acquired. It is at the stage of mastering the advanced objectives that one begins to view family therapy as process and to relate to the process of one's own growth in the adventure of being supervised. The advanced perceptual and conceptual objectives (Cleghorn and Levin, 1973, p. 444) regarding the family are (1) to conceive of symptomatic behaviors as a function of the family system; (2) to assess a family's capacity to change; (3) to recognize that change in the family is more threatening than recognition of the problem; and (4) to define key concepts operationally. The therapist's perceptual and conceptual objectives are (1) to deal with feelings about being a change agent; (2) to become aware of how one's personal characteristics influence one's becoming a family therapist; (3) to assess the effectiveness of one's interventions and explore alternatives; and (4) to articulate rewards to be gained by family members making specific changes. The executive skills objectives involve acquisition of greater technical know-how. Thus the supervisor might role play certain family scenes with the trainee or engage him or her in discussions that start out with "How else might you have handled it?" The executive skills to be mastered are to be able (1) to redefine the therapeutic contact periodically;

(2) to demonstrate relationship between transactions and the symptomatic problem; (3) to be a facilitator of change; (4) to develop a style of interviewing consistent with one's personality; (5) to take control of maladaptive transactions; (6) to work out adaptive behaviors and rewards for them; and (7) to relinquish control of the family when adaptive patterns occur.

As the trainee progresses and tackles more difficult families, the objectives become more subjective; that is, the accumulation of experience leads the therapist to a point of synthesis and integration as he or she becomes less encumbered with anxiety about "how to" and becomes qualitatively better able to conduct therapy. Significantly, the experienced therapist's own seasoning and continued deepening and expansion of diagnostic and treatment skill is ultimately most likely to be fostered if he or she undertakes the role of supervisor and, as such, becomes an active participant with the trainee.

Some Problems Encountered by Supervisors. Increasing numbers of individually oriented therapists have been seeking training in marriage and family counseling. In examining the advantages that family therapy offers, Malone (1974) points out that child psychiatrists who are also trained in family therapy have a greater depth, breadth, and accuracy in evaluating and treating childhood psychopathology. Combined training leads to greater ease in consultation and collaboration with pediatricians and school personnel. A solid grasp of family therapy provides the therapist with a new tool for data collection and research and helps bridge the gap between general and child psychiatry. But training for a psychoanalytic, individual-oriented therapist presents some unique difficulties. Misconceptions about and prejudices against nonanalytic therapy can be barriers to receptivity of new knowledge. Shifting gears creates a tremendous problem for the individual-oriented therapist, who must now focus on the family system; further, the energy expenditure required in treating whole families conjointly is much greater. Characteristically, in family therapy so much data is rapidly elicited by the therapist that he or she may feel inundated and baffled. This can be quite a contrast to the difficulty experienced in getting a single client, especially one who is shy, withdrawn, depressed, or fearful, to share thoughts and feelings. A gifted supervisor can help the trainee see where the real similarities and differences in the two approaches lie and under what circumstances and with what kinds of problems and people each is likely to constitute the treatment of choice. The "ideal supervisor" being described here would not be doctrinaire nor hold that any one treatment modality is a panacea. Rather, he or she would subscribe to a view that each patient constellation has to be viewed in its own terms and that the decision as to the best treatment course to pursue flows from this assessment.

Novak and Busko (1974, p. 14) also address the issue of inducting the individual-oriented practitioner into family therapy training. Their position is that the trainee must "unlearn" many therapeutic behaviors that have become almost automatic. One area to be unlearned involves the orientation to individual psychodynamics and organization around the "disease model of emotional disorder," in which it is typical to see each member of the family as a separate entity, without concern for the whole system as the patient unit, and as being in pain.

Transference and countertransference assume new dimensions when individual-oriented therapists begin to treat couples and families: "Reverberations from the unresolved relationship problems within their own families" may create real barriers to doing family therapy and are a necessary focus during supervision (Novak and Busko, 1974, p. 16). The supervisor should sensitize the trainee to these deeply imbedded idiosyncratic stumbling blocks. Supervisors must be aware of factors such as residual guilt and/or resentment felt to members of one's own family of origin, being pulled into or extruded from the patient family system, and attempts at alliances or to become a party to "confidences," and other perplexing transactions that are likely to be experienced by the student.

Many of these learning objectives can be adapted around the needs of the psychotherapist-trainee to structure his or her relearning to "see" the holistic, homeostatic family system. Supervision, then, encompasses content, technique, and a conversion process oriented to help bridge the gap and facilitate integration.

Techniques and Methods. The *traditional model* of one-to-one supervision has been indirect, consisting of the supervisor meeting with the trainee after a lapse of time following the therapy session(s) (Birchler, 1975, p. 331). The discussion focuses on the case record of the interview—usually a process record for beginners and perhaps a summary record for the more advanced.

The meeting held in the supervisor's office according to a weekly schedule is comfortable, convenient, and routine. The trainee may determine and control the agenda. Disadvantages emanate from the "indirect quality of the model" (Birchler, 1975, p. 332); the trainee's report is based on recall, subjective reporting, and selective remembering. The supervisor learns about the case second-hand. Having no direct observational and experiential contact with the family and its complex system, he or she has little basis for picking up distorted perceptions or the nonverbal behaviors.

A second approach, *cotherapy,* has many advantages as a training and supervision method. It is a particularly effective approach in situations where past conflicts and anxieties are likely to be reactivated in the therapist; the presence of the supervisor as cotherapist can minimize the adverse effects of countertransference phenonema and the number and extent of therapeutic errors. One member of the treatment pair is likely to be reasonably objective at all times. Many arguments have been advanced for the efficacy of the cotherapist team, particularly a heterosexual pair. Kadis and Markowitz (1972) indicate how, just by being there and working together harmoniously or disagreeing constructively, they serve as good current role models for the patients. They also represent a couple who can serve as different kinds of parents and, as such, do some necessary reparenting and reeducating. Also, patients of each sex have someone they can identify with; or, if they are more comfortable with members of the opposite sex, this too is offered. In a sense, the heterosexual cotherapy pair affords "something for everyone"; doubles the number of ears and eyes available for hearing, seeing, and sensing what is going on; ensures that if the patient cannot relate to one therapist he or she is likely to feel fairly positively toward the other; and provides for continuity of treatment in the event that one therapist must miss a session. A note on this technique: The preceptor who doubles as cotherapist must be careful to reserve time to serve as supervisor; this entails allocating more time and energy to the training of each student.

When the supervisor is present and participating, his or her knowledge of the trainee's diagnostic and treatment skill is based on direct observation and shared experience; the selective distortions in a process recording, which may be few or rampant, are not introduced. The fact that the supervisor is willing to risk sharing patients and opening his or her practice to the trainee for observation and participation, question and comment, makes supervision a much more mutual process and is in keeping with the avowed ethos of the field that the masters are willing to be observed and welcome critique and input from viewers. The student "can be exposed to intensive learning by direct observation and participation with the supervisor. Such experiences can be exhilarating and highly productive" (Kaslow, 1972, p. 129).

In family therapy practice, cotherapists of equal stature often team up, and trainees can also be paired together. Working in unison, the therapists have a combined strength in dealing with highly intense, troubled family situations. Other advantages of the cotherapy method are complementarity, support, and a clear communication model. It is also more stimulating and enjoyable for the therapist, a consideration with much merit.

The family therapy training model described by Tucker, Hart, and Liddle (1976) also makes creative use of the cotherapy relationship as a means of supervision. In their program, the cotherapists are all trainees. The reactions of the cotherapists are discussed before the supervisors and other trainees; they are requested to talk about their perceptions and feelings about the family and each other in order to facilitate the learning and growth experience. Supervisory personnel help iron out the issues between cotherapists, moving toward resolution of differences. When cotherapists have a successful relationship, therapy is likely to be more effective: "The supervisors believe that family therapists need to be aware of and sensitive to their own and their cotherapist's emotional state in order to work with families in a facilitative fashion" (Tucker, Hart, and Liddle, 1976, p. 270), and "spending time on the cotherapy relationship in the supervisory sessions helps to improve supervisees' level of functioning with the family and with each other" (p. 272).

Similarly, Sonne and Lincoln (1965) delineated their cotherapy relationship during long-term treatment of a family. Areas of struggle and emotional strain were dealt with as a result of the cotherapy experience. This team was observed by their colleagues through the one-way mirror and utilized feedback received to work out differences and move toward greater unity. The team members felt that "the actual experiential process taking place in our relationship was in itself therapeutic to the family" and that "the total capacity for perception and expression was greater than the sum of our individual capacities" (p. 183).

In concluding this section on cotherapy, it is important to mention that the technique has some disadvantages. Trainees may feel quite overwhelmed by the greater capacity and assertiveness of the supervisor and may perceive that they come off second best. They may repress their own spontaneity and permit the supervisor to carry the major part of the therapeutic action, and they may believe that they should be carbon copies of the supervisor. Hopefully, the supervisor will help them to maintain their individualities, find their own styles, trust their hunches, and gradually feel free to move in more rapidly, so that ultimately the teams will be well balanced. These disadvantages should more than be outweighed by the advantages. Cotherapy experience as part of supervisory method is an investment that yields extensive dividends through improved family treatment; through eliciting the affective reactions of the trainee cotherapist, the supervisor will have greater leverage for promoting growth and learning. Under able supervisory guidance, the cotherapy relationship should yield the derivatives pinpointed by Sonne and Lincoln (1965, pp. 181–182): "As therapists we were able . . . to give the family a clear, unified, and unambivalent presentation of reality. . . . Through our discussions with each other, we maintained a clear and up-to-date understanding of the family . . . having taken the time necessary to communicate with each other in cotherapy conferences, we were not preoccupied with each other in the therapy sessions and could be more occupied in attending to the family."

A third major supervisory method is *direct supervision using delayed feedback*. This has only become possible with the appearance of such hardware as one-way mirrors, films, audio- and videotape recorders and playback equipment, and closed circuit video monitors (Birchler, 1975, pp. 333–334). These enable the supervisor to directly observe the actual therapy session, either while it is occurring or shortly thereafter, on film. Videotaped portions can be rerun for analyses and discussion in supervision. Such on-the-spot observations or full recordings do not permit the omissions or distortions possible in written process records and therefore are much more authentic materials, and therapist or client verbal and nonverbal incongruencies are thus made visible. Based on firsthand knowledge of the case, the supervisor can be much more precise in interpreting dynamics and discussing treatment direction.

However, as with all approaches, this one has its disadvantages as well as advantages. It may be considerably more time consuming and inconvenient for the busy supervisor. Much of the essential equipment is costly. And trainees may feel extremely pressured, knowing they are being watched.

This method, which does not allow for immediate guidance, is found wanting by the proponents of the fourth approach, *direct supervision with instant feedback* (see Birchler, 1975, for fuller discussion). They consider this fourth approach a creative way to combine the best elements of the three models described earlier and to add a new, vibrant dimension—instant feedback. In essence, the supervisor observes the live therapy sessions through a one-way mirror or video monitor. By prearrangement, the supervisor is free to intervene directly, with reasons for such intrusive external input explicated in advance. The form of intervention is contingent on the orientation and objectives of the therapy and the kind of communication system established (Montalvo, 1973). Examples of communication systems are walkie-talkie systems between supervisor and trainee, in which both utilize a citizens' band receiver, and two-telephone hookups with one phone in the observation room and another in the training room. Patient permission is requested (and required) to have an observer present, and an explanation is given that the observer may periodically interrupt to call in questions or observations. The supervisor may intercede to bail out a therapist who is pressing too hard or who appears trapped or to suggest a more fruitful pathway for pursual. Sometimes the observer-expert is summoned or voluntarily enters the session to make an interpretation or statement designed to shock the patients into a system realignment or interactional change (Minuchin, 1974). This verges on psychotherapy of the absurd, as paradoxical injunctions may be given (Whitaker, 1976). The unexpected and unorthodox nature of this approach, combined with its tendency to immediately terminate the previous interaction, may provide the leverage needed to get the patients to modify their transactions and consequently may permit the establishment of more productive ways of relating. It may be essential later in the course of treatment for the expert's intervention to be repeated, or the therapist can remind the patients of it if the destructive pattern of relating is resumed (Birchler, 1975, p. 335).

Another variation is for the therapist to leave the room and go to the supervisor for a brief conference. To me this seems disruptive and potentially undermining of the patients' confidence in the therapist's capability.

Sometimes the observer makes encouraging comments such as "You are on the right track," or provides directions for contract negotiations. I believe that trainees should have as much leeway as possible to proceed on their own, not needing instantaneous praise or help with basic therapeutic tasks such as shaping a contract. Other difficulties seem inherent—battles for control, dependence-independence issues, and feelings of being pawns manipulated on a chessboard. Yet devotees of this method insist that these dangers are outweighed by the advantages of avoiding therapeutic errors, because the supervisor's superior skill can be pressed into service immediately and the trainee has solid support available on call.

A fifth and increasingly popular approach is *group supervision*. Tucker, Hart, and Liddle (1976), in describing their formulations on group supervision used in an educational setting, state that "a basic assumption of their sequential model is that the supervisory process progresses through a series of phases over the course of a semester and/or full year" (p. 269). Each supervisory session also progresses "through an observable, definable, and systematic sequence" (p. 269). Supervision consists of one- to one-and-a-half-hour meetings of ten students with three supervisors, after group observations of two family sessions. Each student participates both as observer and therapist. Cotherapy teams are composed of trainee and trainee, supervisor and supervisor, or supervisor and trainee.

The first goal of the supervisory sequence is to deal with the cotherapists' reactions to each other and to the session. Supervisors discuss these in front of the group, in order to minimize distortions and biases. The cotherapy relationship is viewed as a significant part of therapy; the time involved in working through this area is deemed to yield great benefit.

The second objective in the supervisory sequence is analyzing observed family interactions. This phase of supervision involves diagnosis, evaluation, identification, and hypothesizing the family as a system and is structured to sharpen observation skills and increase the student's capacity; supervisors serve as models to this end. The third goal is to generalize about families and family therapy. Students and supervisors (who now shift to the teacher role) discuss family dynamics by exploring theoretical concepts in the family therapy field. Planning for future sessions with families is the focus in the next phase, in which techniques and approaches are discussed and debated.

Phases Two and Three of the model proposed by Tucker, Hart, and Liddle are focused on the kinds of perceptual and conceptual learning objectives formulated by Cleghorn and Levin (1973) and discussed earlier in this chapter; their Phase Four parallels the latter authors' executive skills objectives. The final phase of the developmental model is the discussion centered on feelings evoked by the previous supervisory sessions, in which the supervisors' function is "one of group facilitator as if in an ongoing sensitivity group." This phase involves feedback, personal feelings, and self-disclosure concerning quality of supervision and sensitive areas of concern to the student. Supervision is aimed at not merely guiding the students but also at leaving room for evolving individual styles. In addition, the cosupervision relationship, like cotherapy, needs to be worked through, and doing so offers growth and learning benefits to the supervisors.

Group supervision serves to reinforce conceptual notions and also has the advantage of helping the trainees build cohesiveness and trust in working with others. The trainees experience relief when they realize that others also feel overwhelmed or ignored by their respective patient families. Often an "aha" phenomenon occurs when a member comments about the similarities between the seminar group's problems and process and that of their patient families. It ultimately tends to ease anxieties about self-exposure while providing a living experience in a small group that in some ways recreates an approximation of a family and reactivates feelings of sibling rivalry and partially repressed attitudes toward authority figures (the supervisors), who represent parent surrogates. In creating an atmosphere in which these emotions are likely to surface and in which they can be dealt with, there is a greater likelihood that unfinished issues from the past will not become unconscious interferences in treating families.

Interestingly, if a nonmember attends as a guest or is added as a new member after the group has gotten underway, the trainees become aware of their sense of belonging; they are likely to perceive and react to the outsider as if the person were a resented intruder. Experiencing this togetherness heightens their awareness of why it is so difficult for a therapist to gain entry into a family, for in this instance it is the new therapist who, no matter how well intentioned, is viewed as the potentially disruptive intruder and whom the family colludes to keep out.

In concluding this encapsulation of group supervision, we turn to Mendelsohn and Ferber (1972), who also consider the group supervisory seminar to be a teaching device in its own right. Their ideology, as reflected in the training program at Bronx State Hospital, promotes (1) eclecticism, as they adapt concepts and techniques from numerous frames of reference and encourage students to be innovative within the dictates of the situation; (2) experimentation first—followed by conceptualization to enable the therapist to intuitively determine how and when to move in and out of the family; (3) commitment to openness in order to bring to light hidden conflicts; (4) scrupulous attention to group process; and (5) trainee responsibility for the family's process, with supervisor responsibility for the training group's development.

A sixth favorite method embodies the use of *role-playing techniques*. The trainees can be asked to reenact what occurred in the therapy hour, taking the part of various patients so as to enable the therapist to obtain a deeper understanding of how it must be and feel for them. Or a trainee may replay his or her own role as therapist and then be instructed to intervene differently. In group supervision, various members can participate in the mini-dramas and, when enacting the therapist, can utilize other treatment strategies conducive to different outcomes. Similarly, the supervisor may familiarize the trainees with family sculpting (Satir, 1972; Duhl, Kantor, and Duhl, 1973), a predominantly nonverbal technique that can be utilized for both diagnosis and treatment. In brief, any member of the family can be asked to sculpt, that is, place the members of the family in a living portrait arrangement—each in a position the sculptor considers characteristic (and revealing) and in a typical family configuration relative to one another. The original sculptor may then be asked to rearrange the family as he or she would like them to be, thus providing an opportunity to convey needs and desires and to make some input into the family's potential change. Or other members may be asked to spatially rearrange the family as they experience it and/or as they would prefer it to be. Thus differential perceptions of the family's alliances and moods are choreographed (Papp, 1976) in a manner intriguing to all present. When trainees are asked to sculpt their own families, involving each other as substitute family members, they not only have an opportunity to utilize the technique before trying it out on patients but also have a chance to see themselves in their own proxy family while emotionally and physically reexperiencing the relationships.

No matter what combination of the aforementioned supervisory techniques is utilized, it is crucial to foster the trainees' self-awareness and a sense of their own histories and intrapsychic and interpersonal dynamics vis-à-vis their own families of origin and, if married, families of creation. One can urge (or require) trainees to make family voyages (Bowen, 1972), that is, home visits to their families of origin to help the trainees reconnect to their parents and siblings and work out unresolved conflicts, become aware of invisible (and not so invisible) loyalties (Nagy and Spark, 1973), and become more cognizant of their own heritage. Having students do genograms (Guerin and Fogarty, 1972), that is, detailed schematic family tree diagrams of at least three generations, is a fascinating pursuit to help them trace their multiple roots and tap into these as a wellspring of strength and understanding. The apprentices can also be asked to bring in and react to family photographs (Kaslow and Friedman, 1977), using these as prods for their memories and as personal projective tools. As the trainees come to grips with who they are and how they came to be that way in their family constellation, they are also gaining mastery of techniques they can translate to use with patients in reconstructing their family histories and for healing old rifts and hurts.

When (in private practice) I am supervising a trainee who is married, part of the training contract calls for the trainee to bring his or her mate along for several counseling sessions. In this way, they experience what it is like to be in the client role, how painful it can be to open up submerged conflict areas, and how difficult it may be to accept interpretations and confrontations. Just as many graduate and professional programs require that students in the process of becoming therapists become analysands or psychotherapy patients, I believe that it is imperative that marriage counselors and family therapists have at least a few treatment sessions, with their close relatives participating.

Slowly, some of the formal educational and training programs are beginning to require that the trainee enter therapy, preferably with spouse and sometimes with family. For example, Jurarsky (1964) reports on running therapy groups for trainees and their spouses for purposes of supervision, didactic education, and analysis of resistances and defenses. The underlying premise is that severe strife in the therapist's own marriage has a negative influence on his or her therapeutic neutrality and effectiveness. Therefore, trainees are expected to be able to work out the difficulties they experience.

The supervisor, sensitive to the particular trainee's personality and professional developmental level, sets the tone and pace of the learning experience. Trainees may express frustration over the gaps in their knowledge, adopt "cookbook" techniques, express insecurities over control of the family, and confront the fear that they may play out their own family problems in the context of the patient's family therapy. Providing the supervisor cares about the trainee's growth and is able to convey this, the group process experience will be enriched by the recognition that the interns are being guided over and through barriers to their development as family therapists. A feeling of success, adequacy, and competence is initially dependent more on the supportive and illuminating quality of the supervision than on the trainee's ability to treat families. Providing this constitutes a major challenge to the supervisor.

Supervision can be summarized as a didactic learning experience that involves the communication of information and provides the necessary foundation for the mastery of theory, technique, and clinical treatment of clients. Too frequently, classroom curricula is aimed at teaching concepts and developing skill but fails to include any concern with value assumptions that undergird clinical interventions. Many teachers and supervisors function along the lines of "do as I say," not "do as I do"—there are glaring inconsistencies between what they preach and what they practice. As Abroms indicates in "Supervision as Metatherapy" (Chapter Four), the trainee is more apt to emulate what the supervisor has modeled in actual on-the-job behavior than to carry out what he or she is told should be done but what in fact is not by the preceptor. As part of the process, the student should be given the opportunity to explore his or her own assumptions, observations, self-perceptions, and creative processes. The supervisor's role should be vitally committed to human and humane values and should encourage learning by strong intellectual and emotional stimulation and by engaging in brainstorming types of emotional problem-solving activities with supervisees. As Price (1976) states, "A humanistic program of clinical supervision focuses upon the student as a complete organic entity rather than a receptacle for learning." He recommends growth enhancement through development of the student's own value system, self-perceptions, and personal ownership of choices.

The supervisory process should enable the apprentice to examine, question, reformulate, and affirm his or her own framework for meaning and value, as these are the intangibles from which therapeutic intervention unfolds. Although a therapist should not presume that his or her values and attitudes are the best and most desirable ones nor superimpose them on the patient, yet the therapist should be completely aware of the value base that he or she holds and be able to communicate it for what it is—pertinent to the therapeutic task. Knowing one's hierarchy of values helps one decide which kinds of problems one is likely to be least effective with and to refer clients presenting these problems to a therapist who is not "turned off" by a specific behavior. For example, a therapist who believes homosexuality or extramarital sex is intrinsically wrong should not undertake to treat people engaging in these behaviors.

Summary: And the Future Cometh

Since so many additional people are trying to become couples therapists and family therapists each year and since the demand for the kinds of services they can ultimately provide is multiplying, the opportunities for experienced clinicians to supervise these trainees in university, medical school, and agency settings are vast. The possibilities of doing so through a family institute or through a specially contracted individual supervisory arrangement are also expanding rapidly. But meaningful and sound supervision can only flow from a broad, in-depth knowledge of (1) the structure and dynamics of couples and families, (2) the theories and techniques of marital and family therapy, (3) the learning process in the context of a training milieu and/or a supervisory relationship, and (4) what teaching and supervisory approaches have proven most efficacious for the particular learning tasks to be mastered.

In this chapter, the history of marital and family therapy has been reviewed and the evolution of training and supervisory programs and models chronicled. The techniques and methods extant in the field have been described and amplified. The *challenges* that exist now and that lie ahead in the near future are (1) the establishment of a strong, central body to function nationally as an accrediting agency for all formal university- and agency-based training programs (the AAMFC has already made commendable and recognized strides in this direction); (2) some standardization as to number of hours and core curriculum for family institute-type training programs; (3) agreement on minimum entrance requirements—both academic background and personality factors; (4) determination of and agreement on the number of didactic, clinical, and supervisory hours necessary before one is sufficiently trained and polished to function in the critical role of a marriage and family therapist; (5) for certification and licensing procedures to protect the public from untrained and/or unethical therapists; and (6) for effectiveness and outcome research comparing different training and supervisory approaches.

This is an exciting, stimulating, and rewarding field; it invites ingenuity, experimentation, and innovation. For these very reasons, it appeals to the more creative free spirits in the therapist ranks. Therefore some defining and standardization for quality without stultification or narrowing are essential. The family is still the most basic institution in our society, and therapists are among those who can help revitalize and enrich family living so that it becomes more satisfying for the members as a group and for each person individually.

CHAPTER 11

Training of
Group Therapists

Erich Coché

Some things cannot be learned well in a classroom—leading a psychotherapy group is one of them. Although students can learn about the history of group psychotherapy, its major theoretical concepts, and some techniques of intervention in the classroom situation, to become group therapists they must apply their knowledge and skill in a working situation. Here supervision is necessary; with it, learning can take place, and patients are protected to some degree from being harmed by the errors of a newcomer to the field.

Supervision can take many forms; the major ones will be discussed later in this chapter. The discussion here is based on the literature and on a variety of approaches my colleagues and I have tried in the training and continuing education of group psychotherapists at Friends Hospital. By experimenting for three years with different training modes used with staff and students alike, we arrived at a model combining didactic work and supervision that has been in existence for two years now but is still open to modifications.

This chapter lists some of the positive and negative aspects of five major forms of supervision as they have been encountered in our experience. There is some discussion of these in the group therapy literature—see McGee (1970) and Yalom (1975)—but these authors have a different emphasis. McGee presents a comparison of four approaches: Dyadic, group, cotherapy, and triadic supervision. He discusses their assets and drawbacks and recommends that the choice of a particular supervisory style should depend on the needs of the supervisors and supervisees. He also sees prior experience with individual therapy and exposure to didactic materials as recommended prerequisites. Yalom (1975) introduces his discussion of supervisory techniques as part of a thoughtfully designed training program for group psychotherapists. Although less detailed in their assessments, in most respects Yalom and McGee have evaluations very similar to mine of the major supervisory techniques. Before we compare the different styles, however, it is worthwhile to look at the goals of supervision.

What do we want the novice to learn?

Goals of Supervision

The acquisition of theoretical concepts, cognitive subject matter—book knowledge—is usually the least important learning goal of the supervisory process. Many group therapy training programs delegate this part to a course that is often taken before the student even begins to work as a therapist. There are times, though, when the supervisor may suggest certain reading matter to the student if it concerns a particular problem he or she may be having.

Another goal is the teaching of skills. The handling of certain situations that repeatedly arise in groups can be learned and practiced. The supervisor can help the student find more effective ways to deal with a crisis, avoid frequent pitfalls, and further the progress of the group and its members.

A better grasp of group dynamics can be another goal of supervision. While the basic principles are relatively easy to learn, their impact in the life of a group is better understood by actually experiencing situations illustrating the principles of group dynamics. Being able to name and to analyze a group's processes makes dealing with them much easier. Yet often even bright and well-educated students can be in the middle of a group process phenomenon, such as scapegoating, and not notice it, mostly because they are so intensely involved. The more detached view of a supervisor can help the trainee to make the connection between his book knowledge and the group interactions.

A knowledge of individual psychodynamics is a prerequisite in most group therapy training programs. But the interaction between two persons' psychopathologies can be baffling. To help the students gain a better grasp of such interactions can be another goal of supervision. Similarly, the transference phenomena known from dyadic therapy are somewhat different in the group, and trainees usually need some help in dealing with these. The most important task of supervision is to help the beginning group therapist use his or her own person as an effective tool in therapy. One needs to learn when to trust one's intuition, how to use the data from within, when to self-disclose and to what extent, when to push, and when to back off.

But is all of this really teachable? Is it not true that there are naturally helpful persons who can do a lot of good just by being as they are? Some people need little training indeed in order to be quite effective, but the majority of students in the mental health field come with little know-how, although they possess some potential and many good intentions. In many students, warmth, empathy, and genuineness exist only as possibilities, which need to be actualized through the supervisory interaction. Other students seem to have had these qualities earlier in their lives, but their development was thwarted because of some misunderstood theoretical concepts. In these cases, the supervisor has to help the students revive hidden talents.

Techniques of Supervision

Reporting to the Supervisor. The trainee meets with his preceptor on a more or less regular basis and discusses the activities of the group in question. One person reports and the other listens, asks questions, suggests, consults, and eventually may evaluate. Of all the techniques described here this is the least cumbersome; there is no need for equipment, and it requires less effort or preparation than most techniques. Teacher and student often develop a relationship that can foster considerable growth on both sides. Furthermore, the student usually has the undivided attention of the teacher, which also enhances the relationship.

The foremost disadvantage of this way of supervision is its susceptibility to distortions. It is natural for the neophyte group therapist to want to make a good impression, which will, however, cause him or her to see events differently from the way in which an independent observer would have seen them. Embarrassing moments go unreported, either willfully or through a process of convenient forgetting. All kinds of defensive techniques come into play, and the student's needs and personal style can give events in the group a different look and an idiosyncratic order of importance. Technical blunders may go unnoticed because the student has not deemed them important enough to talk about.

The supervisor in this situation relies heavily on the student's reports. At times the reports do present an adequate picture of the group process; at other times such a picture can be obtained by careful listening and pointed questioning. But there are times when the view of the group is blocked by the student's personality and defensive makeup, in which case a discussion of the student's needs and defenses may be necessary in order to reopen communications. However, this can lead to a blurring of the distinction between supervision and therapy, with concomitant interpersonal and ethical problems (which will be discussed later).

Many instructors find an easy way out of this dilemma by directing the session so that most of the supervisory time is spent evaluating the individual dynamics of various group members. They choose a safe topic; it requires little effort, and learning is imparted, which means that no one has to feel guilty for not working. After all, something can always be learned by a good discussion of personality dynamics. Yet something gets lost; the actual handling of group situations, the dynamics of the group and transference phenomena between the group and the therapist trainee can remain unspoken for a long time.

Direct Observation, Tapes, and Videotapes. In order to obtain firsthand knowledge of the activities of the group, the preceptor can actually observe the group by sitting silently in the room or behind a one-way screen or can have tape recordings of the group interaction made. There are some obvious technical disadvantages to these methods. Taping and observation rooms require costly and complex equipment that occasionally seems to develop a mind of its own. Having the group leader's "boss" sitting in the room in complete silence is likely to make everyone, including the preceptor, feel very strange and is likely to give the group process an eerie flavor.

Even if he or she is not physically present in the room, the supervisor's presence is felt quite distinctly by some groups. To meet ethical and legal requirements, the leader has to inform the group whenever sessions are being taped or observed. Some group members are likely to raise this as an issue and may even give the leader a difficult time about it. Yet, in most cases, it is the novice leader's own feeling about the matter that arouses the group's reaction, as illustrated in a little vignette presented by Sadock and Kaplan (1971). A resident presented the idea of taping to his group and then reported in his next supervisory session that one of the patients had an extremely strong reaction to this suggestion. An examination of the resident's attitude then showed that the resident had somehow communicated his own strong fears to the group and especially to this one patient. Many group protests about tapes come about as an attempt of the group to help their leader against an unseen "enemy." Leaders who introduce the subject of taping in a relaxed, matter-of-fact tone rarely encounter much reluctance from the group.

At times, the equipment itself seems to resist the observational process: tapes jam, video machines break down, and microphones rattle to the point where the tapes become unintelligible. It becomes frustrating and at times amusing to watch these equipment failures persist. A frank discussion between supervisor and trainee about the feelings connected with being observed can, at times, even help machines to calm down.

The use of a one-way screen and observation room affords not only a clear view of the group but also a direct opportunity for the supervisor with whose style it is consistent to intervene if the situation seems to demand this. Some institutions use telephones or earplugs for the trainer to call in instructions to the neophyte therapist; in others, the supervisor simply walks into the session and takes over. The obvious advantage of this technique is that it allows the preceptor to intervene swiftly when the learner makes mistakes, but the disadvantage is that it undermines the esteem the group has for its leader. The authority with which a leader makes interventions greatly influences their curative value. As Frank (1974) indicates, group members are likely to listen and be influenced by someone they hold in high esteem; their respect drops considerably if the training director barges in and insinuates that the group leader is not very competent. Such direct intervention can do serious harm to the self-esteem of the beginning group leader. Mistakes are natural for a newcomer, but to have them pointed out in front of the group is likely to make him or her more insecure and may eventually lead to even more mistakes.

A completely different way to use observational equipment and one of the most effective is described in Kagan (1973). In his elaborate sequence of techniques, called *interpersonal process recall* (IPR), Kagan uses one setup in which supervisor and student watch the videotape of a session together. The student controls when the tape will be stopped for a discussion of the "inner dialogue" that occurred during the therapy session. The supervisor assumes the role of a "respectful inquirer" (Kagan, 1973); he or she does not push or criticize, but instead gently encourages disclosure of the inner dialogue, the often very emotionally laden patter going on in the leader's head while the group is under way. Although IPR was developed as a technique for counselor education and to supervise individual therapy sessions, at Friends Hospital we have successfully used the elements described here in the supervision of group therapy trainees. The students usually respond favorably to the nonthreatening, nonjudgmental atmosphere. Talking about their feelings during the session can open up many new vistas on the students' feelings toward their group members, their cotherapists, and themselves. Even though one pays little attention to therapy technique in this joint viewing, the students often discover new avenues for intervention after discussing their feelings about their group and themselves.

Cotherapy. In order to assess the usefulness of cotherapy

as a training method, one first needs to look at it as an approach to group leadership. As such, cotherapy has stirred up a lot of controversy. Baron (1975) gives an extensive overview of the status of this controversy in the group therapy literature. It becomes apparent from his analysis that many people have expressed opinions, but research on the many questions raised is extremely sparse. Slavson (1964) and MacLennan (1965) are most critical of cotherapy and leave the reader with the impression that cotherapy is used more for the benefit of the leader than for that of the group. Rosenbaum (1971) points out a major disadvantage in his conclusion that cotherapy often complicates the already complex lines of interaction within a therapy group. Unresolved problems of the cotherapists can surface and lead to a mutual blocking between the coleaders, very much to the group's detriment.

Other authors are more positive in their evaluations; McGee and Schuman (1967) list both advantages and disadvantages. Yalom (1975) points out that cotherapy can provide opportunities for modeling: Patients can observe two people, preferably of opposite sexes, working together in a nonexploitative relationship and working out their differences with mutual respect.

There are some practical advantages in cotherapy. In case a patient storms out of a session, one of the leaders can stay with the group while the other can go and look after the patient, especially if the group is conducted in a hospital setting and there is concern about a patient's suicidal impulses or strong feelings of rejection. Also, the group can continue if one of the therapists becomes ill or is otherwise impeded from coming to the session.

Many authors (Rosenbaum, 1971; Solomon, Loeffler, and Frank, 1953) have noted the diffusion of transference in groups led by more than one therapist. Often, especially with a male-female cotherapy team, the group becomes like a family, and many problems surface more quickly. New behaviors toward the parental and sibling figures can be tried out and familial conflicts can be reenacted and worked through. This similarity to the family structure can provide an opportunity for learning and growth, but it can also be confusing: Typecasting can occur, which can be annoying and impede growth. At best, it costs extra time to work it through; at worst, it stops the group from moving.

Two popular versions of cotherapy are used in training. In

one, the learner works together with his or her teacher in a team; in the other, two students form the team and are then supervised jointly, using one or more of the methods described here.

When paired with a trainee in cotherapy, the preceptor has the opportunity of handling things directly when they get difficult. This may be to the benefit of the group, saving them from the bunglings of a newcomer; but it deprives the learner of the experience of handling troublesome situations alone. Particularly at first, all he or she will get to see is "genius at work," which, via the principle of modeling, can be educational, but which does not foster learning by doing. It depends on the ability of the teacher to hold back, on the student's assertiveness, and on the quality of their relationship, whether the student will slowly grow into an equal-partner role or whether he or she will be permanently stuck in a second-in-command position. The impact of the subordinate role of the trainee on the group depends on its atmosphere. Some groups simply ignore such a cotherapist; others use him as a convenient scapegoat.

Another problem in cotherapy with the supervisor is that the student may be stifled by his or her presence. The student may hesitate to proceed with some good interventions because they involve risk taking or because the patients might not respond to them and the trainee does not want to look foolish. The stifling effect is likely to be heightened by a critique after each session and by grades at the end of the semester.

Stifling can also go the other way. Some supervisors, especially those who are insecure about their role in the group or in the training program, are as likely as students to hesitate before taking risks. Thus, they may end up conducting their groups in a less imaginative fashion than they are capable of. The stifling effect could potentially get worse where two novice therapists work together supervised via taped observations. Yet the opposite is more often true: The two students usually become very supportive of each other, which allows them to be creative and to take risks. This, coupled with a nonjudgmental instructor, can create the right climate for good group therapy and good instruction.

Although most cotherapy teams consist of just two leaders, some groups using teams of three or more therapists exist. One such endeavor is described by Greenberg (1976). In his groups, five to seven team members meet with eight to fourteen patients for a limited number of sessions. Most staff members want this group as a learning experience, but they all participate as full members of the team. Groups of this size are extremely difficult to run meaningfully and tend to fall apart unless the team leader is a charismatic person who gives direction to the whole enterprise. Even then, most therapist learning has to be achieved through the process of modeling and team discussions after the sessions.

It is difficult to evaluate the effects of cotherapy as a training tool because its outcome hinges on so many variables: teacher and student personalities, their relationship to each other, the type of group, and its institutional setting. Depending on these factors, students can potentially become highly competent and confident therapists, or they can end up worried and insecure or mere copies of their masters. Because the outcome of cotherapy depends on so many variables, research evaluating its efficiency is extremely sparse and fraught with problems. Thus there are many opinions to date, but few established facts.

McGee and Schuman (1967, p. 30) stress the importance of the relationship between the cotherapists by stating "There is strongly suggestive evidence that a group's operation and effectiveness are directly related to the quality and vicissitudes of the cotherapists' relationship." Although this statement may be a bit strong and unsupported by research evidence, our own clinical experience attests to its accuracy.

One way of using cotherapy in the supervisory process has recently been described by Tucker, Hart, and Liddle (1976). A major feature of their approach is to elicit reactions of the two student cotherapists to each other. It was felt that making the trainees aware of each other's feelings permitted the removal of issues that might otherwise impede the team's functioning; it also provided some remarkable learning experiences for everyone involved.

Process Group. Many professionals insist that in order to become a good group therapist the student ought to be a member of a group before or while conducting his or her first group. That way the student can feel what it is like and can observe group process while living it. Many processes that occur in the students' groups repeat themselves in the supervisory group, either because the conflicts are universal, because they represent a natural stage of group development, or because the student group leader has a way of provoking or raising the same issues both in his supervisory group and in the one he leads.

The way in which such a process group is conducted differs greatly from one institution to another. In some, the emphasis is on didactic material, and the group spends most of its time discussing concepts of the group therapy literature; the processes of the group are only used peripherally, as they fit into the topics of discussion. At the other extreme are groups that convene for the sole purpose of self-study without utilization of pertinent literature. In his overview, Berger (1969) describes a number of training programs that have employed experiential groups as part of the training program. He lists a number of advantages and desired outcomes of these groups, such as increased interpersonal skills, feedback, and a greater sense of universality, and concludes: "A holistic approach to training for the practice of group psychotherapy should also include the individual's participation as a member in a psychotherapy group or group training experience" (p. 117).

This exhortation is, however, based on Berger's and others' clinical experience but not on any research. Many therapists assert that therapy for the future therapist is an absolutely necessary prerequisite, and psychoanalytic tradition supports this contention. Others, however, claim that this demand is irrational, that the removal of undesired behaviors is a technical skill, comparable to the ability to remove kidney stones, and does not have to be tried out first on the future technician. Although the battle rages and opinions continue to be exchanged, research evidence as to who is right is still lacking.

In our work in supervisory groups at Friends Hospital, we have found that most supervisees want and need a balanced mixture of didactic and process material. We have therefore developed a group style that pays approximately equal attention to literature, self-study, and clinical material from the groups conducted by the trainees. We have found that a group that has spent a good deal of time on theoretical or clinical material will eventually demand a discussion of its own processes, either by direct request or by acting out enough to create a problem that can no longer be disclaimed. Similarly, if the group spends most of its time on self-study, it is likely to eventually request a discussion of the literature on group therapy problems.

We have also seen groups that use one or the other technique as a resistance against having to work either on the group's problems or on a study of the literature. An interpretation of the phenomenon usually gets the group going in a balanced direction again. However, it also depends on the contract under which the group originally convened. Students have a right to resent demands for self-disclosure if they were originally led to believe that they were signing up for a seminar in group theory. If self-study is to be part of the project, that should be made clear to everyone from the start.

The techniques of mixing the components of literature, process, and clinical material can vary. Our groups over the last few years have experimented with a number of modes. For a while we tried weekly alternations but discarded that as too artificial; prestructuring by the group leaders was found to be too rigid unless it was done on an ad hoc basis responding to present needs of the group; and letting the group find its own direction was also only partially successful because of the resistances just mentioned. Presently we are using a combination of on-the-spot guidance, expressed group needs, and maintaining a log that can show real and perceived imbalances. In the log we record the topic of each session and whether we dealt with literature, clinical material, or the group's own process. Favoring of any single component becomes quickly apparent.

The great advantage of process groups as described here is the potential for integration of theoretical and affective learning. Both are needed to help the aspiring therapist develop theoretical knowledge, technical skills, and the personality traits necessary to be effective.

In order to be successful, however, process groups demand a high level of skill on the part of the leader, who must help the group to avoid one-sidedness and resistance. An atmosphere of mutual trust between members is absolutely necessary, which is why such groups may be doomed to fail in institutions in which a high degree of tension prevails. Grading students on their participation in these groups raises yet another set of ethical and other problems that will be discussed later.

Practicing and Role Playing. Practicing and role playing are not exactly supervisory modes in their own right but more frequently serve as an adjunct to the other forms described. There are some situations that are common to most therapy groups and yet can present the beginning therapist with extremely vexing problems: for example, how to begin a session, how to handle highly personal questions from group members, and what to do with monopolizing members. Interventions in these situations can be practiced in supervisory sessions before they occur. This gives the student a chance to try out different responses in a safe setting: Ineffective reactions can be discarded, others can be repeated and improved. Thus the trainee develops a feeling of mastery and a sense of competence beforehand, so that when these situations arise in the group he or she will be able to handle them.

One advocate of such practicing activities is Kagan (1973), who suggests that the novice become familiar with a therapist's "interpersonal nightmares" and prepare for them. Kagan provides motion pictures with which responses to such situations can be tried out. In one of these, he presents actors playing patients who either question the competence of the therapist or arouse his guilt feelings. The students can then try out a variety of responses to these situations, which they can later evaluate as to their therapeutic advisability. Especially when dealing with beginning therapists, practicing responses in this way is highly desirable.

Strotzka (1973) discusses the use of role playing and describes a special form of this approach that he uses in training. Before the students in his course in psychotherapy learn much about group therapy, he sets up a play in which student volunteers play patients having their first group therapy session. Usually this stirs up a great deal of interest in the dynamics of psychotherapy groups, both on an intellectual and on an emotional level.

In dealing with more advanced trainees, role playing can also be a valuable adjunct to the training program. Situations that have come up in their groups can be replayed, with participants giving different responses. The use of role playing within the therapy group itself can also be experimented with in a supervisory group. There a beginner can practice the setting up of role playing, interventions, and modifications of the play.

Combining Different Methods. Most group therapy training institutes use several forms of supervision in combination, as documented by Sadock and Kaplan (1971) in their report on the approaches used in a few training centers throughout the United States. It appears that if the various methods are applied with some forethought they can be integrated into a flexible sequence, which in turn can be adapted to the needs of the institution that sponsors the training program. Yalom (1975) also proposes one sequential arrangement of different training methods, which includes an additional technique not discussed in this paper: the observation of an experienced group therapist by the students—here the beginners sit in an observation room and watch the senior person conduct his or her group.

Ethical and Interpersonal Problems

Inasmuch as group therapy supervision comes in many forms, the ethical problems it can raise have many varieties. Some have clear choices, while others are devoid of any satisfying solution; whatever choice one makes, some uneasiness is bound to remain, as the following examples will show.

The Group and Supervision. Many beginning group therapists hesitate or even decline to let their groups know that they are students or trainees and are being supervised. They fear—and perhaps correctly so—that imparting this knowledge to the group will diminish their authority with their patients. Yet honesty with patients and their right to confidentiality demand that one at least inform them if one is being supervised and is telling another person about what goes on in the group. In fact, it is a salutary habit to tell new group members what the confidentiality rules for the group are and what its limits are. Many trainees have a positive response from their group members if they simply spend a few minutes introducing the supervisor to them. The trainer thereby becomes known as a kind and real human being rather than a mere object of fantasies about some kind of superparent.

Trainee Incompetence. One of the most difficult problems for the supervisor is presented by the seriously incompetent student, particularly the one who is not bright or perceptive enough to understand the group's processes. No one is born an accomplished group therapist, and some errors of judgment are likely to occur. However, if they become too frequent, the group and its members can be hurt. If the problem is only one of lack of training and knowledge, remedial action can usually be taken without serious harm to the student's self-esteem. In some cases, a changeover to a cotherapy training system may be necessary. Intervention on the part of the teacher, however, can at times become quite difficult; if it is direct and incisive, it can severely undermine the novice's self-confidence and lead to a series of further mistakes, but if it is oblique the message may not get through to the learner and improvement may not occur.

Similar problems arise if the student is too aggressive or has some other serious personality problem. Sometimes a frank talk between student and teacher or some concrete injunctions regarding the student's behavior as a therapist can change things. At other times, it may be necessary to advise the trainee to seek therapy for him- or herself.

Occasionally the problems become so serious that the supervisor has to fear for the welfare of the group. A direct intervention, such as taking over the group, is bound to have a devastating effect on the trainee. An additional series of supervisory sessions, some skill-building exercises, or adding a cotherapist may be necessary and sufficient. If not, a more drastic action may be needed, in which case the welfare of the student may indeed be in conflict with the welfare of the patients in the group.

There are cases in which the personality problems of the student are so severe that they impose an ethical obligation on the supervisor to stop the student from pursuing a career in the mental health field. This is one of the most trying tasks for the preceptor, but occasionally it may be essential. Some supervisors try to avoid it by merely informing the student's university setting of their hesitations. But frequently this does not solve the problem; furthermore, the student deserves direct and honest information about his limitations, difficult though that may be for the supervisor. In some such cases, it also turns out that the student has already considered leaving the field and may only need some encouragement to do so.

Cotherapists in Trouble. Cotherapy relationships frequently have a tendency to become highly charged emotionally; they arouse a great deal of feeling in the two cotherapists, which can easily lead to conflict. The two most frequent issues are affection and competition. Two beginning therapists, supervised by a third person, are in a situation that often arouses sibling rivalry; vying for the attention and approval of the supervisor, they can easily feel resentment of the other one, who seems to be in their way. Just as easily, and at times simultaneously, strong feelings of attraction emerge. Few events bind people as effectively to each other as a common crisis, and handling a group can constitute a crisis for two young people who feel like wanderers in the dark, with only each other to lean on. Mutual support gives rise to attraction, and more or less vigorous sexual feelings may complete—and perhaps complicate— the picture.

Some professionals espouse the opinion that it is their job to supervise what goes on in the group but that the relationship of the students to each other is not their business and that prying into it would go beyond the ethical boundaries of supervision. However, if the cotherapists are having difficulties with each other, these are likely to affect the group. Where the attraction between the trainees is so strong that it is frightening to them and they are exhibiting some strange avoidance behaviors, the therapeutic work is likely to suffer; likewise, where competition is too fierce mutual blocking may arise. Thus it is very much in the interest of the group to work out the cotherapy problem. Tucker, Hart, and Liddle (1976) offer some useful suggestions on how this can be done. During the supervisory session, they purposely focus on the reactions of the cotherapists to each other. Feelings that arose during their therapeutic work together can thus be worked through before they become incapacitating. Working on these feelings often becomes a starting point for further learning about the therapeutic process.

Despite efforts such as these, work on cotherapist issues remains an extremely difficult task, requiring a great deal of tact and willingness to be open on all sides. Where this willingness is missing, it may be necessary to dissolve the team. In that case, additional work is necessary to help the group to deal with the crisis precipitated by the dissolution.

Another problem arises if the supervisor is also the cotherapist. In some institutional settings, mechanisms exist by which problems between the two can be handled if they arise; for instance, by assigning a third person to supervise and help both or by having both participate in a self-study group where such issues can frankly be discussed. Where these mechanisms do not exist, a heavy burden is placed on both parties. It may be possible to resolve matters through frank and open talks, but asking a third person to help out is likely to be the more fruitful course of action.

McGee and Schuman (1967) also discuss possible issues in cotherapy in some detail. They present a number of practical hints on how to deal with various problems that are likely to emerge. They also recommend care in matching cotherapists to each other.

Supervision and Therapy. Many supervisors encounter their most difficult problems in setting the border between supervision and therapy, and an investigation of this issue shows that this boundary is indeed set very differently from one trainer to the next. Some prefer to stay completely aloof from the student's personal problems; others practically turn the supervisory hour into a therapy session.

Both extremes entail serious problems: In the first instance, the student is not encouraged to see how his or her own personal quirks enter into perceptions and interventions, nor is the student enabled to overcome blind spots that are hampering his or her work with the group. The other extreme implies a considerable intrusion into the student's personal sphere, and many students are justifiably indignant when it happens. Often resistance sets in so drastically that supervision becomes most difficult. Some students, however, are not indignant at all about the "therapy" style of supervision. They love it and will defend it against all criticisms—but their enthusiasm hardly lessens the ethical problems of this mode.

The demand for self-examination on the part of the student is most explicit among psychoanalytically oriented supervisors, who usually favor some form of therapy for the neophyte therapist. Berger (1969) follows a similar line of reasoning when he recommends participation in a psychotherapy group as part of the training of future therapists. Recommending therapy, however, is still different from using supervision for this purpose.

The dilemma becomes even more acute in the group mode of supervision. For the reasons just described, such a technique—desirable as it is—is bound to lead to situations in which the personal problems of the trainees surface. To avoid them, then, would completely undermine the purpose of this supervisory model. But in order for them to be successfully worked through, a fair degree of self-disclosure is necessary. Without it, little learning is likely to take place. But what can the leader do to encourage self-disclosure? There is at least one training program of which I am aware in which participants receive their course grade depending on the degree of self-disclosure they have shown. That practice—in my opinion—is unethical and potentially harmful.

In our supervision group at Friends Hospital, we have made participation voluntary, and we establish a clear contract at the outset. This contract states that we will, among other activities, examine our own group process but that we will not delve into past personal histories and that the degree of self-disclosure on the part of the participants is fully determined by the individuals.

Sadock and Kaplan (1971) have a different outlook in this regard. In their group therapy training program for psychiatric residents, some kind of group experience as a patient is mandatory for the psychiatric resident. This can take place in the institution or in an outside therapy group. The resident enters a therapeutic contract with the therapist, and a high value is placed on openness and frankness. The program is highly structured but seems to make much less use of the group process phenomena than does Yalom's model (1975) or the Friends Hospital program.

Teaching Ethics. Like many other aspects of group therapy, its ethics too are best taught by a combination of literature study, self-discovery, and modeling by the supervisor. A logical requirement is that the student be familiar with the ethical code of the profession. The tentative guidelines proposed by Gazda (1975) and some of the papers he cites are worthwhile further readings.

Self-discovery about ethical dilemmas usually begins quickly. Difficulties arise in the group—often in the very first session—that demand ethical choices. Sometimes there is sufficient time to really think about it before the choice is made; more often, there is no time, a decision is needed on the spot, and deliberations can be held afterward. These dilemmas can be painful, but they are always enlightening, and they contribute to the maturation of the new group therapist, as illustrated in the following example.

One afternoon, one of our cotherapy teams, on its way to the group session, was confronted by a male and a female patient who with a mixture of glee and shame reported that they had had sexual relations with each other the night before. They then told the therapists that under no circumstances did they want this information relayed to the group and made veiled threats as to the consequences of such disclosure. The therapists were clearly in a dilemma. There was little time to discuss the issue; if they disclosed the information, they would lose these patients' trust and risk the threatened consequences of their leaving the group. If they did not talk about it, they would have the burden of a secret impeding their work, and they would violate their own principle that self-disclosure and the open discussion of relationships among the patients are major curative forces.

On the spot, the two therapists, one senior person and one psychologist intern, decided to allow the two patients to keep their secret. They felt uneasy about their decision and were less effective than usual during the session. Afterward they discussed the matter again with the two patients, who then on their own decided to raise the matter in the group. The therapists reported on the event in their supervisory group, where a fruitful discussion of secrets in group therapy ensued.

Much learning of ethics is accomplished by emulating the standards of the supervisor. Here lies one of the supervisor's most responsible functions; his or her ethical behaviors, deliberations in staff meetings, and example in other professional activities provide a model for the trainees.

The Supervisor as a Role Model

Despite the differences between therapy and supervision I have mentioned, there are many similarities between the two activities, and in many ways the supervisor acts as a model not only for the way in which the student will eventually conduct supervision but also for the student's therapeutic work. By supervisory style, often more than by words, the trainer communicates many attitudes and beliefs about human nature. If the supervisor is basically misanthropic, students are likely to notice and—if they respect him or her highly—to adopt a similar stance. On the other hand, if the teacher is basically optimistic and believes in people's willingness to change despite their fears in order to escape their miseries, he or she is likely to teach that to the students by words and interactions.

If one agrees with the opinion that accurate empathy, genuineness, and nonpossessive warmth are important therapist qualities and—to a degree—teachable, then it follows that a supervisor can augment these in students by modeling these qualities in interactions with them. Of course, there are some excellent therapists who had cold and distant trainers, but if we ask students about their finest moments in supervision, we will often hear about incidents of sharing or other strongly personal interactions.

Interpersonal risk taking is a good example of such modeling. Where the supervisor is willing to take risks in dealing with the student, in mode and degree of self-disclosure, or in willingness to try out novel techniques, he or she sets an example and conveys the message that, even though the consequences can at times be embarrassing or otherwise unpleasant, the rewards in deepening relationships are ultimately worth the risk.

If we want our students to grow during their supervision years, we have to be open to growth ourselves. This can occur only if we are willing to listen to feedback. Most students need some encouragement in order to go so far as to give feedback to their preceptors. Yet without it supervision becomes a one-way street, and the experience is likely to be less meaningful than it could be.

Many students like to be very intellectual when asked about their most influential experiences during their professional training and about why they chose one therapeutic style over the other. When asked again a few years later, however, they will often point to one or two specific instructors who were "somehow different" from the others, who were more personal and more direct, and who shaped their thinking and therapeutic style a great deal. This potential influence on the next generation of therapists places much responsibility on the supervisor and is at the same time one of the greatest rewards.

CHAPTER 12

Criminal Justice Settings

Stanley L. Brodsky

Supervisors in justice agencies are invariably the object of great criticism, abuse, suspicion, and praise. They are granted near-absolute authority but, as Ambrose Bierce ([1911] 1958) observed of all plenipotentiaries, only on the condition they never exert it. This chapter examines supervisors caught in just such dilemmas in two settings: law enforcement and corrections.

The Supervisory Task

There are a great variety of uniformed employees in these two occupational groups. Within corrections alone, there will be kitchen supervisors whose tasks are much more akin to those of any cafeteria supervisor than with prison guards. In penal settings, wide differences exist between the laundry supervisors, officers assigned in guard towers, shoe repair experts, vocational trainers, tailors, administrators, classification specialists, yard officers, drivers, and others. Many police serve as correctional officers as well, in maintaining county and small-town jails (jails in large cities usually have their own separate correctional staff).

In prisons and jails, there is an expansion of the number of persons directly supervised as one goes down the supervisory chain of command, with one important difference from industrial settings. At the very bottom of the employment ladder, the entry level, there are a large number of persons conducting supervision of confined persons. In most industries, there are no persons conducting supervision at the bottom tier of the organization. For police and correctional officers, the lowest rank has the greatest degree of citizen contact.

The line correctional and police officer is actually a supervisor; in prison and jail settings, the jobs require management skills, often in situations of high stress. There are two levels of supervision: supervision of confined persons (inmates or residents) and supervision of other police and correctional officers. To the extent that the same issues are involved, they will be discussed together.

Transient Personnel

A first distinction between industrial and justice settings is the turnover in supervisees. At the line officer level, the turnover in supervisees is frequently over 100 percent per year. That is, the average prison sentence actually served is well under a year. While a few inmates serve long sentences, the number of inmates admitted and released is greater than the total inmate population. The same turnover exists for correctional officers in some states. For example, in Louisiana in 1974, there was a 103 percent turnover of guards. While this is higher than in most states, turnover percentages of 30 percent to 50 percent are frequent.

This high turnover rate interferes with the stability of long-term relationships and negatively affects the entire organizational milieu. McGregor's (1960) analysis of organizational types provides a context in which this effect may be examined. Theory X organizations assume that employees dislike their work and responsibilities and that coercion, threat, and control are primary management techniques. Theory Y organizations assume that employees are self-directed, seek responsibility, and share organizational goals in creative and imaginative ways. Supervisors whose style is based on Theory Y organization—that is, on mutual trust and self-motivation—are frustrated by parades of new employees. The necessity of starting over and over again impairs the establishment of collaborative working relationships. The instability promotes Theory X thinking; the officers are seen as transients of uncertain loyalty, reluctant to accept organizational goals, who must be carefully monitored and promptly punished for poor efforts. In corrections and law enforcement, where legal coercion is always an element, such background notes have the potential for becoming the whole orchestral score. Theory X assumptions rule. Fear is omnipresent. Every discussion with correctional officers eventually produces the observation that inmates truly run the prison and that if they really wanted to the inmates could take it over at any time. There is a cumulative impact of social control functions, high staff and client turnover, and Theory X coercive modes, which have a distinctive character in justice agencies.

Administrative Structures

Several issues in supervision and management of criminal justice agencies are not present in other organizations. Indeed, an underlying rationale for preparation of a special chapter on supervision in criminal justice settings is that these principles and applications do differ. Comparative research is skimpy, but there is some support for this rationale. One study reported that *consideration* and *initiating structure* in police supervision depart from the body of knowledge in supervision and attitudes (Brief, Aldag, and Wallden, 1976). In supervision, *consideration* is defined as trust, warmth, and mutual friendship. The term *initiating structure* refers to achievement-oriented supervision that results in well-defined organizational patterns. In the Brief, Aldag, and Wallden (1976) study of these orthogonal variables among seventy-five police officers, *consideration* in supervision was unrelated to job satisfaction, involvement, or faith in people. In numerous studies of industrial organizations, *consideration* and job satisfaction were interrelated. On the other hand, *initiating structure,* which typically was found to be negatively related to job satisfaction in corporations, yielded just the opposite finding among police. Among the police it was related positively to job satisfaction, involvement, and commitment, meaningfulness of the job, faith in people, and a less defensive posture.

What accounts for the differences? Police have much role ambiguity in their jobs and are confronted by much situational uncertainty, and initiating structure may well provide a comforting security and order. The military model in police and correctional organizations maintains a basic soldier or warrior conceptualization of the job (Brodsky, 1975). Consideration is of little importance in many military organizations in which fear of the commanding officer is greater than the fear of the enemy (Brodsky and Eggleston, 1970).

Supervision Stressors

Justice agencies have pervasive "low-trust, high-control" patterns with their clientele and with their employees, sometimes with good reasons. In the case of apprehending a suspect or guarding a prison gate, the job demands control and distrust. In other situations, however, there are mixed objectives. The so-called treatment-custody dichotomy has been debated and delineated for several decades in corrections, and the role of the line officer is always on the edge of the barbed wire fence separating the concern for the client from the protection of society (Johnson, 1971).

The distrust and overcontrol of justice agencies' employees has led to poor supervision being identified as a major source of psychological stress for police and correctional officers. In training sessions as well as informal discussions, one of the most frequent topics of conversation is the frustration created by administrative policies and supervisory personnel. Virtually all officers complain bitterly about insensitive supervisors and unfair department policies. Eisenberg (1975, p. 28) distinguished between normal "bitching

and griping" and the more serious stress factors attendant on poor
supervision. He observed, "The supervisor who always 'goes by the
book,' is never available on a complicated or delicate street situation,
is overly demanding, tends not to back up a subordinate when
conditions justify such support, or who fails to attend to a subordinate's personal needs represents a supervisor who can substantially
contribute to the psychological stress of his subordinates." As part
of training state troopers in human relations effectiveness, Brodsky
and Danish (1973) studied the relative weighting of fifteen occupational stressors. Unjust supervisory criticism and poor management practices were identified as stressful and traumatic by troopers
at all levels in the organization.

The effect of poor supervisory practices combined with other
occupational stressors can be severe. The annual suicide rate in
police in Tennessee was 69.1 per 100,000, third highest among
twenty-four occupations for which data were available (Richard
and Fell, 1975). Similarly, police were found to have high rates of
premature death and hospitalizations for circulatory and digestive
disorders. Di-Gel and Bufferin are standard equipment in most
patrol cars and station desks.

Supervisors and supervisory practices represent just one element in the complex factors that influence law enforcement and correctional officers and their clients. Nevertheless, they are important
factors, in which much subjectivity is present, in assigning criteria
for good supervisory performance.

Performance Criteria

The assessment of satisfactory supervision depends on examining the meaning of "satisfactory" at both the supervisory and
line officer levels. This judgment may be from the view of the
concerned officers, of the clients with whom they work, of the administration of the agency, or lastly, from the independent perspective of a theoretical or societal overview. The performance objective
about which most controversy storms is that of reformation in the
correctional setting. Glaser (1964) studied which correctional personnel have the greatest influence on the lives and postprison experiences of released offenders; the results indicate by far the most

significant number of inmates were affected by correctional officers.

The goal of successful correctional officer activities is often not prisoner reform. The distinction has been made between cure and care of correctional clients. A cure orientation assumes a disease entity and a personality exorcism or change function for the officer. On the other hand, a care objective assumes that offering reasonable and humane care is the prime function of officers; if individuals change, they do so in the context of nourishing and positive surroundings. Whether or not individuals change is contingent on their relationships with other people.

The key element is justice. When clients or line officers feel that they are being treated unjustly, all other factors pale. If a basic sense of fairness and justice is experienced, then even unpleasant and inconsiderate supervisors and officers are tolerated and sometimes tolerated quite well. The repeated theme is heard of the admired, "tough but fair" officer or administrator. Fairness and justice seem to work independently of other traits. Dean and Morgan (1975, p. 26) report that inmates respect fairness above all other characteristics of officers and that "being fair and friendly does not interfere with his [the officer's] job of maintaining security and control."

In this context, there are the problems of moral discontinuities of helpers—the discontinuities between what they ought to be and what they are, between their stated role as helpers on the side of the client and their true role as agents of the court or agency. When officers artificially seek to establish friendships without having learned that status, they are quickly seen as phonies and devalued.

The justice setting calls for the experience of fairness, of the officer having heard the clients, of the supervisor having heard the line personnel. In the Kansas City preventive patrol experiment (Kelling, 1974) the efficiency of solving crimes had nothing to do with citizen ratings of police. Rather, it was the speed with which the officers answered calls and how well they listened to and recorded the citizen complaint that led to favorable evaluations. The same principle applies to client satisfaction with their attorneys. The Missouri Bar Study (*Lawyers Practice Manual*, 1964) indicated that results and knowledge of the law were seen by attorneys as most important in dealing with clients; however, thousands of clients themselves stated that the most important factors were what transpired between attorney and client. Courtesy, listening well, and taking the time to work with the client were most favorably assessed.

In many settings, the cry by male employees and clientele to "be treated like a man" represents a form of adolescent, chest-thumping hypermasculinity, an overcompensating need to affirm manhood because of feelings of inadequacy. In justice settings, this is also true to some degree. However, it reflects more fully the striving for fair treatment. Thus, Dean and Morgan (1975, p. 27) write, "Inmates respect the officer who conducts himself like a real man. The officer carries the authority of the correctional institution on his shoulders. He does not have to be a bully to let this be known. The inmates know it well. The officer must act like a man and treat inmates like men."

Occupational Socialization and Supervision

Occupational socialization is the process of acquiring attitudes, beliefs, and behaviors common to members of any occupation. These acquired attitudes and behaviors typically serve the employee in adapting to the special role demands and person-job fit of that occupation. Thus surgeons in training quickly learn ways of adapting to the constant ever-present possibility of patient deaths. High school teachers take on patterns of formality in relationships with students. In the mental health professions, a series of socializations similarly occur, first in graduate studies and later in applied practice.

The socialization of nurses to their "bedside manner" has been described by Jourard (1971, pp. 179–180) as "a peculiar kind of inauthentic behavior that I believe does more harm than good. Some nurses always smile, others hum, and still others answer all patients' questions about medication with the automatic phrase, 'this will make you feel better.' The 'bedside manner' appears to be something which the nurse puts on when she dons her uniform. The performance sometimes functions as an emetic for perceptive patients." Some of the automatic responses of mental health professionals include the reflexive head nod, and the ready "uh-huh" or "mmm-hmmm." Within criminal justice agencies, there are a series of equally pervasive and automatic behavior adaptations.

In his book *Behind the Shield*, Neiderhoffer (1967) suggested that cynicism is the predominant characteristic of police socialization. Police (and correctional officers as well) enter their work for reasons of job security and with neutral or sometimes mildly idealistic commitments to the notions of justice and helping others. While in training, a socialization process begins that is accelerated during the first year of employment; doubts and distrust emerge about agency goals and citizen worth. One college professor of criminology spent five months as a police officer (Kirkham, 1975, p. 198). He reported that in place of his Berkeley-educated radical-liberal philosophy, he acquired a series of altogether new attitudes and behaviors: "punitiveness, pervasive cynicism and mistrust of others, chronic irritability and free-floating anxiety, racism, a diffuse personal anxiety over the menace of crime and criminals that seemed at times to border on the obsessive."

In correctional settings, this transformation has been studied less than it has in police agencies. Still, a parallel process seems to be present in which officers become vociferous advocates of capital punishment and severe disciplinary procedures and convinced of the malevolent and untrustworthy nature of confined persons. The Stanford Prison Experiment (Haney, Banks, and Zimbardo, 1973) dramatically illustrated the metamorphosis in correctional employees. In a simulated prison, over one third of the college students chosen to play guards became punitive, angry, and brutal. These students had been selected for participation in the experiment because they were healthy and well-adjusted. The implications of this Stanford study and the Kirkham report are that the occupational demands, the stimulus pull of working in corrections, are what transform persons. Individuals do not seek out correctional employment as a vehicle for aggressive and sadistic tendencies. Rather, some become that way on the job because of the nature of the job and as a result of a realistic appraisal of the harmful or aggressive nature of groups within their client population.

Staff Development Recommendations

The problems associated with occupational socialization and poor supervision have led to a series of behavioral science programs and proposals. We will examine several of these possible remedies.

Modeling. How can a supervisor establish and encourage positive and productive behaviors in line personnel? Indeed, the question is not limited to criminal justice settings; it applies to the training of physicians, teachers, and artists as well. One school of thought is founded in a "doing-is-learning" philosophy. The story has been told of the time Sinclair Lewis, the noted writer, had been invited to address an audience of aspiring novelists for a generous fee. He walked on the stage and immediately asked for a show of hands of how many in the audience wished to be successful writers. All raised their hands. He then exhorted, "In that case, go home and write," and left the stage. There is increasing reason to believe that if he had invited a few authors to sit with him and discuss what he did as he wrote, Lewis would have been a more successful teacher of writing skills. The imitation of models is a powerful and successful means of acquiring new behaviors.

In one study in a correctional setting for delinquent youth, three training approaches were employed: instructions, daily graphic feedback, and modeling (Maloney and others, 1975). Live modeling, as well as modeling of appropriate positive behaviors on videotape, led to increases in the four categories of positive behaviors. Instruction plus feedback plus modeling was the most effective condition. The authors concluded that "the use of conglomerate training 'packages' may actually benefit staff more and thus provide the best possible care to juvenile offenders in the shortest possible time" (p. 212). Sarason (1968) has also presented a program in which delinquents effectively learn socially appropriate skills through role playing and modeling.

Staff development through modeling requires a series of steps:

1. Identification of the targeted desired behavior to be modeled. A study of agency and supervisory objectives will help determine what the goal-related behavior of the supervisors should be.
   goal-related behavior of the supervisors should be.
2. Selection of those supervisors who possess the required characteristics and who know how to structure situations that elicit these desired characteristics.

3. Creation of high-visibility opportunities for the clients to observe the modeled behaviors. Any agency offers a wide range of potential exposure of key persons to others. The supervisors selected should be placed in these readily observable positions.
4. Synthesis of modeling with training. The models should display the targeted behaviors in structured educational situations in which the trainees have the opportunity to watch in order to learn and then to try out the modeled behaviors.
5. Sensitivity to possible problems in the person-model fit. Some modeled behaviors will not fit well for trainees with very discrepant life-styles. Be prepared to have several "good" models that can fit with a variety of trainee styles.
6. Follow-up behavior observations of the models and the trainees. The models may change as a result of the explicit assignment as model supervisors and of being observed. The trainees may assimilate traits of the models that are divergent from the desired ones.
7. A return to the originally stated goals of the agency and the supervisory objectives and assessment of the modeling training has contributed to achievement of these goals.

Self-Esteem Enhancement Through Organizational Change. Stotland (1975, p. 12) identified stress as particularly affiliated with the felt low status and low sense of competence of police. He sees the officer as "in the lowest position in an ostensibly quasi-military organization," which leads to low self-esteem. The low status may lead to a compensatory reaction: The officer sometimes tries overly hard to regain his self-esteem through unnecessary aggression. Stotland suggests that supervisory practices will be enhanced through change in the structure of the agency. Status differences in particular should be minimized: Too great a distance exists from top to bottom in most departments. The hierarchy should be compressed to the minimum number of levels. Military ranks artificially exaggerate the status distance and should also be dropped. Improved supervision would result from the loosening of the inflexible bonds of the hierarchical rank structure.

Peer Feedback. Toch, Grant, and Galvin (1975) and Stotland (1975) have proposed a peer supervisory and feedback procedure. Toch and his colleagues found that officers with records of violence were very responsive to peer evaluations of their behaviors. The rate of charges for resisting arrest and assault on an officer dropped significantly among these thirty-two Oakland, California officers. Stotland proposes that each squad meet for two hours a month of self-criticism, without sergeants being present. This approach seems to work because the meetings are relatively nonthreatening. Thus undesirable behavior may be removed and constructive alternatives added, without fear of reprimand or punishment from a superior officer. The officers seek and assume more personal responsibility for their own actions and those of their peers. Even without the formal structure of peer supervision, fellow officers are extremely influential through both praise and criticism in affecting other officers.

The mechanics of implementing a peer supervision process follow several stages. To begin, organizational permission and encouragement must be developed. This encouragement needs to be presented as a positive opportunity for officers and any suggestion of mutual blame avoided. Small, naturally associated groups should be utilized, rather than structuring the groups into a forced or arbitrary composition. The fact that officer unions may consider such a program suspect should be anticipated, and mutually agreed-on objectives and procedures should be planned well in advance. The peer supervisory group should meet regularly, and the group should have an accountability element, in which attainment of objectives is assessed periodically by parties acceptable to both team members and to management.

Peer supervision and feedback provide unusually powerful behavioral impact in ways that are desired by many line officers. The National Advisory Commission on Criminal Justice Standards and Goals, in its 1973 report on corrections, has recommended a parallel process of participatory management, in which policy is formulated jointly by staff and supervisors. The military superstructure is bypassed, and the officers experience a high degree of participation in events related to their job performance and well-being. However, it is just that circumnavigation of command chains that has made the program reports suggested by Toch and his colleagues so rare and so threatening to traditional agencies.

Training in Supervision. The effects of criminal justice agency supervision have been described earlier as a source of considerable stress. Training programs represent one course of action to improve the quality of supervision and reduce the subsequent stress.

A variety of approaches have been followed to train supervisors in human service and corporate settings. However, relatively few of these approaches have been targeted particularly for use in justice agencies. As part of one training program directed at Illinois State Police supervisors, Brodsky and Danish (1973) elicited key stress situations for supervisors and supervisees. A series of brief film vignettes were prepared in a "subjective camera" technique, in which the actor on the screen appears to talk directly to the trainee in the audience. In one such vignette, the subordinate whose patrol car is being inspected speaks: "I don't know, but—when we came out of the same class together, we used to be buddies—and you weren't a bad Joe then. But it seems now, since you got this rank, you're goin' a little bit, like—rank happy, like the rest of these guys—trying to throw it around, and make everybody's job and life rough. I remember when you were on the road, your car was used for personal uses—I know damn well it was! And you're not kiddin' me—because I know whose ass you had to kiss to get those bars." In two others dealing with supervisor's roles, the supervisor speaks: "Okay, dammit. I think I've listened long enough. This is the fourth time you've come in, and I've tried to sit down and listen to you. But what you're bringing from the classroom doesn't apply in the real world." In the second vignette: "You don't have to ask me why you're in here. You know why you're here. You're in here all the time. Every time that something goes wrong, I know who to call—I know who to bring in here—and so does everybody else. No matter how hard I try to work with ya'—no matter how much information we give ya'—no matter how much help I try to give ya'—it's the same damn story! It's you, all the time. You're always foulin' up. Everything's always screwed up, and you're always at the bottom of it. People who have to work with ya,' me, everybody—it's always you! You're the guy! You're just no damn good!"

Following each vignette, up to one hour was used discussing the situation, role playing possible responses and supervisory methods, and developing leader-guided peer consensus on the desired goals and outcomes. An assessment of the training effectiveness indicated that line officers and supervisors alike viewed the training as relevant and effective. It should be added that the line officers felt the training was important for all supervisors. The supervisors in training, however, felt it was important for the *other* supervisors, those not in training.

Over a period of five years, the Southeastern Correctional Manpower Training Council at the University of Georgia has offered advanced training for correctional supervisors, administrators, and trainers in short-term institutes. These three- to five-day workshops have been positively assessed by the correctional agencies and have produced several publications directed at improving correctional management.

Career Development. Career development opportunities in justice agencies are major factors that affect the quality of supervisory personnel. We have observed that superior police officers, for example, have few options for remaining in direct citizen contact in law enforcement; if they are skilled and able, they are promoted. Officers in both law enforcement and correctional settings are promoted into supervisory positions because there is only one career ladder available. Officers who are successful in direct dealings with citizenry and correctional clients are frequently unsuccessful as supervisors. The Peter Principle applies: Individuals *do* rise to their levels of incompetence in an organizational hierarchy. Once at the level at which they are ineffective, they cease rising and remain at that level, frustrated, frustrating to others, and without adequate skills in supervisory performance.

One possible action to combat this managerial incompetence is the changing of career ladders. The modification of career ladders begins with promotion opportunities for line officers so a person can rise in rank and perhaps responsibility and still maintain direct citizen and client contact. One ladder still ascends through traditional supervisory channels. A second ladder maintains direct client contact and service activities. A third employment structure is possible for civilians to fill clerical positions; however, this proposal has the disadvantage of reducing placement possibilities for those officers with poor interpersonal skills whose performances are insufficiently bad to merit dismissal.

Summary

The task of a police or correctional officer supervisor is difficult. The supervisor is responsible for men and women in an inherently stressful and frequently unpleasant occupation. The line officers work with end products, with persons who have failed and have harmed others and been harmed repeatedly in their lives. The supervisor has the responsibility to protect these officers from unfair criticism and support them, and at the same time to ensure that the officers do not arbitrarily exercise their powers of social control over the lives of others. The supervisor has the responsibility of being just, of organizing a problem-oriented structure, and of presenting a constructive and inspiring role model. And the supervisor is likely to be seen or felt as a cause of the officers' ulcers, headaches, and marital problems.

The suggestions presented here include structural changes in supervisory practices. Peer supervision, hierarchy reductions, and alternate career ladders are organizational changes, not changes in individuals. Potent contributory roles are available for modifying transactions between people, in the form of training exercises and modeling procedures. However, only in the context of organizations amenable to change can the supervisor's role become positive, appreciated, and nourishing.

CHAPTER 13

Community
Mental Health Centers

Florence Whiteman Kaslow

The prevailing model in most human service settings has been that one receives training and supervision from senior, higher-status members of one's own profession. Thus, during one's residency in psychiatry, one is precepted by full-fledged psychiatrists and teaching analysts. Similarly, graduate departments of psychology and schools of social work draw their faculties almost totally from members of their respective professions. Such inbreeding is further perpetuated by licensing and certification requirements that one must have been supervised for a given number of hours by a member of the profession in which one is seeking credentialing. This in turn reinforces compartmentalization between professions in agencies, clinics, and hospitals. In order to understand the departure from this tradition in community mental health centers, it is important to summarize the reasons for their creation and the forces that led to their acceptance and expansion as an integral part of the human service agency network. Some of the points made earlier in Finch's Chapter Three, "The Role of the Organization," are illustrated and hopefully illuminated in this chapter, particularly in regard to role ambiguity and professional identity.

With the passage of the Mental Health Act in 1963 (established under U.S. Congress Public Law 88–164), the mental health movement swung into high gear. The original five essential services mandated for inclusion before any center could receive a bounty in the form of federal funds were: in-patient, partial hospitalization, out-patient, consultation and education, and twenty-four-hour emergency care. Because of the kind of package thus legislated, community mental health clinics tended to be created by existing hospitals or to come into being and immediately seek an affiliation with a nearby hospital in order to be able to provide in-patient and emergency services. Thus the medical model seemed likely to prevail, and physicians expected to move into prominence and top positions. But their supremacy was challenged by other mental health professionals and caregivers. Psychologists and social workers had also been active in working for the passage of this legislation and had a deep commitment to being an important part of the staff and to playing a key role in the decision making about center functioning and service delivery.

The reverberations of the civil rights movement of the 1950s and 1960s were still at a crest; practitioners from minority groups were intent on equal rights as staff members and on seeing that people from their communities received first-class, high-quality services. "Black power" became a popular slogan and ghetto politics a potent force (Warren, 1969). Community leaders wanted input from the residents, and so separate community advisory boards were set up; these often rivaled the authority of existing more traditional and conservative boards of directors, which generally were drawn from the wider community and tended to be composed of older and wealthier individuals. Outspoken community leaders were also instrumental in pressing for the hiring of indigenous workers, paraprofessionals from within the catchment area, who, by virtue of their familiarity with the neighbors and neighborhood and their similarity of life-style, brought with them a special kind of understanding and empathy for the patients (Richan, 1972). They also insisted that those served not be called *patients,* since this term connoted illness. Instead, the term *consumer of services* was coined. Where this was not accepted, *client* was preferable to *patient.* In many quarters, the medical model was denigrated.

The community mental health movement was clearly born of widespread social discontent and ferment, and the pressure for egalitarianism in staff relationships and even between client and therapist was great. Programs such as New York's Mobilization for Youth, a storefront program that maximized input from the consumers it served and thrived on outspoken participatory decision making and challenging the establishment, had become famous or infamous—depending on one's reaction to them (Rein and Miller, 1964). The entire climate militated against ascribed roles and vertical hierarchical patterns in staff relationships. The push to bring services out into the community, where they were more readily and easily accessible, meant that potential clients from previously unserved segments of the population would find their way to the clinic. It also meant that those clamoring to see that the *community* emphasis in the Mental Health Act was enforced could maintain some surveillance.

Given this atmosphere, many changes from prevailing norms were permissible. The concept of treatment was refined and subdivided into three levels of therapeutic intervention (Kaslow, 1976), described as follows. First, *primary prevention* is an intervention strategy that predicts who may be most susceptible to a malady and then tries to lower the risk of illness for that segment of the population. It is focused not on a specific person, but rather on reducing noxious influences conducive to mental illness and on creating healthier environments. Often such action programs must be inaugurated rapidly because of immediate pressing needs, but epidemiological studies should be carried on concurrently to refine and validate lists of etiological factors. Primary prevention revolves around determining factors operating widely in the community in a specific segment of the population and around determining factors likely to be amenable to alteration by preventive programs. It emphasizes goals quickly attainable.

Next, *secondary prevention* entails lessening the likelihood or the severity of a mental disorder through early and adequate treatment and nonspecific mental health education. This approach, which is often the one preferred by therapists, includes the traditional gamut of therapies offered by psychiatric clinics, social agencies, and private practitioners.

Last, *tertiary prevention* is instituted long after the onset of the disorder and is concerned with rehabilitation and offsetting permanent impairment or invalidism. It occurs mostly in in-patient facilities or daycare centers. At community mental health centers, because they offer out-patient, partial hospitalization, and in-patient services, treatment geared to all three levels of prevention is practiced.

As community mental health centers began to be established, a concept that received a great deal of attention in the deliberations of such bodies as the Council of Social Work Education and the American Psychological Association was that of career ladders. It was stressed that there were tasks at different levels of difficulty, that people should be deployed in positions consonant with interest and training levels, and that upward mobility should be made possible as knowledge and experience were gained. Although many professionals originally perceived the entrance of indigenous workers into their sacred terrain as an intrusion, some of the tension between paraprofessionals and professionals gradually abated as they participated together on teams. The indigenous workers made unique contributions, and the "pros" learned from them; conversely, many paraprofessionals absorbed the new knowledge they were exposed to and began functioning more like their more highly educated peers. In the vocabulary of the decade, some indigenous workers became co-opted by the system and lost their potency as change agents as they modeled themselves after the professionals and became more distant from their community peers.

At the same time, and on a parallel level, psychologists and social workers challenged the concept that the center director must invariably be a psychiatrist and that only medically trained therapists could serve as head of a treatment team. In some communities, the dislike of the medical model and its implicit doctor-patient connotations led community boards to select nonmedically trained therapists as unit heads and as directors. Henry's book *The Fifth Profession* (1971) presented the thesis that clinicians from the four major helping disciplines of psychiatry, psychology, social work, and psychoanalysis have more in common with each other than they do with the nonclinicians in their own disciplines and that a fifth profession of psychotherapy was emerging that cut across the helping fields. In many centers, roles became interchangeable; clients were assigned to whomever on the staff had open treatment time and was skilled in the modality determined to be the treatment of choice. Method and competence became as important as background. The ideas that the psychiatrist administers the medication and electroconvulsive therapy and is the master psychotherapist, that the psychologist administers tests and leads groups, and that the social worker takes the family history were recognized as much too arbitrary and became obsolete.

Some homogenization of roles occurred as psychiatry, heretofore a field concerned mainly with treating individuals, exploded into being concerned about community psychiatry, as psychologists insisted on their right to be therapists and community consultants, and social workers let it be known that they were more than handmaidens who could take histories, counsel parents while another therapist treated the child, and dispense relief. Out of the turbulence, a new egalitarianism did emerge in many centers—born in turmoil and engendering resentment and defensiveness.

The pure psychoanalytic method did not seem adaptable to short-term treatment, which was the only form that many inner-city residents could tolerate and sustain. Rather, we began to speak of treatment contracts specifying number of sessions and contingency clauses about renegotiating. Open-ended statements such as "I don't know how long it will take—perhaps several years" were not destined to be favorably received by the kinds of clients for whom service was to be provided in many catchment areas. For them, survival *this* week, in the midst of poverty and many other serious problems, precluded such long-range commitments. "Here-and-now" and crisis-oriented approaches came to the fore, often bringing in their wake much staff confusion and conflict, as unanimity of staff philosophy became a thing of the past. Different schools of thought and treatment methodologies competed to become agency philosophy and practice approaches. These were heady, stimulating times for some and unhappy ones for others. Sadly, some of the vital and unique characteristics of the various professions became too completely submerged in the effort to become similar, and in the 1970s we have seen some attempts to take another look at how they really are similar and still leave room for healthy differences and special functions.

The Emergence of an Interdisciplinary Training Model

Within such a climate, it no longer made sense to insist that only a social worker could supervise a social work student or a beginning worker. Psychiatric residents and psychology interns found that their preceptor might be from a sister discipline. If a social work student was carrying a family and the family therapy supervisor was a psychologist by training, then that psychologist was appointed to supervise the case. This wreaked havoc at many of the schools of social work, which were still insisting that only a social worker could supervise their students. These sharp demarcations were reenforced by the several professions, because certification requirements specify a certain number of supervisory hours by a certified member of the same profession. But the staffing patterns of the agencies often did not lend themselves to these divisions. For instance, a clinic might have two half-time psychiatrists and six psychiatric residents; some trainees might be there on days the senior psychiatrists were not. Thus the precepting would have to be carried, at least in part, by psychologists and social workers. In many settings, there was and continues to be strong "snobbery" opposed to this—a sense that the doctoral psychologist who has had ten years of college and graduate school and much clinical training and experience is still inferior to his or her medical counterpart. Yet the exigencies of the clinic situation necessitated an interdisciplinary mix, and often it was found to work, and quite well. This became increasingly true in specialties such as family and group therapies, behavior modification, transactional analysis, and other newer approaches in which no one discipline can lay claim to a monopoly. Students from each field wanted the best supervision they could find, even if it was not from someone in their own discipline. And some of the barriers slowly tumbled—

at least insofar as the newer and less doctrinaire staff members were concerned.

Unfortunately, nonmedical personnel in a medical setting often feel somewhat disenfranchised. In an effort to compensate for this, some have gone along with permitting clients to assume they are doctors, afraid that if they reveal their true identity or level of education the client may insist on seeing a "real" doctor. To complicate the student or nonmedical staff members' dilemma, some patients insist on using the title of *Dr.* even when they have been told it is inaccurate; it seems to make the patient feel more important. Some supervisors not only go along with this but encourage it. This makes it impossible for trainees to request a supplementary interview of their patients by their supervisors (Schuster, Sandt, and Thaler, 1972), for in order to do this they would have to disclose their trainee status. Such behavior is unethical and unprofessional, and everyone involved in perpetrating such deceptions is liable to charges of misrepresentation.

Also pertinent from both an ethical and treatment perspective is the issue of honesty and authenticity. There is a blatant incongruity between a therapist's words in telling a patient "for me to help you, you have to be honest with me—even when it is painful" and his or her own behavior when perpetrating a misconception about identity. Although the temptation to acquire the title of *Dr.* without having fully earned the degree may be particularly tempting in a medical environment, the supervisor, regardless of discipline, should exemplify genuineness in all behavior, as students and trainees are apt to emulate their mentors and to learn far more from their actions and comportment than from their minilectures. Gaining the trust of patients is urgent in therapy—and how can a patient trust a therapist who falsifies?

Another part of the emerging scene has been the provision of several supervisors—one for each modality. This can afford the requisite number of supervised hours under someone from the same profession and still permit the trainee or junior staff member to seek additional supervision from other staff members who are specialists in a particular approach or technique. For the purists who were trained more than fifteen years ago, many of these ideas were almost heretical. In schools of social work, one was only permitted to have one supervisor, and any effort by the student to change who this was or to supplement the relationship was seen as a resistance and interpreted as very manipulative behavior. It was thought that if a student related to more than one supervisor he or she would be tempted to play them off against one another and perhaps to get caught between two philosophies and treatment approaches. Yet in the centers with which I am familiar that utilize interdisciplinary supervision and permit trainees and staff to have more than one supervisor, the model appears to work quite well, and the feared competition between supervisors or the pitting them against one another seems minimal.

This type of freedom is encouraged at the Hahnemann Community Mental Health Center Clinics, day treatment center, and in-patient unit at Hahnemann Hospital and Medical College in Philadelphia. By way of example, I am currently supervising a second-year resident on two cases; she also is in supervision with two psychiatrists on other individual cases and sees a fourth faculty member for supervision in group therapy. Everyone seems quite clear as to their area of responsibility, and at no point have I sensed any infringement or competition. Rather, the learning package seems well rounded. The same holds true for our doctoral psychology students, who frequently have at least two supervisors—one for psychodiagnosis (testing) and another for therapy.

Some other factors necessitated and augmented the cross fertilization and cross pollination. One of the goals of the community mental health movement was to release as many patients as possible from mental hospitals to live within their own communities and receive whatever assistance they needed from out-patient or day treatment centers. Despite the use of psychotropic drugs since their introduction in 1955, many ex-hospital patients still needed a great deal of care and many support services from a variety of agencies. Social workers, who were probably the group most conversant with the network of resources available in their community, became valuable as staff trainers who could teach others how to make referrals, establish eligibility for service quickly, cut through red tape, and see that referrals were solidified; who could lead in smoothing the way for interagency cooperation and who could orient other staff members to the vast array of services existing in their community, the quality of each, how to gain access to them for patients, and what to do by way of follow-up. Since everyone on staff had to acquire this knowledge, the composition of staff-training groups was interdisciplinary instead of segregated by disciplines.

A corollary goal of the community mental health movement was to prevent hospitalization through primary and secondary prevention. Thus many quite dysfunctional and disturbed individuals, who in an earlier era would have been hospitalized, were now being treated, along with not fully recuperated ex-patients, in community-based facilities. This meant that many patients were on medication and the nonmedical therapists had to go to their colleagues to prescribe and monitor medication. Many psychologists and social workers, intellectually and professionally curious, wanted to learn more about the different categories of antidepressants, sedatives, and other drugs and asked their medical colleagues to engage in staff training on the subject of psychopharmacology.

In many community mental health centers, psychiatrists led ongoing diagnostic and treatment case conferences, which were open to all professional staff as a vehicle for continuous training. With staff being drawn from more varied socioeconomic, cultural, ethnic, and racial backgrounds, the kinds of questions and answers were less directed by expert to novice and more involved collegial probing and disagreeing. Theories had to truly describe reality or be discarded; techniques that were applicable with neurotic middle-class patients but that did not prove useful with people with character and personality disorders or psychotic conditions had to be supplemented or replaced with more viable ones. Short-term problem-solving approaches, reality-oriented therapies, social learning and educational therapy models, and sociotherapy and environmental modification approaches were brought in by nonanalytic psychologists and social workers to take their place along with insight-oriented techniques, and concepts such as treatment of choice and beginning with the patient at his or her level of readiness took root. Whoever led the case conferences and staff-training workshops had to identify his or her own theoretical position and be willing to accept input or disagreement from those with other orientations. Thus the trainers had to be flexible and able to maintain their own perspective while being able to accept that there is more than one theory and technique of therapy that can be efficacious. This caused a ripple effect regarding the supervisor—if one might decide one case would respond best to operant conditioning techniques and a second to psychoanalytic psychotherapy, it might well be that no one supervisor was proficient in both of these approaches and that therefore the logical move would be to assign different supervisors to the two cases. This is what occurred, and the expansion of horizons followed for many; professional ethnocentrism seemed indefensible.

In a similar vein, the psychologist brought to the team his or her special skill in psychodiagnosis utilizing psychological tests. Since neither social workers nor psychiatrists are trained in test administration and interpretation, this was one of the roles the psychologist was expected to fill. It was crucial that other staff members referring patients to the psychologist for testing know how to utilize the test reports they received, and this too led to inter-disciplinary staff-training sessions. Also, psychologists had become involved in family and group therapies, behavior modification, and biofeedback and often were employed as consultants or staff trainers in these approaches. Staff psychologists also were assigned to supervise students and other staff from sister disciplines in all treatment modalities in which they had greater expertise.

Out of this ferment also came a reaction against labeling, since it became evident that what might be termed *psychotic* in one culture was accepted as normal in another. For example, an American Indian who was taken to a mental hospital in California was diagnosed as schizophrenic because of his long silences, general failure to communicate, and withdrawn behavior. After he was there for some months, an American Indian resident from the same tribe came into the ward as part of his psychiatric rotation. He talked with the patient, decided that he was suffering more from a case of cultural shock in the alien city than from a psychosis, and that his behavior would look quite typical back on the reservation. The man was discharged, and follow-up a month later indicated that he was functioning reasonably well back home. From experiences such as this and from the reality-oriented interpretations proffered by colleagues with different class and ethnic backgrounds, concepts of normalcy have expanded, some diagnosis is less rigid, and social as well as psychological and biological determinants of behavior are receiving more attention from supervisors and staff trainers who have moved beyond a "there is only one right way to interpret and treat" stance.

At its best, this interdisciplinary model makes a major contribution to enhancing interdisciplinary collaboration and understanding. It also fosters mutual respect. It is stimulating and exciting for the students, broadening their exposure and preventing overdependence on one supervisor or getting locked into a destructive, all-encompassing relationship. At its worst, it stirs up professional rivalry and factionalism, and the clients suffer as staff compete for territorial rights. Where status hierarchies still exist, the resident assigned to a psychologist for precepting may feel that he or she is being treated as a second-class citizen and may complain to the residency training director; it is appropriate that such arrogance be worked out early in one's training if team cooperation and collaboration are to be meaningful and feasible.

Power Issues

The struggle is perhaps an unending one, as more groups enter the scene wanting to share it. Mental health nursing is emerging as a strong force (Sloboda, 1976). Associate programs in the community colleges and bachelor-level programs are training mental health technicians and technologists. As Kutzik indicated in Chapter Two, many schools of social work now offer B.S.W.s, and some accept this as the entry level of practice. So, while some are insisting that virtually untrained indigenous workers and people with A.A. or B.A. degrees can function effectively in certain therapeutic roles under appropriate supervision (Gottesfeld, Rhee, and Parker, 1970), the professions of psychology and psychiatry are requiring longer periods of training and are raising their requirements for certification and licensure. Are we all jet-propelled on a collision course? Perhaps.

As of now, most community mental health centers are multidisciplinary in staff composition, and supervision cuts across the strict lines of disciplines. And currents of fresh air enter sometimes gently, other times with gale force. Nonetheless, where issues of authority, power, and control are omnipresent, even though superficially glossed over, the egalitarianism is likely to be more fiction than fact. Status differentials based on length and kind of training and experience are realities; one need only to look at salary scales to see the wide disparities between the different groups. Can one person's input be valued as equal when he or she earns half of what another person does? Is this really possible in a society in which individual professional worth is closely connected to monetary remuneration? Why do we perpetuate the myth of egalitarianism, when the status and salary picture contradicts it so clearly? Perhaps because what we articulate comes closer to our ideals and makes us feel better and prouder.

It is imperative never to lose sight of the *community* base of the mental health center. This represents another power segment, one that is intent on monitoring programs and holding administrators, supervisors, and service delivery staff accountable for actions and expenditures. Partially because community expectations and demands regarding needs for service and desires for power do not always coincide with those of the professional staff, confrontation as a strategy has surged to the fore. It therefore behooves the supervisor in this setting to teach apprentices the techniques of bargaining, trade-off, negotiation, and confrontation and to affirm their validity and value in the mental health professional's method of operating.

The supervisor or trainer in the community mental health center needs to be adept in the strategies of confrontation and negotiation, relatively new ones in the helping professional's armamentarium, because he must be able to convey the value and the use of these techniques to his supervisees. The same holds true in settings such as prisons and residential treatment centers, wherever militant populations are likely to band together to insist vociferously that their demands be met. A passive, nondirective approach, in which one responds to nonnegotiable demands with "You seem to be feeling hostile today," is simply inappropriate and is guaranteed to be ineffective. Instead one must respond nondefensively and with strength, assessing if violence is intended, what the merits of the demands are, which ones can viably be met, and what the consequences of failure to comply will be. Strategies of confrontation can be shown using videotapes and films; experiential techniques such as role playing or precipitating confrontations to be worked through in group training sessions also usually prove worthwhile. Leopold, in *The Psychiatrist as Negotiator* (1971, p. 195), states that

> Negotiation as a major function of the community mental health center psychiatrist requires special attention in connection with the growing demands of the consumer community for involvement in the community mental health center's planning and operation. Obviously this role is threatening to professional leadership but, obviously also, if the community mental health center is to remain in effective existence, it can neither abrogate professional competence nor allow professional arrogance to risk loss of the community's acceptance and respect. Problems in relations between the white majority and various racial and ethnic minorities . . . may exacerbate the difficulties of reconciling the community's and the professional's demands, which . . . must be accommodated within the legislative mandate on which the community mental health center depends for its major funding. In brief, community involvement is an area where perhaps the psychiatrist feels most the need for skills in negotiation.

I concur with Leopold's analysis but feel it is imperative to add that these same skills are essential tools for all community mental health center staff members. Since these skills are rarely taught in formal classes, it is incumbent on supervisors and staff trainers to see that those receiving their tutelage become proficient in the art of negotiation as well as that of confrontation.

Since supervision in the numerous treatment modalities has been well covered in earlier chapters, it is not necessary to repeat the material on "how to" here. Suffice it to say that all of the techniques described earlier are utilized alone or in combinations in individual and group supervision and in staff training at different community mental health centers throughout the country. Perhaps one of the greatest and least recognized contributions of the community mental health center has been the fostering of interdisciplinary supervision and training and consequently of respect and collaboration. It remains to be seen how the advent of peer review within each profession might reverse the gains made in interdisciplinary teaching, learning, and practice.

CHAPTER 14

Private Practitioners

Eugene Cohen

Historically most private practice in psychotherapy[1] is conducted by psychiatrists, psychologists, and clinical social workers, the latter having entered independent practice most recently. Whereas until the past decade, the status and order in the hierarchy of the psychotherapist[2] was a major factor in determining whose help was to be utilized, today this is no longer as true, although it still often is a significant factor in patient choice. The title "Dr." may be generalized as attesting to one's qualifications and is often preferred; those with an M.S.W. or M.A. are at a disadvantage because they do not carry the prestigious "Dr." designation. However, increasingly, more weight is attached to the specific therapist's level of competence, reputation, and the extent to which he or she is perceived to have been helpful to patients.[3]

Traditionally, the original kind of service offered by private practitioners and the progressive new services that they now deliver parallel the development of similar services in community agencies and organizations.[4] Both private and agency practitioners began with offering psychotherapy. The initial treatment modality was individual adult or child therapy; then clinicians proceeded to add group, marital, family, divorce, adolescent, and sex therapies, in keeping with new knowledge and the particular therapist's training and preferences as well as his or her formulation of what would constitute the treatment of choice. Private practice became synonymous with psychotherapy. The next step was for private practitioners to provide consultation to community health care and welfare agencies, both public and private, in modalities in which they had become expert.

Although consultants are often chosen from among those who are faculty members of universities, particularly professional and graduate schools, there has been an expansion in choices to include competent, well-known private practitioners. Thus the emphasis is being placed less on affiliation and the institution's reputation and more on the potential consultant's ability to perform the requisite tasks. This is encouraging, because it is an indication of the field's increasing maturity, namely, acting on the relevant and valid criteria of efficiency and effectiveness of the service delivered.

An additional rarely discussed special use of private practitioners has been in relation to other clinicians, both to those working in agencies and to those in private practice. This function, too, has gone through its own development. First it entailed therapy for the therapist-patient; subsequently, therapists began seeking consultation from a respected private practitioner on professional matters such as a difficult case, or refining their therapeutic skills, or how to set up or expand a private practice.

A highly innovative new service among those being sought voluntarily, mainly by private practitioners from more experienced private therapists, is supervision, a process that is distinctly different than consultation. Such clinicians recognize their own learning needs and responsibly seek to have these met. This is in contrast to supervision sought because it is required in order to qualify for membership in an organization—such as the International Transactional Analysis Association (ITAA) and the American Association of Marriage and Family Counselors (AAMFC)—which requires a certain number of supervised hours of clinical practice in the specialty and which can be contracted for with one of their teaching members (ITAA) or approved supervisors (AAMFC). Eidelberg (1968, pp. 423–424) describes the supervision required of candidates of psychoanalytic institutes by senior members of such institutes. These latter requirements constitute an externally imposed standard, while the former is an internally experienced desire. The considerable difference between required supervision in an agency and voluntary supervision of private practitioners, with the latter's dynamic potential, will be highlighted later.

This chapter explores the various functions just mentioned that some clinicians now perform, with special emphasis on those provided to other private practitioners.

The Private Practitioner: An Overview

When a psychotherapist enters private practice, it is assumed that he or she possesses a sufficiently high level of knowledge and skill to function autonomously. The qualifications are generally set by the professional association of the discipline in which one is trained and/or by state law. Many professions require either board certification and/or state licensure. Once practitioners meet these requirements, they are usually permitted to establish and continue in private practice unless they blatantly violate the law, or their professions' codes of ethics. Another stipulation by some professions is participation in continuing education and amassing requisite credits. Even though this can be done without a commensurate increase in skill, it is assumed that continuing education does contribute to professional growth, awareness of new techniques and trends, additional knowledge of research findings and implications, and thus to greater competence.

Clinicians who enter independent practice do so for various reasons. Many therapists are employed by public and community agencies. Lengthy careers may have been spent in such settings, and, after a period of time, desiring a change of pace and greater freedom, the therapists decide to establish a private practice. Others combine part-time employment with part-time private practice to increase the diversity of their activities and supplement their income. Whichever path is chosen, there continue to be opportunities to shift from one alternative to another. Therefore, those who remain in private practice have concluded that for them the advantages outweigh the disadvantages.

Among the advantages is that one is free to make one's own decisions regarding one's practice—the kinds of services offered, treatment modalities to be used, types of patients to be seen, structure, policies, procedures, office location, days and hours of work, and fees. Some therapists do not like being part of an agency with myriad regulations, procedures, and hierarchial relationships. For those who prefer to be more independent, masters of their own professional careers, private practice affords an excellent opportunity. Status and prestige are also considerations. Higher income is a significant factor. *Psychotherapy Economics* (1977, pp. 1–2) reports that the most frequent range of fees is $30 to $50 for an individual therapy session of forty-five minutes to an hour and from $15 to $25 for a group therapy session. The fee depends largely on the clinician's reputation, years of experience, academic degree, and geographic locale.

The disadvantages are the other side of the same coin. There is greater risk, unpredictability, and insecurity regarding income. Setting up one's own practice requires not only an understanding of and skill in the services to be given but also a knowledge of business management. There is stress resulting from the greater responsibility of being totally on one's own. Frequently there is a sense of isolation and loneliness. An attempt to reduce this has been made by those who establish group practices. However, most private practitioners still function alone and after a period of time feel the need for an exchange of ideas and experiences with colleagues.

Various channels are pursued to afford this exchange, such as attending meetings of professional organizations, seminars, workshops, formal courses, and informal "rap" sessions. Nevertheless, many private clinicians have found that any or all of these still are not enough, particularly when there is a specific case "stumping" them, when they become aware of a troublesome pattern in their practice, or when they are dissatisfied with the results they have obtained. At such times, more and more, psychotherapists seek individualized assistance via consultation and through voluntary supervisory arrangements.

The Private Practitioner as Psychotherapist

Numerous social workers, psychologists, and psychiatrists enter therapy to obtain assistance in resolving personal problems and functioning more effectively. This is true of many who have had previous therapy; new areas of concern emerge, or they wish to reexplore unfinished matters from the past. The very nature of the clinician's training, experience, and job is apt to contribute to or exacerbate his or her personal dilemmas. Modlin (1976, pp. 12–13) gives the following examples: Intense relationships with patients produce emotional strain and drain that sometimes leaves the therapist little to offer his or her own family; the ethical prohibition of discussing patients with the therapist's own family; the difficulty in staying within his role as husband and father (or wife and mother) in his or her own family rather than as psychotherapist; a feeling of giving much and receiving little to meet his or her own needs. Conflict between empathizing or identifying and overidentifying is a source of stress for the conscientious clinician. Frustrations in failing to help some patients add further dissatisfaction. Spensley and Blacker (1976, pp. 542–545) also comment on the need for psychotherapists to be aware of the stresses they experience and their sources, noting that therapists have not devoted sufficient time and effort to accomplishing this and then to utilizing this information in their own behalf. Luthman and Kirschenbaum (1974, p. 225) state that they have not seen anything written about the stress of doing therapy. Often the common difficulty of admitting the need for and seeking treatment is compounded by the fact that clinicians are helping professionals who give the same service to others. This frequently results in their feeling that they should be able to identify, assess, and resolve their own problems in view of their understanding of human behavior and their treatment skills. Although many, if not all, know intellectually that this is an unrealistic expectation, this notion exists; the difficulty in resolving this feeling is directly proportional to the degree of its pervasiveness and chronicity.

Therefore it is necessary for the treating therapist to be aware of the messages that reveal this complex data and to be especially sensitive to it, no matter how subtle or misleading the therapist-patient's statements may be. Dynamically utilizing such thinking and feeling may make the difference between being or not being helpful. It is a serious mistake to assume that because one's patient is himself a psychotherapist he does not have difficulty in accepting that he has significant problems, has been unable to resolve them, and therefore requires treatment. McCarley (1975, p. 221) points out that "There are formidable internal and external forces opposing the mature practicing psychotherapist's return to therapy or analysis. The internal factors include the feeling of humiliation or embarrassment at again identifying oneself as a 'patient' and the reluctance to assume a dependent role. The external deterrents include the problem of having social relationships with the colleagues to whom one might choose to go for therapy." These are but a sampling of obstacles encountered by clinicians seeking professional help.

Therapist-patients' problems run the same gamut as those of nontherapist-patients—self-esteem; marital, parent-child, and family conflicts; job-related problems; social adjustment; and sexual difficulties. Perpetual recognition that clinicians are people and thus are human and fallible is also essential. Such a statement seems ridiculously simple, but too often we lose sight of elemental truths in our daily efforts and struggles and in living as the "healers," who can help people restructure their personalities. We who nourish others also need to be nourished!

The foundation in treatment is precarious if the patient's feeling about his or her problems and self-esteem as a result of having difficulties is not dealt with adequately. It can best be addressed by relating it to the verbal and nonverbal data presented by the patient rather than merely in general conceptual terms—thus the treating therapist should recognize the importance of the therapist being sensitive to and perceptive of such indicators and the therapist-patient's superior skill at camouflaging and masking deep feelings.

One of the clues to how the therapist-patient feels about being in treatment is whether he or she keeps it a secret from the family, other relatives, friends, and/or colleagues. When this information is not revealed in the initial sessions, it is easy enough to elicit it merely by asking who knows about the therapy. Frequently there are signs, such as arriving for the session in such a way that he or she does not have to wait and be seen in the waiting room, asking for appointment times that decrease the likelihood of being seen, or asking that his or her therapist not telephone (or write to) him or her at work or at home, and if the therapist must do so, that he not identify his relationship to the patient. Once this significant data is out in the open, it can be dealt with in terms of its implications, not only for the patient's self-concept but also regarding receptivity and commitment to treatment.

Throughout the years, my practice has included numerous therapists as patients. Although our focus was on the patient's personal problems, the growth he or she attained extended into the professional realm. While this is not surprising, because a person's kind of functioning and integration is similar in both personal and professional areas and therefore we can expect such growth to be reflected in both spheres, nonetheless the oft-repeated stark evidence and the extent of the development made a strong impact on me. Obviously, an improved self-image and increased self-confidence and assertiveness would not be expressed only in interaction with one's family and in social relationships but also would permeate one's professional activities.

However, there has been another aspect that is frequently forgotten or ignored. That is the model of the treating therapist, in his role with the therapist-patient, who simultaneously is both a severe critic and a keen appreciator of skilled practice. Thus therapist-patients often have pridefully informed me of their utilization, with successful results, in their own practice of approaches that they experienced in our sessions and that they found had been helpful to them. Conversely, the psychotherapist also sometimes inadvertently serves as a negative model of what not to do, how not to do it, and when not to do it! We need to be more aware of this aspect, too.

The practitioner who treats other psychotherapists not only needs to be highly skilled but also should have much confidence in his professional efficacy and be able to accept realistically his own limitations without defensiveness, discomfort, or embarrassment. This is a sine qua non in order to be effective in treating clinicians. I have found psychotherapist-patients to be the most difficult, challenging, and rewarding of all my patients.

The Private Practitioner as Consultant

Private practitioners are engaged to serve as consultants to health care, social, and welfare agencies; to educational institutions; to industry; and, most recently, to other private practitioners. In this role, they undertake several different functions.

An outstanding feature of consultation is the lack of authority entailed in terms of the consultee being accountable to the consultant. The consultee is free to accept or reject any or all of the consultant's formulations, opinions, and/or recommendations. This is in sharp contrast to supervision, where the supervisee is definitely accountable to the supervisor for decisions and performance. Consultation is entirely educational in nature, while supervision encompasses administrative, supportive, and educational components. As Kaslow (1972, p. 134) notes, a consultant does not carry line power of administrative authority to evaluate or promote. Neither can he hire nor fire. The authority inherent in a consultant is his expertise, competence, and comportment. Consultation is offered to individuals and to groups. When offered to private practitioners, it is generally on an individual basis in the consultant's office; when provided to agency staff, it may be on an individual or group basis and usually takes place in the agency. The following case example outlines a typical consultation situation.[5]

Case Example

Referral Source: Self. Mr. M. chose the specific consultant as a result of being favorably impressed by him through contacts at professional association and committee meetings.

Presenting Problem: Inability to administer family agency due to staff's resentment at his recent appointment, from the outside, as executive director.

Goal: To resolve the problematic relationship with staff so that he could effectively fulfill his responsibilities.

Focus: Mr. M.'s managerial style and related factors such as his value system and career goals.

Contract: Sixteen one-hour sessions to be held in consultant's office (at consultee's request, because he was not ready to let staff know that he needed and was receiving help). Criteria and procedure regarding broken and canceled appointments were established, as was the fee. Mutual responsibilities of consultant and consultee were agreed on. These included goals, focus, and methodology; provision for task assignments and feedback; specific measurable behavior changes; a basis for evaluation of results in terms of goal achievement; assessment of Mr. M.'s utilization of consultation; and recommendations on termination.

Background: Previous executive director resigned to accept a position in another area and recommended Mr. M., a friend, to the board of directors as executive director. He was appointed nine months ago. The agency provides premarital counseling, marriage counseling, family therapy, and family life education. Staff consists of, in addition to Mr. M. (forty years of age, twenty years experience), one supervisor (forty-five years old, female, with agency entire career of twenty years), six social workers (ranging in ages from twenty-five to forty, three males and three females, with agency from one to fifteen years, some with experience in other agencies), one secretary, one receptionist-telephone operator, and two typists. Good relationships exist among them (except with Mr. M.). The supervisor had not been considered by the board for promotion to executive director due to their policy of appointing a person from outside the agency to this position. While staff disagreed with this policy, they were determined, in the interest of service delivery, to give Mr. M. an opportunity to demonstrate his competence and contribution. The previous executive director had not achieved even mediocrity and had not had a good relationship with staff.

Assessment: Considering himself knowledgeable and capable managerially as well as in supervision and counseling, Mr. M. was unable to see himself accurately. The most he could admit was that he needed to sharpen his considerable skill rather than recognize the necessity for making some basic changes. His managerial style was highly authoritative, with little concern for staff. Although he occasionally utilized some staff input, he did so almost by accident and never conveyed appreciation for input to staff. Communication was sporadic and almost always consisted of instructions or criticism. Mr. M. was unconcerned about the emotional climate in agency, since he saw no connection between it and qualitative and quantitative productivity. He believed that since employees were receiving a good salary and had an opportunity to help people— that should be enough! Mr. M. did not sufficiently value his staff members' abilities and performance and therefore could not convey appreciation of them.

Outcome: Once Mr. M. recognized the effect of his administrative philosophy and practice on agency staff, he accepted that he would have to inject something different in order to obtain a different response from those with whom he worked. Readings on management were assigned and discussed, particularly regarding the rationale and the experience of others. As Mr. M. conscientiously identified his values, he was able to understand how they influenced his view of and behavior toward agency staff. As difficult as it was, he was determined to "pay the cost" in order to obtain the "payoff," namely a better-functioning agency, with the resultant advantages for him of being a successful executive. Mr. M. reached out to agency staff, expressing his dissatisfaction and acknowledging theirs too. He involved all staff in taking stock of what existed and what needed to be done by each, including himself. He enlisted the supervisor's ongoing assistance, giving her special recognition. Mr. M. established a mechanism for continuous communication and an atmosphere conducive to openness. This was made possible by his conveying his sincerity and investment in improving services, their common purpose. Although Mr. M. did not really become a humanistic administrator, he made those changes in order to achieve his goal. The brief period of consultation was not sufficient to attempt to achieve changes in basic values. Nonetheless, a beginning was made with a loosening of long-held values, which opened the door for further subsequent changes, as Mr. M. was highly satisfied with his achievement, which contributed to increased self-esteem and esteem by others.

Recommendations Made: Continuing to focus on common goals with staff, to utilize staff's expertise toward achieving that end, to recognize staff's performance, to expand open communication, and to obtain further formal training in administration for himself.

Obtaining consultation is a "natural" for private clinicians, because it is consistent with and supportive of their autonomy. At the same time, it offers the consultee an opportunity to enrich his thinking and practice. It is less likely that struggles of will and competition will take place in a consultative arrangement than in a supervisory one, since the former is less threatening. There is usually greater receptivity to the stimulation offered because the request was initiated by the private practitioner-consultee and is at his own expense. In contrast, agency staff do not pay the consultant themselves and may not even desire consultation; it may have been the agency administrators' idea. A private practitioner's focus in consultation generally is on a specific case and the clinician's handling of it. Often the necessary data includes the consultee-therapist's emotional blocks, attitudes, and values related to his patient and the case situation, but this is to be focused on only if the consultee concurs and it is part of their contract. Thus the need for assistance with a case must be recognized by the private practitioner because there is nobody else involved to point this out to him. Therefore the private practitioner has a greater responsibility to identify his own professional needs and to take the steps to obtain appropriate help. On the other hand, the consultant should be aware of and dynamically employ these built-in positives to maximize his being utilized effectively.

The selection of a consultant may be based on a number of factors, some of which are relevant and valid, while others are not. Logically, the overriding factor should be the consultant's level of competence in the area of difficulty and how likely he is to be able to transmit his knowledge and in other pertinent ways to be helpful to the consultee. This is sometimes determined by obtaining opinions about potential consultants based on direct or indirect experience, from discerning colleagues, or knowledgeable friends. The consultant's reputation is also a consideration, although not necessarily a reliable one. He may choose as consultant someone who he believes has special expertise in the area needed, someone who was impressive while presenting a paper or whose articles and/or books made a favorable impression, a highly regarded former professor, or an extremely capable colleague with whom he has a comparatively distant relationship and with whom he has become acquainted through professional organizations. Another factor is the consultant's ability to teach, since simply possessing knowledge is not enough. Middleman (1974) recommends that the consultant's value orientation should be considered. Mendes (1977) suggests that the consultant should have a value premise different from that of the consultee, to avoid the possible strengthening of existing biases. A consultant's values certainly are significant. However, equally important are the ability and willingness of the consultant and consultee to sincerely, thoughtfully, and thoroughly consider their agreement and differences in value premises and the implications for the job to be done. It is infrequent that the disagreements are so pervasive that consultant and consultee are a mismatch.

The most common criterion used in selecting a consultant is that his amount of experience in the focal area is considerably greater than the consultee's. Three of the least valid criteria for choosing a consultant are personal friendship; political considerations, such as job and client referrals; or mere expediency, such as physical proximity of their offices. Wolberg (1967) considers, and I concur, that the consultant needs to be knowledgeable about community organization, social planning, organizational management, administration, public relations, public health, individual and group dynamics, research, legal and legislative matters, teaching, supervision, social psychology, cultural anthropology, sociology, and political action.

First there should be an exploratory meeting to determine whether a specific potential consultant is appropriate. If so, a contract is agreed on, specifying the mutual expectations and responsibilities, methodology, number of sessions, options for renegotiations, and other pertinent matters. The more detailed and clear the contract, the greater its potential contribution to the consultative process and results and the more possible it will be to evaluate not only the outcome but also the extent to which both consultant and consultee have fulfilled their respective responsibilities.

Another special use of a consultant is as a trainer for a particular segment of staff, such as administrators, supervisors, therapists, or diagnostic staff. Under these circumstances, the consultant is engaged to provide a seminar, workshop, or course in a specific substantive area such as a treatment modality, diagnosis, dynamics of behavior, staff relationships, or collaboration. Frequently the in-service training is provided on a continuous basis, although each topical unit is decided on and contracted for in discrete units. This is the traditional and best-known type of arrangement and is utilized by such agencies as the Veterans Administration, Catholic Social Services, and departments of public welfare.

An alternative is for an agency to assign one of its own staff members as an "in-house," in-service trainer. Even when this is done, outside consultants are often also utilized and integrated into the overall training program. A significant advantage of an external trainer-consultant is that staff feel less threatened by him or her and therefore are freer and more open to learning. Another advantage is the "outside" view, which frequently brings a different and a fresh perspective. Probably the external trainer's lesser familiarity with the agency, and its personnel, compared to an internal trainer, is both a disadvantage and an advantage. The lack of knowledge of specifics is offset by the noninvolvement in agency politics and factionalism.

Another kind of arrangement that has existed for many years is the designation of trainers who are part of and specified by a professional association as approved trainers, preceptors, or supervisors for potential members. These organizations require applicants for membership who are not fully qualified to receive a specified amount of training under one of their sanctioned senior member supervisors in order to be accepted into the association. This is in contrast to an arrangement with an individually sought supervisor whom a therapist contacts in order to enhance his dynamic understanding and treatment skills. The latter is distinguished by the therapist trainee deciding voluntarily, without being required to do so by anyone, to obtain the appropriate supervision necessary for increasing pertinent knowledge and competence in order to be more effective. He takes full responsibility for initiating the process. The therapist (or potential therapist) who enters training or supervision to fulfill requirements to qualify for admission to a professional organization or to graduate from a program, on the other hand, has this generally as his primary goal, with the increase in professional competence being a corollary.

The Private Practitioner as Educator

Education in the helping professions has been left, for the main part, to educators who are usually on the faculty of graduate and professional schools. Clinical practice is performed and experience is obtained in social agencies, health facilities, and correctional institutions,[6] where teaching is generally done by staff members who are conversant with the material to be taught, because they are directly involved in service delivery and daily operations.

A growing trend has been for graduate and professional schools to use agency staff (often called *field faculty* or *adjunct faculty*) as instructors to teach certain courses in which they have great knowledge and capacity. To only a slight extent in social work, as evidenced by the paucity in the literature, have private practitioners been included in this development. In departments of psychiatry and psychology in medical schools, many respected private practitioners have adjunct or clinical faculty appointments; these titles signify a part-time affiliation and are given in exchange for teaching and/or supervising several hours a week. Although these often are unpaid appointments, they are desired because of the status conferred by the title, the stimulation of being on a medical school faculty, and the opportunity to help educate future therapists.

Graduate schools of social work and departments of psychology do not utilize private practitioners as professors to any significant extent. Yet this resource pool could provide considerable benefit to their students. With all the talk about the need for sound innovations in professional education to keep abreast of the times, action lags far behind. The advantage of adding underutilized, readily available talent for the direct benefit of the students and the indirect benefit of the field would be a logical step toward fulfilling education's charge and responsibility. Private practitioners' vast, rich, valuable clinical experience should not be allowed to remain virtually untapped. Professional qualifications and procedures for selecting private practitioners as faculty members could be comparable to those presently in use for others appointed to faculty positions. In this way, education could incorporate more of the "grass roots" of practice, thus becoming more responsive to changes in kinds of problems and patterns patients present and current "treatment of choice" possibilities. Continuing education, which is required in some professions and undoubtedly will become mandatory in the others in the not too distant future, would thus add this important resource. It is long past due that formal education expand its boundaries by incorporating the various integral parts of the field in practice as much as in verbalization.

The Private Practitioner as Supervisor

The most recent, exciting, innovative development, still in its embryonic stage, is voluntary supervision provided by a private practitioner to a less-experienced private clinician. Because of the nature of supervision, by definition it appears at first glance to be a contradiction in terms. Contrary to consultation, inherent in supervision, particularly in social work, authority is endowed in the supervisor by the agency. It is this authority that has always been considered an absolute necessity for supervision to be successful. The strength and even force of the agency, with its implied threat, constitutes the basis for the arrangement and provides the ultimate motivation. Even where staff members are well-motivated to learn and to accept help to enable them to increase their competence and where staff truly agree with the need for accountability, they are aware that they do not determine *whether* there will be supervision or by whom. Staff may determine *how,* or indeed even whether, they will *use* supervision, but they know that if they do not meet the minimum requirements in this regard, whatever they may be, they are open to dismissal. Thus the decision by staff to comply with the requirement to be supervised is not really a free choice, since the alternative is even worse. Under these circumstances, maximum productive use of supervision cannot realistically be expected.

Using Kadushin's (1976) frame of reference of the supervisor's power, we find that whereas an agency supervisor has both formal and functional power, the private practitioner-supervisor has only the functional power. The formal power is related to the office of supervisor, namely the authority with which the position or title is invested, such as positional and reward and punishment power; the functional power includes expertise and referent power, namely, what the supervisor knows, is, and can do. This functional power is the basis for the most positive approach to and use of supervision. It is the essence of private-practitioner supervision.

Thus, contrary to required supervision, supervision voluntarily sought out of felt need and under relatively nonthreatening circumstances is far more likely to be well utilized. This is what is happening in private practice, a surprise in view of the strong feeling in the field of social work against supervision of experienced, competent psychotherapists: In psychology and psychiatry, there has been a stronger inclination of fledgling therapists to eagerly seek tutelage from their "masters" until they are licensed or board certified.

Social work has traditionally been the profession that has most strongly advocated the need for ongoing supervision and integrated it as a process in its own right consistent with the purposes of social work. Smalley (1967) presents this viewpoint. Supervision has historically been required of even experienced social workers over periods of many years. This led to charges that supervisees were being infantilized and kept dependent. Cohen (1972) and Kadushin (1976) make the salient point that it is not the inherent nature of supervision that causes dependency and infantilization, but rather it is poor supervision that does so! Both of these authors recommend better formal training for supervision to upgrade its quality.

This point appears to be borne out by the fact that clinicians in private practice are seeking and committing themselves to supervision rather than to consultation. Apparently they perceive supervision as more nearly meeting their needs or as providing an additional means in conjunction with other opportunities. Private practitioners who are concerned and interested in improving their effectiveness seek other private practitioners from whom they believe they can learn, using essentially the same criteria as for consultants as described earlier. This effort is in keeping with their code of ethics and with the increasing thrust toward continuing education.

It is interesting to note how a supervisory arrangement is made between two autonomous private clinicians. A contract is negotiated that spells out not only the objectives and the problem areas to be resolved but also the mutual responsibilities consistent with achieving those specified aims. Crucial parts of the contract are the conferring by the supervisee on the supervisor of the necessary authority to follow up on agreed tasks and the overall use being made of the supervisor. In effect, the supervisee is making himself accountable to the supervisor, thus adding of his own volition an element otherwise missing by virtue of the nature of the reality, namely the lack of positional (formal) authority. The frequency and duration of supervision; days and hours of the sessions; ground rules regarding changing, canceling, or breaking appointments (for both parties); and fees are among the essential details of the contract. This builds in a time limit on supervision, a concept somewhat similar to that advocated by Wax (1963, p. 37) who believes it should "be planned sequentially with individualized goals tied to defined stages or steps in the educational process. . . . It should have an end point."

The question arises as to why an independent psychotherapist would voluntarily partly surrender his autonomy. Obviously, the supervisee thinks that it is to his own advantage professionally and thus also on his patients' behalf. He is actually telling the supervisor that he wants more than simply opinions and recommendations, the latter being consultation. He wants help both with an aspect of his practice and with increasing his ability to implement his new learning. Particularly the latter is a problem, at least periodically, for even experienced, highly skilled therapists. An isolated repetitious practice, in spite of a variety of types of patients, can lull one into taking an easy path without even realizing it, until suddenly one day it becomes obvious.

If the supervisee demands more from the private supervisor, due to the very nature of supervision, then the latter must decide whether he is able and willing to give that extra assistance. Again, in spite of the voluntary assignment of authority by the supervisee, it can be expected that he will struggle against it at times. To hold the supervisee to the contractual stipulation regarding authority demands much clarity and understanding from the supervisor. Supervision is a more difficult and stress-producing process than is consultation. Nonetheless, some private practitioners accept this role because it is a service needed that they have the expertise to offer. Another reason is that the deeper, more intense involvement in supervision, as compared to consultation, results in greater gratification from success. Contributing to this is the built-in feedback from the supervisee, which is an integral aspect of supervision.

Case Example

Referral Data: Self. Mrs. A. chose specific supervisor on recommendation of close friend, a psychologist, who had been in therapy with this private practitioner.

Identifying Data: Mrs. A. is a thirty-six-year-old social worker with seven years professional (post-M.S.W.) experience as a psychotherapist in a community mental health center, with a part-time private practice for the past year.

Presenting Problem: Frequent inability to utilize the initial interview to maintain contact, resulting in abortive termination.

Goal: To increase skill in establishing a connection in the first interview conducive to sustaining a professional relationship.

Focus: Clinician's therapeutic philosophy, base, purpose, expectations, approach, formulations, and emotional climate in initial sessions.

Contract: Twelve weekly one-hour sessions, held in supervisor's office, with one follow-up conference six months after completion. Responsibilities and expectations of supervisee and supervisor; goals; focus; methodology; task assignments and how they would be utilized; criteria for evaluation of results regarding goal achievement; basis for results; assessment of Mrs. A.'s use of supervision; and recommendations on completion of the twelve supervisory conferences. A crucial integral provision, which must be present, was the granting by Mrs. A. and the acceptance by the supervisor of positional authority in addition to the inherent functional authority; this was expressed in the supervisee being accountable to the supervisor for fulfilling her agreed-on responsibilities, including a constructive use of supervision.

Assessment: Mrs. A. had carried over, to an exaggerated extent, from her community mental health center experience, a strong emphasis on obtaining much history material and formulating a psychosocial diagnosis in the initial session. She saw this as her purpose, which enabled her to make specific recommendations regarding treatment. Unfortunately, she was so intent on that aspect that she failed to relate to her patients as people. Instead, although she very much wanted to help them, she used the patients as a means to accomplish her more immediate purpose, namely, obtaining an understanding of them and formulating a therapy plan. Mrs. A.'s approach was not blatant, and indeed she did at times demonstrate feeling for her patients, but she was so determined to complete her self-assigned task that she felt under pressure and had little time to really listen, empathize, or "stay with" her patients. She had not yet developed the ability to find a balance in this respect. Those who needed to feel that Mrs. A. really cared and was "human" were the ones who ended precipitously; others, who were favorably impressed with Mrs. A.'s efficiency and diagnostic skill, continued into therapy with her. Mrs. A. was functioning on a consultative basis at the community mental health center, and her dropout rate was comparable to other therapists there, particularly since her primary assignment was psychotherapy, with only minimal intake responsibilities.

Use of Supervision: In spite of her strong desire to resolve the problem of "losing" too many patients in the initial contact, Mrs. A. at first fervently held to the validity of her purpose and approach, unable to accept that it was possible to obtain necessary data by relating to her patients and thus laying the foundation for being helpful. The first requisite was that they return, and the approach suggested by the supervisor made that more likely for some patients. Mrs. A. struggled against giving up the known and comfortable for something new and very different for her. Utilizing pertinent readings on this aspect, tapes of her initial interviews, and role modeling of both approaches in supervising Mrs. A. combined to "move" her to try this different approach. The impact of one particular conference, in which negative role modeling by the supervisor was emphasized, in marked contrast to his usual style, contributed significantly to Mrs. A.'s decision to take the risk.

Outcome: Mrs. A.'s own experience in receiving help in two contrasting forms demonstrated to her the importance of conveying to her patients the feeling that she really had, of truly hearing them by "staying with them," and of incorporating them more in the planning by "loosening the atmosphere." As the series of supervisory conferences neared completion, Mrs. A. had already begun to obtain her desired results with some regularity.

Recommendations Made: In her private practice, Mrs. A. was to continue taping all initial and ending interviews for three months for her own assessment of her practice. In the community mental health center, she was to make regular use of the consultation available to her, the frequency to be mutually decided by Mrs. A. and agency.

As more private practitioners experience and benefit from supervision, both supervisees and supervisors, we can look forward to its greater usage. This is one of the most unanticipated and innovative developments in the past decade. Some have voluntarily come back full circle to a point from which so many other psychotherapists have been fleeing! This new development reaffirms the importance of judiciously sought quality supervision when the need for a sounding board and tutor arises.

Summary

Private practitioners offer a variety of services, not only to the general public but also to members of the helping professions. A rich resource, well-utilized in some respects, private practitioners as a whole are underutilized in others. While well known as psychotherapists, consultants, trainers and educators, they are less known as supervisors for other, less-experienced private practitioners and graduate students. Providing voluntarily sought and individually contracted supervision is a recent development that has considerable potential for making a significant contribution to psychotherapists directly and to patients indirectly. This is an indication of the growing maturity of the field that augurs well for the helping professions and for the patients we serve.

Notes

1. The terms *psychotherapy, therapy,* and *counseling* are used synonymously in this chapter.

2. The terms *psychotherapist, therapist, counselor, clinician, private practitioner,* and *independent practitioner* are used synonymously.

3. The terms *patients* and *clients* are used interchangeably.

4. My perspective is primarily from the field of social work, the discipline in which I received my formal graduate education and with which I am most familiar.

5. Case examples do not represent actual persons or agencies; rather, they are disguised amalgams.

6. The term *agency* will henceforth be used to subsume and include *agency, health facility,* and *institution.*

Future Trends

Florence Whiteman Kaslow

଼ଡ଼

Then said a teacher, Speak to us of Teaching.
And he said:
No man can reveal to you aught but that which already lies half asleep
in the dawning of your knowledge.
The teacher who walks in the shadow of the temple, among his fol-
lowers, gives not of his wisdom but rather of his faith and his
lovingness.
If he is indeed wise, he does not bid you enter the house of his wisdom,
but rather leads you to the threshold of your own mind.
The astronomer may speak to you of his understanding of space, but
he cannot give you his understanding.
The musician may sing to you of the rhythm which is in all space, but
he cannot give you the ear which arrests the rhythm nor the voice
that echoes it.
And he who is versed in the science of numbers can tell of the regions
of weight and measure, but he cannot conduct you thither.
For the vision of one man lends not its wings to another man.

The Prophet, Kahlil Gibran

It is to teachers, supervisors, trainers, and consultants who know the essential truth so beautifully expressed in this passage from Gibran that we expect this book will have the most meaning. Perhaps the most salient ingredient in the three processes with which this book has been concerned is the *relationship* of supervisors, trainers, or consultants to their trainees. We therefore emphasize, as does Gibran, the folly of trying to impart wisdom alone and the importance of giving generously of one's faith and caring and of leading students to explore their own thoughts, feelings, and intuitions and to experiment with what works for them. Indeed, each helping professional must be inspired by his preceptors and teachers to become attuned to his clients, his trainers, and the agency of which he is a part and to still listen to the rhythm of his own inner drumbeat.

Before we project into the future, we will give a brief recapitulation by way of summarizing where the field is today. The impact of the organization on practice is receiving increased recognition, and there is more awareness of the ecosystem in which helping professionals operate. One-to-one supervision is still probably the most widely practiced model because of the close contact it offers, the clarity of roles and mutual expectations, the greater familiarity with this approach than with any other, and the number of excellent supervisors for individuals available. Still, it is costly, can foster excessive dependence if carried on for a prolonged period and in a controlling fashion, and it can become monotonous. This approach has been joined by group supervision, a technique gaining in popularity as more supervisors gain greater proficiency in its usage, as agencies find it cost effective, and as participants find the input from other group members stimulating. Group supervision has been initiated in many educational programs and agencies for some of the same reasons that have led to greater usage of staff training and consultation with small and large groups of staff members. In addition, these latter two processes permit an agency to augment the available staff expertise in the form of hiring outside specialists to perform specific tasks with the expectation that they will be informative, provocative, and refreshing. Their ability to function outside of the political machinations in the agency or organization leaves them much freer to concentrate all of their energies on the job to be done.

We have shown that there is now a tremendous variety of techniques in usage for carrying out the three processes. These include discussion of process or tape recordings and verbal accounts of sessions with clients; observation of live sessions over one-way mirrors or on videotape followed by discussion of these after a given period of time has elapsed; cotherapy, in which the trainee is paired up with the supervisor as a team to discuss their interaction and the treatment after each session; observation and direct, immediate feedback, in which the preceptor watching through a one-way screen either calls in suggestions or enters the room and takes over the treatment session; having the supervisor do a special session with the patient(s) in order to meet them and have a chance to formulate his own impressions as well as model how to intervene therapeutically; role playing and other psychodrama approaches; problem solving and brainstorming; and confrontation.

Several authors in this book talk about goal setting and contracting. This happens as much between supervisor or trainer and supervisee as between therapist or group leader and patient or group member. It is in keeping with the thrust toward clear and open communication and involvement of trainees in formulating what it is they want to gain from their supervisor; the joint determination of objectives parallels the process that therapists set in motion when they engage in specifying goals and contracting with the consumers of their services.

In some specialties, such as marriage and family counseling, as in some settings such as community mental health centers, some strides have been made toward interdisciplinary supervision and training. These remain more the exception than the rule, as professionals cling to their separate identities.

A Forward Look

Too often, in the past, clinicians moved into supervisory slots because there were vacancies and because going into administrative positions meant salary increases and more prestige. Because a clinician was a good therapist or group worker and leader, it was frequently assumed that he or she would therefore be a fine supervisor. Conversely, the opposite assumption also was made: If someone was not a very able therapist but was well organized, efficient, and intellectually knowledgeable, perhaps that person's contribution might be in the area of supervision. Too rarely has specific training in supervision, staff development, or consultation been a prerequisite for being appointed to such a position. Thus the "how to" formula was narrowly based on the supervisor's own previous experiences as a supervisee—emulating what was valuable and appealing, rebelling against and trying to do the opposite of what was found to be distasteful or counterproductive. Added to this has been (and should be) trial-and-error efforts, also called *innovations*. Both of these constitute valid but not sufficient bases on which to build one's own supervisory endeavors. What is needed is sound grounding in the theoretical formulations about learning processes and goals, supervisor-supervisee relationships, the gamut of techniques and methodologies that have been developed, the rational use of authority, and the importance of professional accountability. Only by such depth and breadth can the use of supervisory and consultative time be maximized. Supervisors, consultants, and trainers should be provocative, stimulating, and challenging mentors who find these tasks exciting and can convey their enthusiasm for and belief in the changes, minuscule and monumental, that can be wrought through attentive listening, sensitive responses, and strategic interventions in the various kinds of client units we service—individual, couple, family, group, community, and institution.

The fact that supervisors serve as role models has been emphasized in the chapters by Abroms, Cohen, Gitterman and Miller, Kaslow, and Melchiode. Both transference and identification may be occurring, either simultaneously or sequentially. Supervisors need to be aware of this and to use the halo effect in a constructive way for all concerned, and must not confuse transference phenomena with positive identification with what they, as teachers and supervisors in the current reality, are and do.

From all this flow both the hope and our first prognostication that more and more residency training programs as well as psychology, social work, and nursing graduate education programs will begin to offer courses in supervision and consultation, either in the final year of the program or for postgraduates as part of continuing education. The continuing education approach has much in its favor, since one should be firmly rooted in clinical practice before attempting to supervise another's interpreting of behavioral dynamics, interpersonal relationships, transference and countertransference phenomena, and therapeutic strategies.

Clearly, there is no unanimity on how to define the terms *supervision, consultation,* and *staff training,* nor on what one is to be educated to do in any of these roles. Generally, the dividing line (to the extent that any consensus was achieved by the authors of this book) between the first two seems to revolve around whether or not administrative authority is lodged in the senior person. When it is and when he or she can hold the trainee accountable, the process is termed *supervision;* when authority is lacking and the process has a quality that suggests "this is what I have to offer and you are free to take it or leave it," it is dubbed *consultation.* Confusion sometimes results because some group supervision closely resembles staff training—perhaps here the decisive factor is whether the focus is on the process of how trainees are conducting therapy, in which event it is usually designated *group supervision,* or whether the focus is on teaching substantive material, in which instance it is labeled *staff training.* Of the three, staff training is the most cognitive process and entails the most highly structured format. Usually there is specific didactic content to be absorbed. Supervision is geared to increasing the supervisee's awareness of his or her role as a practitioner as well as his or her skill, competence, and confidence. Consultation often has a more specific problem focus.

Thus one can predict, as the second trend and as a corollary to the first, increased efforts in academe, agencies, and professional organizations to clarify the nature of these three somewhat overlapping and certainly complementary processes so that there will be less ambiguity as to a person's function and its parameters when he or she is hired for any of these supervisory tasks. People will then have a clearer idea of what to expect when contracting for supervision versus for consultation, and there will be greater agreement about the meaning of terms in applications that mental health professionals fill out for jobs or for licensure. Clearer definitions and demarcations should eliminate much of the semantic fuzziness that has caused misinterpretations of processes, functions, and procedures.

A third trend is the quest for greater freedom on the part of trainees to have some say in the selection of a supervisor. Supervisors must continue to be rationally firm about their expectations and know when to deal with negative reactions as resistances or countertransferences, when to decide they are involved in a poor supervisor-supervisee pairing and to arrange for a transfer, and when to raise serious question about the student's inability to accept another's authority position and greater knowledge. Closely related as a fourth trend, we foresee research in the area of supervisor-supervisee match, similar to that being conducted in the area of therapist-patient match. Hopefully, if the findings yield significant differences in terms of trainee knowledge and skill when matches are made (using certain variables), then these findings will be utilized in making more advantageous assignments of supervisors. This type of selection factor, albeit informal, is already operative in private arrangements such as those described by Cohen and Kaslow.

Traditionally, teachers and supervisors have graded or in other ways evaluated their supervisees. Despite some efforts to standardize criteria and grading systems, tremendous variations and much latitude exist. Assessment and feedback are essential if one is to provide the trainee with data about his progress, strengths, and weaknesses and whether he seems suitable for the chosen field and to provide input into the larger program as to the student's level of competence and knowledge and skills gaps. Evaluations by different supervisors and educators should be conducted, using similar dimensions and criteria, so that when necessary they can be compared and tabulated in some meaningful way. Refinement and standardization of the supervisor's evaluative tools are greatly needed, which leads us to predict, as a fifth trend, more concerted efforts to devise, test out, and standardize such forms.

Another development likely to escalate, related to evaluation of supervisees' work, is the soliciting of input from patients or consumers regarding whether their goals in coming for help have been realized and whether the professional's interventions have been effective. In truth, who knows better than the clients if they have received what they think is needed? And, if we really respect our clients, can we disregard their evaluation? The helping professions have been reluctant to ask the recipients of their services to assess the quality of what they receive, but, given the scarcity of funds and greater sophistication in the lay public regarding mental health and social services, tolerance of inferior services is likely to diminish. Enlightened supervisors might well be expected to seek such input as part of the total assessment of their supervisees' work.

Lagging far in the rear of standardized ways of evaluating supervisees are systematic guidelines for assessing supervisors and trainers. Usually evaluation forms are distributed the last day of a class's or group's existence, or the group may periodically be encouraged to discuss their reactions. But, whether written or verbal, it is often possible for the trainer to obtain the answers desired. For example, if a trainer makes up his own forms and is seeking primarily positive comments, knowing that these will be utilized in deciding whether to rehire or promote him or her, the form can be designed accordingly, to ask questions such as "What did you find most useful in the course?" Queries that elicit negative comments can be avoided. Reactions are only comparable and valid if all groups in a given setting go through a similar evaluation process.

Just as supervisors should discuss (and sign) reports on a trainee with the trainee himself and provide an opportunity to append comments if there is a disagreement, so too trainees evaluating a supervisor or consultant should be accountable for what they write by signing their names to evaluations and being willing to discuss them. The anonymity that currently abounds is conducive to distortions as well as to candor and can be a protective screen for destructive maneuvers.

A promising subtrend in the evaluation of supervision may be self-assessment. Just as videotapes and films are being extensively used to help clients see and hear themselves and to supervise trainees based on direct observations of their work, we encourage supervisors to tape their sessions with trainees for self-critiquing and for discussion with valued colleagues as a way of assessing and improving performance.

When a supervisor or consultant repeatedly receives negative evaluations and these have been gone over with him, and when no improvement over time is noted, one can only wonder why he is retained in this post. If evaluations are utilized merely to provide an aura of participation, it is dishonest to pretend that they have any significance, and they had best be dropped. We can only hope that, as peer review and the stronger push for accountability at all performance levels take hold, department chairmen, training directors, and agency administrators will become courageous enough to not continue using those who consistently are rated poor.

A program tends to have a "good reputation" if its training faculty are renowned by virtue of being well published and/or because its graduates make laudatory comments and do well after graduation. But more is needed in the arena of program evaluation, and only after goals are stated in measurable, observable, and operationalizable terms will we begin to be able to evaluate and compare training programs. This, too, will come to pass in the not-too-distant future.

Moving away from evaluation into the area of heightened sensitivity, now that the metatherapy elements of supervision have been highlighted by Abroms, one can speculate that more understanding of the metatalk in training, teaching, and consultation will follow and that mental health professionals will be able to pick up and cope with these messages and try to eliminate the dissonance, just as therapists try to minimize double-bind communications. Perhaps we will never achieve agreement between those such as Abroms, who present a cogent case for including therapeutic elements in supervision, and Finch and Richan, who are at the far distant pole, feeling these to be necessarily separate and distinct. Such divergence constitutes dynamic tension, which is healthy, as it keeps dialogue alive and periodically leads to new and better syntheses of ideas, methods, and systems.

In the area of supervisory and training techniques, our forward glance visualizes expanded usage of role-playing and psychodrama techniques such as those described by Gitterman, Miller, and Kaslow. These have been shown to be excellent for helping trainees empathize with and act out different roles, to literally try to get into another person's skin and see what it must feel like to be and think as that other does. When it comes to providing trainees with a method for trying out possible future behaviors, role rehearsal can prove fruitful. In addition, such experiential techniques maximize trainee involvement in their own learning process. Moving in this direction will require greater flexibility and ingenuity on the part of training personnel.

The increasing utilization of multiple and interdisciplinary supervisors, highlighted most prominently in the chapter on community mental health centers, is a phenomena we think will and should spread. As more techniques of therapy are permitted to coexist in the same settings, it is improbable that any one person will be proficient in all. Thus trainees will be precepted in different modalities by specialists in each particular approach. We see this as a laudable trend that should prevent narrowness and myopia in the helping professions. But, as this occurs, it will be important to lodge responsibility in one of the supervisors for the coordination of the training and overall assessment of the supervisees' performance. The multidisciplinary supervisory and training programs should also push the professions to look toward interdisciplinary educational programs in graduate and professional schools with shared faculty, students from different disciplines taking classes together, and some joint curriculum planning. Only then will full collaboration become a reality.

Another trend emerges from the realization that not everyone needs similar amounts of supervision and that therefore the rigid, weekly schedule might be adhered to when appropriate, while more flexible and less frequent scheduling can be adapted for intermediate and senior staff. At the advanced-practitioner level, peer consultation sought voluntarily, when needed, could well become the preferred model (Kaslow, 1972). Similarly, in settings where frequent crises occur—such as acute wards of mental hospitals, foster care agencies, drug treatment programs, and prisons—access to on-the-spot crisis supervision should be available, for if a conference is not scheduled until the following week, it may simply be too late!

Most of the professions are moving toward or are already requiring continuing education credits (Kutzik, Chapters One and Two), and this is a trend we heartily endorse. Perhaps the professional organizations might consider formal individual arrangements for supervision and consultation as sufficiently meritorious to award

credit for these as well as for work taken in educational programs and at institutes and conferences. This impetus for ever-increasing knowledge and competence is to be hailed.

It is likely that the trend Cohen pinpointed of private practitioners from all the helping disciplines voluntarily contracting for precepting and tutelage to acquire more knowledge and new competencies will continue, whether or not continuing education credits are awarded for such study. For we are an achievement-oriented professional culture.

In drawing to a close, we sincerely hope more "superstar" helping professionals will utilize their skills in working in and training others to work in underserved, unglamorous settings such as the prisons so accurately depicted by Brodsky or the mental hospitals mentioned by Coché. Inner-city clinics and settlements, departments of probation, and public welfare agencies are in the same category. If such positions do not provide sufficient monetary rewards and professional stimulation and satisfaction to warrant a full-time investment, then a part-time arrangement that allows such professionals to live out their own commitments to social justice is often possible. Only when supervisors, educators, and trainers have some investment in the lower-status agencies will they be sanctioning such involvement on the part of their supervisees.

We conclude this chapter as we began it—with a quote from

The Prophet:

And a man said, Speak to us of Self Knowledge.
And he answered, saying:
Your hearts know in silence the secrets of the days and the nights.
But your ears thirst for the sound of your heart's knowledge.
You would know in words that which you have always known in thought.
You would touch with your fingers the naked body of your dreams.

References

ABELS, P. "On the Nature of Supervision: The Medium Is the Group." *Child Welfare,* 1970, *49* (6), 305–307.

ABELS, P. *The New Practice of Supervision and Staff Development.* New York: Association Press, 1976.

ABELS, S. "Utilization of Grounded Theory as a Methodological and Substantive Approach to the Education of Social Work Practitioners." Paper presented at Council on Social Work Education Conference, Phoenix, 1977.

ABRAHAMSON, A. C. *Group Methods in Supervision and Staff Development.* New York: Harper & Row, 1959.

ABRAHAMSON, M. *The Professional in the Organization.* Chicago: Rand McNally, 1967.

ABROMS, G. M. "Persuasion in Psychotherapy." *American Journal of Psychiatry,* 1968a, *124,* 98–105.

ABROMS, G. M. "Setting Limits." *Archives of General Psychiatry,* 1968b, *19,* 113–119.

ABROMS, G. M. "Defining Milieu Therapy." *Archives of General Psychiatry,* 1969, *21,* 553–560.

ABROMS, G. M. "Psychiatric Ethicism." Unpublished manuscript, 1973.

ABROMS, G. M., and GREENFIELD, N. S. (Eds.). *The New Hospital Psychiatry.* New York: Academic Press, 1971.

313

Accreditation Committee. "AAMFC Accredited Degree Programs and Approved Training Centers." *Journal of Marriage and Family Counseling,* 1977, *3* (1), 95.

Ackerman Institute. Ackerman Institute brochures. New York: Ackerman Institute, 1977.

ACKERMAN, N. "Some Considerations for Training in Family Therapy." In *Career Directions.* Vol. 2. East Hanover, N.J.: Sandoz Pharmaceuticals, D. J. Publications, 1973.

ACKERMAN, N., BEATMAN, F., and SHERMAN, S. (Eds.). *Exploring the Base for Family Therapy.* New York: Family Service Association of America, 1961.

ALMY, F. "The Problem of Charity." *Charities Review,* 1895, *4* (4), 169–180.

ALTMAN, L. L. *The Dream in Psychoanalysis.* New York: International Universities Press, 1969.

American Association of Marriage and Family Counselors. Membership brochure. Claremont, Calif.: American Association of Marriage and Family Counselors, 1976a.

American Association of Marriage and Family Counselors. *The Approved Supervisor.* Claremont, Calif.: American Association of Marriage and Family Counselors, 1976b.

APTEKAR, H. "The Continued Education of Experienced Workers." *Child Welfare,* 1959, *38* (2), 7–12.

AUSTIN, L. N. "Supervision in Social Work." In R. H. Kurtz (Ed.), *Social Work Year Book.* Vol. 13. New York: National Association of Social Workers, 1957.

AUSTIN, L. N. "Supervision in Social Work." In R. H. Kurtz (Ed.), *Social Work Year Book.* Vol. 14. New York: National Association of Social Workers, 1960.

AUSTIN, L. N. "The Changing Role of the Supervisor." *Smith College Studies in Social Work,* 1961, *31* (3), 179–195.

BABCOCK, C. "Social Work as Work." *Social Casework,* 1955, *34* (10), 415–422.

BALES, R., and STRODRTBECK, F. "Phases in Group Problem Solving." *Journal of Abnormal and Social Psychology,* 1965, *45.*

BARBER, B. "The Sociology of the Professions." In K. S. Lynn (Ed.), *The Professions in America.* Boston: Houghton Mifflin, 1965.

BARON, P. S. "Co-Therapy in Group Treatment: Critical Issues." Unpublished master's thesis, Hahnemann Medical College, 1975.

BECKER, D. G. "The Visitor to the New York City Poor, 1843–1920." *Social Service Review*, 1961, *35* (4), 382–396.

BECKER, S., and NEUHAUSER, D. *The Efficient Organization*. New York: Elsevier, 1975.

BENNIS, W., and SHEPHERD, H. A. "A Theory of Group Development." *Human Relations*, 1956, *9* (4), 415.

BERGER, M. M. "Experiential and Didactic Aspects of Training in Therapeutic Group Approaches." *American Journal of Psychiatry*, 1969, *126*, 845–850.

BERKELEY, G. *The Administrative Revolution: Notes on the Passing of Organization Man*. Englewood Cliffs, N.J.: Prentice-Hall, 1971.

BIERCE, A. *The Devil's Dictionary*. New York: Dover, 1958. (Originally published 1911.)

BION, W. R. *Experiences in Groups*. New York: Basic Books, 1961.

BIRCHLER, G. R. "Live Supervision and Instant Feedback in Marriage and Family Therapy." *Journal of Marriage and Family Counseling*, 1975, *1* (4), 331–342.

BLAU, P. "Critical Remarks on Weber's Theory of Authority." In P. Blau (Ed.), *On the Nature of Organizations*. New York: Wiley, 1974a.

BLAU, P. "Statistical Records of Performance." In P. Blau (Ed.), *On the Nature of Organizations*. New York: Wiley, 1974b.

BLOOM, B. L. *Community Mental Health: A Historical and Critical Analysis*. Morristown, N.J.: General Learning Press, 1973.

BOTT, E. *Family and Social Network*. (2nd ed.) London: Tavistock, 1971.

BOWEN, M. "On the Differentiation of Self in One's Own Family." In J. Framo (Ed.), *Family Interaction: A Dialogue Between Family Researchers and Family Therapists*. New York: Springer, 1972.

BRAGER, G. "The Indigenous Worker: A New Approach to the Social Work Technician." *Social Work*, 1965, *10* (2), 33–40.

BRAGER, G. "Institutional Change: Perimeters of the Possible." *Social Work,* 1967, *12* (1), 59–69.

BRAGER, G., and SPECHT, H. *Community Organization.* New York: Columbia University Press, 1973.

BRIAR, S. "Social Casework and Social Group Work: Historical Foundations." In R. Morris (Ed.), *Encyclopedia of Social Work.* (16th issue.) New York: National Association of Social Workers Press, 1971.

BRIEF, A. P., ALDAG, R. J., and WALLDEN, R. A. "Correlates of Supervisory Style Among Policemen." *Criminal Justice and Behavior,* 1976 (3), 263–271.

BRODSKY, S. L. "Situation-Specific Stressors and Training for Police." In W. H. Kroes and J. J. Harrell (Eds.), *Job Stress and the Police Officer: Identifying Stress Reduction Techniques.* Cincinnati: National Institute for Occupational Safety and Health, 1975.

BRODSKY, S. L., and DANISH, S. J. *Final Report: Human Relations Training Project for Illinois State Police.* Carbondale, Ill.: Southern Illinois University and Illinois State Police, 1973.

BRODSKY, S. L., and EGGLESTON, N. (Eds.). *The Military Prison: Theory, Research and Programs.* Carbondale, Ill.: Southern Illinois University Press, 1970.

BROWN, W. *Explorations in Management.* New York: Wiley, 1960.

BRUNER, J. *On Knowing: Essays on the Left Hand.* Cambridge, Mass.: Harvard University Press, 1966.

BRUNER, J. *Toward a Theory of Instruction.* New York: Norton, 1968.

BULLOUGH, V. L. *The Development of Medicine as a Profession.* New York: Hafner, 1966.

BURNS, M. E. "Supervision in Social Work." In H. L. Lurie (Ed.), *Encyclopedia of Social Work.* (15th issue.) New York: National Association of Social Workers Press, 1965.

CAPLAN, G. *The Theory and Practice of Mental Health Consultation.* New York: Basic Books, 1970.

CARR-SAUNDERS, A. M., and WILSON, P. A. *The Professions.* London: Cass, 1964. (Originally published 1933.)

CATHELL, D. W. *Book on the Physician Himself.* (10th ed.) Philadelphia: Davis, 1895.

Charity Organization Society of the City of New York, Tenth Annual Report for the Year 1891. New York: Charity Organization Society, 1892.

CLEGHORN, J. M., and LEVIN, S. "Training Family Therapists by Setting Learning Objectives." *American Journal of Orthopsychiatry,* 1973, *43* (3), 439–446.

COHEN, E. "Supervision in a Large Federal Agency Psychiatric Setting." In F. W. Kaslow and Associates, *Issues in Human Services: A Sourcebook for Supervision and Staff Development.* San Francisco: Jossey-Bass, 1972.

COLLINS, A. H., and PANCOAST, D. L. *Natural Helping Networks.* New York: National Association of Social Workers, 1976.

CRUSER, R. W. "Opinions on Supervision: A Chapter Study." *Social Work,* 1958, *3* (1), 18–25.

DAVIES, P. M. *Medical Terminology in Hospital Practice.* London: Heinemann Medical, 1969.

DEAN, C. W., and MORGAN, D. I. *Correctional Officer Training Manual.* Columbus, S.C.: South Carolina Department of Corrections, 1975.

DEUTSCH, F., and MURPHY, W. F. *The Clinical Interview.* New York: International Universities Press, 1955.

DEVINE, E. T. "The Relief and Care of the Poor in Their Homes." *Charities Review,* 1900, *10* (3), 118–128.

DEVIS, D. A. "Teaching and Administrative Functions in Supervision." *Social Work,* 1965, *10* (2), 83–89.

DEWEY, J. *Experience and Education.* New York: Macmillan [1938], 1947.

DEWEY, J. *The Child and the Curriculum and the School and the Society.* Chicago: Phoenix, 1966.

DIMOCK, H. S., and TRECKER, H. B. *The Supervision of Group Work and Recreation.* New York: Association Press, 1949.

DORNBUSCH, S. M., and SCOTT, W. R. *Evaluation and the Exercise of Authority: A Theory of Control Applied to Diverse Organizations.* San Francisco: Jossey-Bass, 1975.

DRAKE, D. *Practical Essays on Medical Education and the Medical Profession in the United States.* Baltimore: Johns Hopkins University Press, 1952. (Originally published 1832.)

DUHL, F. J., KANTOR, D., and DUHL, B. S. "Learning, Space, and Action in Family Therapy: A Primer of Sculpture." In

D. Block (Ed.), *Techniques of Family Psychotherapy*. New York: Grune & Stratton, 1973.

EIDELBERG, L. *Encyclopedia of Psychoanalysis*. New York: Free Press, 1968.

EISENBERG, S. *Supervision in the Changing Field of Social Work*. Philadelphia: University of Pennsylvania and Jewish Family Service of Philadelphia, 1956.

EISENBERG, T. "Job Stress and the Police Officer: Identifying Stress Reduction Techniques." In W. H. Kroes and J. J. Harrell (Eds.), *Job Stress and the Police Officer: Identifying Stress Reduction Techniques*. Cincinnati: National Institute for Occupational Safety and Health, 1975.

EKSTEIN, R., and WALLENSTEIN, R. S. *The Teaching and Learning of Psychotherapy*. New York: Basic Books, 1963.

ETZIONI, A. "Organizational Control Structures." In J. March (Ed.), *Handbook of Organizations*. Chicago: Rand McNally, 1965.

FAIRBAIRN, W. R. D. Object-Relations Theory of the Personality. New York: Basic Books, 1954.

FENSTERHEIM, H., and BAER, J. *Don't Say Yes When You Want to Say No*. New York: Dell, 1975.

FERBER, A., MENDELSOHN, M., and NAPIER, A. (Eds.). *The Book of Family Therapy*. New York: Science House, 1972.

FIELDS, J. T. *How to Help the Poor*. Boston: Houghton Mifflin, 1885.

FINCH, W. "Education and Jobs: A Study of the Performance of Social Service Tasks in Public Welfare." Unpublished doctoral dissertation, School of Social Welfare, University of California at Berkeley, 1974.

FINCH, W. "Paraprofessionals in Public Welfare: A Utilization Study." *Public Welfare*, 1976a, *34* (1), 52–57.

FINCH, W. "Social Workers Versus Bureaucracy." *Social Work*, 1976b, *21* (5), 370–375.

FINE, S. *Guidelines for the Design of New Careers*. Kalamazoo, Mich.: W. E. Upjohn Institute for Employment Research, 1967.

FIZDALE, R. "Peer Group Supervision." *Social Casework*, 1958, *39* (8), 443–450.

FLEXNER, A. *Medical Education in the United States and Canada.* New York: Arno [1910], 1972.

FLOMENHAFT, N., and CARTER, R. "Family Therapy Training: A Statewide Program for Mental Health Centers." *Hospital and Community Psychiatry,* 1974, *25* (12), 789–791.

FOLLETT, M. "Constructive Conflict." In G. Metcalf (Ed.), *Scientific Foundation of Business Administration.* New York: Harper & Row, 1940.

FRANK, J. D. "Systematic Preparation of Patients for Psychotherapy." *Journal of Psychiatric Research,* 1964, *2,* 267–281.

FRANK, J. D. *Persuasion and Healing.* Baltimore, Md.: Johns Hopkins University Press, 1961; New York: Schocken, 1974.

FREUD, A. *The Ego and the Mechanisms of Defense.* New York: International Universities Press, 1967. (Originally published 1936.)

FREUD, S. "Analysis of a Phobia in a Five Year Old Boy." *The Standard Edition of the Complete Psychological Works of Sigmund Freud.* Vol. 10. London: Hogarth Press, 1955. (Originally published 1909.)

FROEBEL, F. *The Education of Man.* (W. M. Hailmann, Trans.) New York: Appleton-Century-Crofts, 1887.

GARLAND, J., KOLODNY, J. H., and KOLODNY, R. "A Model for Stages in the Development of Social Groups." In S. Bernstein (Ed.), *Explorations in Group Work.* Boston: University of Boston, 1966.

GARTH, S. *The Dispensary.* London: H. Hills, 1709.

GARTNER, A., NIXON, R. A., and RIESSMAN, F. (Eds.). *Public Service Employment: An Analysis of Its History, Problems and Prospects.* New York: Praeger, 1973.

GAZDA, G. M. "Some Tentative Guidelines for Ethical Practice by Group Work Practitioners." In G. M. Gazda (Ed.), *Basic Approaches to Group Psychotherapy and Group Counseling.* (2nd ed.) Springfield, Ill.: Thomas, 1975.

GETZEL, G. S., GOLDBERG, J. R., and SALMON, R. "Supervising in Groups as a Model for Today." *Social Casework,* 1971, *52* (3), 154–163.

GIBRAN, K. *The Prophet.* New York: Knopf, 1975. (Originally published 1923.)

GILBERT, N. "Assessing Service Delivery Methods." *Welfare in Review,* 1972, *10* (3), 25–33.

GITTERMAN, A. "Comparison of Educational Models and Their Influences on Supervision." In F. W. Kaslow and Associates, *Issues in Human Services: A Sourcebook for Supervision and Staff Development.* San Francisco: Jossey-Bass, 1972.

GLASER, D. *Effectiveness of a Prison and Parole System.* Indianapolis: Bobbs-Merrill, 1964.

GOIN, M. K., and KLINE, F. "Countertransference: A Neglected Subject in Clinical Supervision." *American Journal of Psychiatry,* 1976, *133* (1), 41.

GOODE, W. J. "The Theoretical Limits of Professionalization." In A. Etzioni (Ed.), *The Semiprofessions and Their Organization.* New York: Free Press, 1965.

GOSS, M. E. W. "Influence and Authority Among Physicians in an Outpatient Clinic." *American Sociological Review,* 1961, *26* (1), 39–50.

GOTTESFELD, H., RHEE, C., and PARKER, G. "A Study of the Role of Paraprofessionals in Community Mental Health." *Community Mental Health Journal,* 1970, 6 (4), 693–712.

GREENACRE, P. "On Reconstruction." *Journal of the American Psychoanalytic Association,* 1975, *23* (4).

GREENBERG, M. "Brief Therapy for the Parents of Hospitalized Adolescents." *Gruppenpsychotherapie und Gruppendynamik* [*Group Psychotherapy and Group Dynamics*], 1976, *9,* 310–311.

GREENSON, R. *The Technique and Practice of Psychoanalysis.* New York: International Universities Press, 1967.

GROSSER, C., HENRY, W. E., and KELLY, J. G. (Eds.). *Nonprofessionals in the Human Services.* San Francisco: Jossey-Bass, 1969.

Group for the Advancement of Psychiatry. *The Field of Family Therapy.* GAP Report 78. New York: 1970.

GUERIN, P., and FOGARTY, T. "Study Your Own Family." In A. Ferber, M. Mendelsohn, and A. Napier (Eds.), *The Book of Family Therapy.* New York: Science House, 1972.

HAGE, J., and AIKER, M. "Program Change and Organizational Properties." *American Journal of Sociology,* 1967, *72,* 503–518.

HALEY, J. *Strategies of Psychotherapy.* New York: Grune & Stratton, 1963.

HALEY, J., and HOFFMAN, L. *Techniques of Family Therapy.* New York: Basic Books, 1967.

HALLOWITZ, E. "Use of Non Professional Staff: Issues and Strategies." In W. C. Richan (Ed.), *Human Services and Social Work Responsibility.* New York: National Association of Social Workers, 1969.

HAMILTON, G. "Social Case Work." In R. H. Kurtz (Ed.), *Social Work Year Book.* New York: Russell Sage Foundation, 1939.

HANEY, C., BANKS, C., and ZIMBARDO, P. "Interpersonal Dynamics in a Simulated Prison." *The International Journal of Criminology and Penology,* 1973, *1,* 69–97.

HANLAN, A. "Changing Function and Structures." In F. W. Kaslow and Associates, *Issues in Human Services: A Sourcebook for Supervision and Staff Development.* San Francisco: Jossey-Bass, 1972.

HARE, R. T., and FRANKENA, S. "Peer Group Supervision." *American Journal of Orthopsychiatry,* 1972, *42* (3), 527–529.

HENRY, W. E., SIMS, J. H., and SPRAY, S. L. *The Fifth Profession: Becoming a Psychotherapist.* San Francisco: Jossey-Bass, 1971.

HERBART, F. J. *A Textbook in Psychology.* New York: Appleton-Century-Crofts, 1945.

HERTZ, M. L. "Mutual Self-Help as a Framework for the Training of Paraprofessionals for Work in the Human Services." Unpublished master's thesis, School of Social Administration, Temple University, 1972.

HOLMES, D. T. *A Guide for the Presentation and Submission of Proposals for Federal and Private Support.* Atlanta: United Board for College Development, 1971.

HUGHES, E. C. "Professions." In K. S. Lynn (Ed.), *The Professions in America.* Boston: Houghton Mifflin, 1965.

ILLICH, I. *Tools for Conviviality.* New York: Harper & Row, 1973.

JOHNSON, E. H. *Crime, Correction, and Society.* (Rev. ed.) Homewood, Ill.: Dorsey, 1971.

JOURARD, S. M. *The Transparent Self.* (Rev. ed.) New York: D. Van Nostrand, 1971.

JUNG, C. G. *Synchronicity.* Bollingen Series. Princeton, N.J.: Princeton University Press, 1973. (Originally published 1952.)

JURARSKY, J. A. "A Sit-In Method for Training Family Group Therapists." *Journal of Psychoanalysis in Groups,* 1964, *1,* 109-114.

KADIS, A., and MARKOWITZ, M. "Short-Term Analytic Treatment of Married Couples in a Group by a Therapist Couple." In C. Sager and H. Kaplan (Eds.), *Progress in Group and Family Therapy.* New York: Brunner/Mazel, 1972.

KADUSHIN, A. "Supervisor-Supervisee: A Survey." *Social Work,* 1974, *19* (3), 288–297.

KADUSHIN, A. *Supervision in Social Work.* New York: Columbia University Press, 1976.

KAGAN, N. "Influencing Human Interaction: Eleven Years of IPR." East Lansing: Michigan State University, 1973. (Mimeographed manuscript.)

KAMERMAN, S. B., and KAHN, A. J. *Social Services in the United States.* Philadelphia: Temple University Press, 1976.

KASLOW, F. W. "Group Supervision." In F. W. Kaslow and Associates, *Issues in Human Services: A Sourcebook for Supervision and Staff Development.* San Francisco: Jossey-Bass, 1972.

KASLOW, F. W. "Marital Therapy, Monogamy and Menages." *Journal of Marriage and Family Counseling,* 1975, *1* (3), 281–287.

KASLOW, F. W. "Crisis Intervention Theory and Technique." *Intellect Magazine,* 1976, *104* (2371), 316–317.

KASLOW, F. W., and ASSOCIATES. *Issues in Human Services: A Sourcebook for Supervision and Staff Development.* San Francisco: Jossey-Bass, 1972.

KASLOW, F. W., and FRIEDMAN, J. "Utilization of Family Photos and Movies in Family Therapy." *Journal of Marriage and Family Counseling,* 1977, *3* (1), 19–25.

KAUFMAN, H. *Administrative Feedback.* Washington, D.C.: Brookings Institution, 1973.

KELLING, G. L. *Kansas City Preventive Patrol Experiment: A Summary Report.* Washington, D.C.: Police Foundation, 1974.

KENNEDY, A. J., and FARRA, K. *Social Settlements in New York City.* New York: Columbia University Press, 1935.

KERNBERG, O. "The Treatment of Patients with Borderline Personality Organization." *International Journal of Psychoanalysis,* 1968, *49,* 600–619.

KING, L. S. *The Medical World of the Eighteenth Century.* Chicago: University of Chicago Press, 1958.

KIRKHAM, G. "The Metamorphosis." In W. H. Kroes and J. J. Harrell (Eds.), *Job Stress and the Police Officer: Identifying Stress Reduction Techniques.* Cincinnati: National Institute for Occupational Safety and Health, 1975.

KISSICK, W. L. "Medical Education, History." In L. C. Deighton (Ed.), *The Encyclopedia of Education.* Vol. 6. New York: Macmillan and Free Press, 1971.

KOBERG, D., and BAGNALL, J. *The Universal Traveler.* Los Altos, Calif.: Kaufman, 1972.

KOHLBERG, L. "Stage and Sequence: The Cognitive Development Approach to Socialization." In D. Goslin (Ed.), *Handbook of Socialization: Theory and Research.* New York: Rand McNally, 1969.

KOHLBERG, L. *The Just Community Approach to Corrections: A Manual.* Cambridge, Mass.: Harvard University Press, 1970.

KOHLBERG, L. "From Is to Ought." In T. Mishel (Ed.), *Cognitive Development and Epistemology.* New York: Academic Press, 1971.

KOHUT, H. *The Analysis of the Self.* New York: International Universities Press, 1971.

KUHN, T. S. *The Structure of Scientific Revolutions.* Chicago: University of Chicago Press, 1970.

KUTZIK, A. J. *Guidelines for Student Training in the Philadelphia Settlements.* Philadelphia: Delaware Valley Settlement Alliance, 1967.

KUTZIK, A. J. "Class and Ethnic Factors." In F. W. Kaslow and Associates, *Issues in Human Services: A Sourcebook for Supervision and Staff Development.* San Francisco: Jossey-Bass, 1972.

LACQUER, M. P. "Multiple Family Therapy." In A. Ferber, M. Mendelsohn, and A. Napier (Eds.), *The Book of Family Therapy.* New York: Science House, 1972.

LANDAU, M. "On the Concept of Self-Correcting Organization." Paper presented under the auspices of the Albert Schweitzer

Chair in Humanities at the Maxwell School, Syracuse University, Syracuse, New York, April 13, 1972.

LATHAM, E. "Hierarchy and Hieratics." In L. Gawthrop (Ed.), *The Administrative Process and Democratic Theory*. Boston: Houghton Mifflin, 1970.

Lawyers Practice Manual, A, Based on the Missouri Bar—Prentice-Hall Survey. Englewood Cliffs, N.J.: Prentice-Hall, 1964.

LEADER, A. "New Directions in Supervision." *Social Casework,* 1957, *38* (9), 462–468.

LEAKE, C. D. *Percival's Medical Ethics.* Baltimore: Williams and Wilkins, 1927.

LEJEUNE, F., and BUNJES, W. E. *German-English, English-German Dictionary for Physicians.* Stuttgart: Thieme, 1969.

LEOPOLD, R. L. "The Psychoanalyst at Work in the Community Mental Health Center: Special Contributions." *Community Mental Health Journal,* 1971, *7* (3), 189–197.

LEVINE, M. "Trends in Professional Employment." In E. E. Schwartz (Ed.), *Manpower in Social Welfare: Research Perspectives.* New York: National Association of Social Workers, 1966.

LEVINSON, E. A. *The Fallacy of Understanding.* New York: Basic Books, 1972.

LEVI-STRAUSS, C. "Social Structure." Quoted in P. Bohannon and M. Glazer (Eds.), *High Points in Anthropology.* New York: Knopf, 1973.

LEWIN, K. "Group Decision and Social Change." In T. Newcomb and E. Hartley (Eds.), *Readings in Social Psychology.* New York: Holt, Rinehart and Winston, 1952.

LEWIS, M. O. (Ed.). *The Foundation Directory.* New York: Foundation Center, 1975.

LEYENDECKER, G. "A Critique of Current Trends in Supervision." In *Casework Papers, National Conference on Social Work.* New York: Family Service Association of America, 1959.

LINDENBERG, S. *Supervision in Social Group Work.* New York: Association Press, 1939.

"List of Accredited Training Programs." *Journal of Marriage and Family Counselors,* 1977, *3* (1), 95.

LOCKE, J. *An Essay Concerning Human Understanding.* New York: Dover [1889], 1959.

LONG, N. "Administrative Communication." In S. Mailik and E. Van Ness (Eds.), *Concepts and Issues in Administrative Behavior.* Englewood Cliffs, N.J.: Prentice-Hall, 1962.

LUBOVE, R. *The Professional Altruist: The Emergence of Social Work as a Career.* Cambridge, Mass.: Harvard University Press, 1965.

LUTHMAN, S. G., and KIRSCHENBAUM, M. *The Dynamic Family.* Palo Alto, Calif.: Science and Behavior Books, 1974.

MCCARLEY, T. "The Psychotherapist's Search for Renewal." *The American Journal of Psychiatry,* 1975, *132* (3), 221–224.

MCGEE, T. "Supervision in Group Psychotherapy: A Comparison of Four Approaches." *International Journal of Group Psychotherapy,* 1970, *20*, 165–176.

MCGEE, T., and SCHUMAN, B. N. "The Nature of the Cotherapy Relationship." *International Journal of Group Psychotherapy,* 1967, *17*, 25–36.

MCGREGOR, D. *The Human Side of Enterprise.* New York: McGraw-Hill, 1960.

MCLEAN, F. H. *The Family Society.* New York: American Association for Organizing Family Work, 1927.

MACLENNAN, B. W. "Co-Therapy." *International Journal of Group Psychotherapy,* 1965, *15*, 154–156.

MAGER, R., and PIPE, P. *Analyzing Performance Problems or "You Really Oughta Wanna."* Belmont, Calif.: Fearon, 1970.

MAIN, J. W. "Restructuring Social Work Education: Knowledge, Curriculum, Instruction." *Journal of Education for Social Work,* 1971, *7* (2), 31–38.

MALONE, C. A. "Observations on the Role of Family Therapy in Child Psychiatry Training." *Journal of American Academy of Child Psychiatry,* 1974, *13* (3), 437–458.

MALONEY, D. M., and OTHERS. "Training Techniques for Staff in Group Homes for Juvenile Offenders: An Analysis." *Criminal Justice and Behavior,* 1975, *2*, 195–216.

MARCH, J., and SIMON, H. *Organizations.* New York: Wiley, 1958.

MARCUS, G. "How Casework Training May Be Adapted to Meet Workers' Personal Problems." In *Proceedings of the National Conference of Social Work.* Chicago: University of Chicago Press, 1927.

MENDELSOHN, M., and FERBER, A. "Is Everybody Watchin'?" In A. Ferber, M. Mendelsohn, and A. Napier (Eds.), *The Book of Family Therapy*. New York: Science House, 1972.

MENDES, H. "Countertransferences and Counter-Culture Clients." *Social Casework*, 1977, *58* (3), 163.

MERTON, R. K. "Some Preliminaries to a Sociology of Medical Education." In R. K. Merton, G. Reeder, and L. Kendall (Eds.), *The Student Physician*. Cambridge, Mass.: Harvard University Press, 1957.

METCALF, H., and URWICK, L. (Eds.). *Dynamic Administration: The Collected Papers of Mary Parker Follett*. New York: Harper & Row, 1940.

MEYER, H. J. "Sociological Comments." In C. Grosser, W. E. Henry, J. G. Kelly (Eds.). *Nonprofessionals in the Human Services*. San Francisco: Jossey-Bass, 1969.

MIDDLEMAN, R. "A Consultant Thinks About Choosing a Consultant." *Bucks County Drug and Alcohol News*, 1974, *1*.

MILLER, I. "Distinctive Characteristics of Supervision in Group Work." *Social Work*, 1960, *5* (1), 69–76.

MILLER, I. "Supervision in Social Work." In R. Morris (Ed.), *Encyclopedia of Social Work*. (16th issue.) New York: National Association of Social Workers, 1971.

MILLER, R., and PODELL, L. *Role Conflict in Public Social Services*. New York: Office of Community Affairs, State of New York, 1970.

MILLS, T. M. *Group Transformation*. Englewood Cliffs, N.J.: Prentice-Hall, 1964.

MINUCHIN, S. *Families and Family Therapy*. Cambridge, Mass.: Harvard University Press, 1974.

MINUCHIN, S., and OTHERS. *Families of the Slums*. New York: Basic Books, 1967.

MODLIN, H. "The Psychiatrist and His Family. . . . Not All Understanding and Insight." *Menninger Perspective*, 1976, *7* (3), 12–13.

MONTALVO, B. "Aspects of Live Supervision." *Family Process*, 1973, *12*, 343–359.

MUDD, E. H. "Marriage Counseling and the Related Professions." Paper presented at meeting of College of Physicians, Philadelphia, November 1974.

NAGY, I. B., and SPARK, G. M. *Invisible Loyalties*. New York: Harper & Row, 1973.

NAPIER, R. W., and GERSHENFELD, M. K. *Groups: Theory and Experience*. Boston: Houghton Mifflin, 1973.

National Association of Social Workers. "Working Definition of Social Work Practice." *Social Work,* 1958, *3* (2), 5–9.

National Association of Social Workers. *Standards for Social Service Manpower*. New York: National Association of Social Workers, 1973.

NEFF, W. *Work and Human Behavior*. New York: Atherton Press, 1968.

NEIDERHOFFER, A. *Behind the Shield*. Englewood Cliffs, N.J.: Prentice-Hall, 1967.

NOVAK, D. W., and BUSKO, B. P. "Teaching Old Dogs New Tricks: Issues in the Training of Family Therapists." *The Psychiatric Forum,* 1974, *14* (2), 14–20.

OLMSTEAD, J. *Organizational Structure and Climate: Implications for Agencies*. Working Papers No. 2. Washington, D.C.: Social and Rehabilitation Service, U.S. Department of Health, Education and Welfare, 1973.

OLMSTEAD, J., and CHRISTENSEN, H. *Study of Agency Work Contexts: Implications for Supervision*. Program Application Report No. 1. Washington, D.C.: Social and Rehabilitation Service, U.S. Department of Health, Education and Welfare, 1973.

PAPP, P. "Family Choreography." In P. Guerin (Ed.), *Family Therapy: Theory and Practice*. New York: Gardner Press, 1976.

PEARL, A., and RIESSMAN, F. *New Careers for the Poor*. New York: Free Press, 1965.

PEARLIN, L. K. "Alienation from Work: A Study of Nursing Personnel." *American Sociological Review,* 1962, *27* (3), 314–326.

PERLMUTTER, F. "Barometer of Professional Change." In F. W. Kaslow and Associates, *Issues in Human Services: A Sourcebook for Supervision and Staff Development*. San Francisco: Jossey-Bass, 1972.

PETTES, E. D. *Supervision in Social Work*. London: Allen & Unwin, 1967.

PFEIFFER, J. W., and JONES, J. E. *Annual Handbook for Group*

Facilitators. La Jolla, Calif.: University Associates Publishers, 1974.

PORTER, L. "Communication: Structure and Process." In H. Fromkin and J. Sherwood (Eds.), *Integrating the Organization.* New York: Free Press, 1974.

PORTER, L., LAWLER, E., and HACKMAN, J. *Behavior in Organizations.* New York: McGraw-Hill, 1975.

PRICE, J. L. "Value Assumptions in Humanistic Clinical Supervision." Paper presented at the American Association of Marriage and Family Counselors National Conference, Philadelphia, October 1976.

PRINCE, G. M. *The Practice of Creativity: A Manual for Dynamic Group Problem Solving.* New York: Harper & Row, 1970.

Psychotherapy Economics. Special Report. 1977, *4* (2), 1–2.

RABINOWITZ, C. "The Caseworker and the Private Practitioner in Psychotherapy." *Jewish Social Service Quarterly,* 1953, *30* (2), 166–178.

RAIA, A. P. *Managing by Objectives.* Glenview, Ill.: Scott, Foresman, 1974.

RAPOPORT, L. *Consultation in Social Work Practice.* New York: National Association of Social Workers, 1963.

RAPOPORT, L. "Consultation in Social Work." In R. Morris (Ed.), *Encyclopedia of Social Work.* (16th issue.) New York: National Association of Social Workers, 1971.

REIN, M., and MILLER, S. M. "The Demonstration as a Strategy for Change." Paper delivered at the Columbia University Mobilization for Youth Training Institute Workshop, New York, April 1964.

REYNOLDS, B. *Learning and Teaching in the Practice of Social Work.* New York: Farrar and Rinehart, 1965.

RICHAN, W. C. "A Theoretical Scheme for Determining Professional and Nonprofessional Roles." *Social Work,* 1961, *6* (4), 22–28.

RICHAN, W. C. *Human Services and Social Work Responsibility.* New York: National Association of Social Workers, 1969.

RICHAN, W. C. "Indigenous Paraprofessional Staff." In F. W. Kaslow and Associates, *Issues in Human Services: A Sourcebook for Supervision and Staff Development.* San Francisco: Jossey-Bass, 1972.

RICHARD, W. C., and FELL, R. D. "Health Factors in Police Job Stress." In W. H. Kroes and J. J. Harrell (Eds.), *Job Stress and the Police Officer: Identifying Stress Reduction Techniques.* Cincinnati: National Institute of Occupational Safety and Health, 1975.

RICHMOND, M. E. *Social Diagnosis.* New York: Russell Sage Foundation, 1917.

RIESMAN, D. *The Story of Medicine in the Middle Ages.* New York: Hoeber, 1935.

RIOCH, M. J. "The Work of Wilfred Bion on Groups." In M. Kissen (Ed.), *From Group Dynamics to Group Psychoanalysis.* New York: Wiley, 1976.

ROBINSON, V. P. *Supervision in Social Casework.* Chapel Hill: University of North Carolina Press, 1936.

ROSENBAUM, M. "Co-Therapy." In H. I. Kaplan and B. J. Sadock (Eds.), *Comprehensive Group Psychotherapy.* Baltimore, Md.: Williams and Wilkins, 1971.

ROTHSTEIN, W. G. *American Physicians in the Nineteenth Century.* Baltimore, Md.: Johns Hopkins University Press, 1972.

ROWLEY, C. M., and FAUX, E. J. "The Team Approach to Supervision." *Mental Hygiene,* 1966, *50* (1), 60–65.

RYLE, G. *The Concept of Mind.* London: Hutchinson University Library, 1949.

SADOCK, B. J., and KAPLAN, H. I. "Training and Standards in Group Psychotherapy." In H. I. Kaplan and B. J. Sadock (Eds.), *Comprehensive Group Psychotherapy.* Baltimore, Md.: Williams and Wilkins, 1971.

SANAZARO, P. J. "Physician Support Personnel in the 1970s." *Journal of the American Medical Association,* 1970, *214* (4), 98–100.

SARASON, I. G. "Verbal Learning, Modelling, and Juvenile Delinquency." *American Psychologist,* 1968, *23,* 254–266.

SARRI, R., and GALINSKI, M. *A Conceptual Framework for Teaching Group Development in Social Group Work.* New York: Council on Social Work Education Conference, 1969.

SATIR, V. "The Quest for Survival: A Training Program for Family Diagnosis and Treatment." *Acta Psychotherapeutica Et Psychosomatica,* 1963, *11,* 33–38.

SATIR, V. *Peoplemaking*. Palo Alto, Calif.: Science and Behavior Books, 1972.

SCHERZ, F. H. "A Concept of Supervision Based on Definitions of Job Responsibility." *Social Casework*, 1958, *39* (8), 435–443.

SCHOUR, E. "Helping Social Workers Handle Work Stress." *Social Casework*, 1953, *34* (10), 423–428.

SCHUSTER, D. B., SANDT, J. J., and THALER, O. F. *Clinical Supervision of the Psychiatric Resident*. New York: Brunner/Mazel, 1972.

SCHWARTZ, W. "The Social Worker in the Group." In *The Social Welfare Forum*. Official proceedings, National Conference on Social Welfare. New York: Columbia University Press, 1961.

SHAH, I. *The Sufis*. New York: Anchor Books, 1964.

SHAPIRA, M. "Reflections on the Preparation of Social Workers for Executive Positions." *Journal of Education for Social Work*, 1971, *7* (1), 55–68.

SILVER, H. K. "New Allied Health Professionals: Implications of the Colorado Child Health Associate Law." *New England Journal of Medicine*, February 11, 1971, *284* (6), 304–307.

SLAVSON, S. R. *A Textbook in Analytic Group Psychotherapy*. New York: International Universities Press, 1964.

SLOANE, P. "The Technique of Supervised Analysis." *Journal of the American Psychoanalytic Association*, 1957, *5*, 539–547.

SLOBODA, S. B. "What Are Mental Health Nurses Doing?" *Journal of Psychiatric Nursing*, 1976, *14* (4), 24–27.

SMALLEY, R. *Theory for Social Work Practice*. New York: Columbia University Press, 1967.

SMITH, Z. D. "Volunteer Visiting: The Organization to Make It Effective." In I. C. Barrow (Ed.), *Proceedings of the National Conference of Charities and Correction 1884*. Boston: George Ellis, 1885.

SMITH, Z. D. "How to Get and Keep Visitors." In I. C. Barrows (Ed.), *Proceedings of the National Conference of Charities and Correction. 1887* Boston: George Ellis, 1887.

SOLOMON, A., LOEFFLER, F. J., and FRANK, G. H. "An Analysis of Co-Therapist Interaction in Group Psychotherapy." *International Journal of Group Psychotherapy*, 1953, *3*, 171–180.

SONNE, J. C., and LINCOLN, G. "Heterosexual Co-Therapy Team Experiences During Family Therapy." *Family Process,* 1965, *4* (2), 177–197.

SPECHT, H. "The Deprofessionalization of Social Work." *Social Work,* 1972, *17* (2), 3–15.

SPECK, R., and ATTNEAVE, C. "Social Network Intervention." In C. Sager and H. Kaplan (Eds.), *Progress in Group and Family Therapy.* New York: Brunner/Mazel, 1972.

SPENSLEY, J., and BLACKER, K. "Feelings of the Psychotherapist." *American Journal of Orthopsychiatry,* 1976, *46* (3), 542–545.

STARBUCK, W. H. "Organizations and Their Environments." In M. Dunnette (Ed.), *Handbook of Industrial and Organizational Psychology.* Chicago: Rand McNally, 1976.

STEDMAN, T. H. *Stedman's Medical Dictionary.* Baltimore, Md.: Williams and Wilkins, 1966.

STERNBACH, R. A., ABROMS, G. M., and RICE, D. G. "Clinical Responsibility and the Psychologist." *Psychiatry,* 1969, *32,* 165–173.

STEVENSON, I. "The Psychiatric Interview." In S. Arieti (Ed.), *American Handbook of Psychiatry.* New York: Basic Books, 1959.

STOTLAND, E. "Self-Esteem and Stress in Police Work." In W. H. Kroes and J. J. Harrell (Eds.), *Job Stress and the Police Officer: Identifying Stress Reduction Techniques.* Cincinnati: National Institute for Occupational Safety and Health, 1975.

STROTZKA, H. "Das Rollenspiel als Ausbildungmethode." *Gruppenpsychotherapie und Gruppendynamik [Group Psychotherapy and Group Dynamics],* 1973, *6,* 286–293.

STRUPP, H. H. "On the Technology of Psychotherapy." *Archives of General Psychiatry,* 1972, *26,* 270–278.

SWIFT, L. B. "Social Work as a Profession." In R. H. Kurtz (Ed.), *Social Work Year Book, 1939.* New York: Russell Sage Foundation, 1939.

TARACHOW, S. *An Introduction to Psychotherapy.* New York: International Universities Press, 1963.

THELEN, H. *Education and the Human Quest.* New York: Harper & Row, 1960.

TOCH, H., GRANT, J. D., and GALVIN, R. T. *Agents of Change: A Study of Police Reform.* New York: Wiley, 1975.

TOREN, N. *Social Work: The Case of a Semi-Profession.* Beverly Hills, Calif.: Sage Publications, 1972.

TOWLE, C. "The Place of Help in Supervision." *Social Service Review,* 1963, *37* (4), 405–415.

TUCKER, B. S., HART, G., and LIDDLE, H. A. "Supervision in Family Therapy: A Developmental Perspective." *Journal of Marriage and Family Counseling,* 1976, *2* (3), 260–276.

TUCKMAN, B. W. "Developmental Sequence in Small Groups." *Psychological Bulletin,* 1965, *62* (6), 384.

UDY, S. *Work in Traditional and Modern Society.* Englewood Cliffs, N.J.: Prentice-Hall, 1970.

United States Task Force on Social Work Education and Manpower. *Closing the Gap . . . in Social Work Manpower.* Washington, D.C.: U.S. Department of Health, Education and Welfare, 1965.

VEBLEN, T. *The Theory of the Leisure Class.* New York: New American Library, 1953. (Originally published 1899.)

VINTER, R. D. "The Social Structure of Service." In A. J. Kahn (Ed.), *Issues in American Social Work.* New York: Columbia University Press, 1959.

WAELDER, R. *Basic Theory of Psychoanalysis.* New York: International Universities Press, 1960.

WARNER, A. G. *American Charities.* New York: Crowell, 1919. (Originally published 1894; second edition, 1908.)

WARREN, R. L. (Ed.). *Politics and the Ghettos.* New York: Atherton Press, 1969.

WATSON, F. D. *The Charity Organization Movement in the United States.* New York: Macmillan, 1922.

WAX, J. "Time-Limited Supervision." *Social Work,* 1963, *8* (3), 37–43.

WEINER, M. L. *The Cognitive Unconscious.* Davis, Calif.: California International Psychological Press, 1975.

WHITAKER, C. A. "Psychotherapy of the Absurd: With a Special Emphasis on the Psychotherapy of Aggression." *Family Process,* 1976, *14* (1), 1–16.

WHITAKER, C. A., and ABROMS, G. M. "New Approaches to Residency

Training in Psychiatry." In G. Farwell, N. Gamsky, and P. Mathieu-Coughlan (Eds.), *The Counselor's Handbook.* New York: Intext Educational, 1974.

WHITE, R., and LIPPIT, R. "Leader Behavior and Member Reaction in Three Social Climates." In D. Cartwright and A. Zander (Eds.), *Group Dynamics.* New York: Harper & Row, 1960.

WHOLEY, J. S., and OTHERS. *Federal Evaluation Policy.* Washington, D.C.: Urban Institute, 1970.

WILENSKY, H. L., and LEBEAUX, C. N. *Industrial Society and Social Welfare.* New York: Russell Sage Foundation, 1958.

WILENSKY, H. L., and LEBEAUX, C. N. *Industrial Society and Social Welfare.* New York: Free Press, 1965.

WILLIAMSON, B. *Supervision.* New York: Woman's Press, 1950.

WILLIAMSON, B. *Supervision: New Patterns and Processes.* New York: Association Press, 1961.

WISEMAN, M., and SILVERMAN, G. "Evaluating Social Services: Did the General Accounting Office Help?" *Social Service Review,* 1974, *48,* 315–326.

WOLBERG, L. *The Technique of Psychotherapy.* New York: Grune & Stratton, 1967.

WOODS, R. A., and KENNEDY, A. J. *The Settlement Horizon.* New York: Russell Sage Foundation, 1922.

YALOM, I. D. *The Theory and Practice of Group Psychotherapy.* (2nd ed.) New York: Basic Books, 1975.

Index

334

improvement over time is noted, one can only wonder why he is retained in this post. If evaluations are utilized merely to provide an aura of participation, it is dishonest to pretend that they have any significance, and they had best be dropped. We can only hope that, as peer review and the stronger push for accountability at all performance levels take hold, department chairmen, training directors, and agency administrators will become courageous enough to not continue using those who consistently are rated poor.

A program tends to have a "good reputation" if its training faculty are renowned by virtue of being well published and/or because its graduates make laudatory comments and do well after graduation. But more is needed in the arena of program evaluation, and only after goals are stated in measurable, observable, and operationalizable terms will we begin to be able to evaluate and compare training programs. This, too, will come to pass in the not-too-distant future.

Moving away from evaluation into the area of heightened sensitivity, now that the metatherapy elements of supervision have been highlighted by Abroms, one can speculate that more understanding of the metatalk in training, teaching, and consultation will follow and that mental health professionals will be able to pick up and cope with these messages and try to eliminate the dissonance, just as therapists try to minimize double-bind communications. Perhaps we will never achieve agreement between those such as Abroms, who present a cogent case for including therapeutic elements in supervision, and Finch and Richan, who are at the far distant pole, feeling these to be necessarily separate and distinct. Such divergence constitutes dynamic tension, which is healthy, as it keeps dialogue alive and periodically leads to new and better syntheses of ideas, methods, and systems.

In the area of supervisory and training techniques, our forward glance visualizes expanded usage of role-playing and psychodrama techniques such as those described by Gitterman, Miller, and Kaslow. These have been shown to be excellent for helping trainees empathize with and act out different roles, to literally try to get into another person's skin and see what it must feel like to be and think as that other does. When it comes to providing trainees with a method for trying out possible future behaviors, role rehearsal can prove fruitful. In addition, such experiential techniques maximize trainee involvement in their own learning process. Moving in this direction will require greater flexibility and ingenuity on the part of training personnel.

The increasing utilization of multiple and interdisciplinary supervisors, highlighted most prominently in the chapter on community mental health centers, is a phenomena we think will and should spread. As more techniques of therapy are permitted to coexist in the same settings, it is improbable that any one person will be proficient in all. Thus trainees will be precepted in different modalities by specialists in each particular approach. We see this as a laudable trend that should prevent narrowness and myopia in the helping professions. But, as this occurs, it will be important to lodge responsibility in one of the supervisors for the coordination of the training and overall assessment of the supervisees' performance. The multidisciplinary supervisory and training programs should also push the professions to look toward interdisciplinary educational programs in graduate and professional schools with shared faculty, students from different disciplines taking classes together, and some joint curriculum planning. Only then will full collaboration become a reality.

Another trend emerges from the realization that not everyone needs similar amounts of supervision and that therefore the rigid, weekly schedule might be adhered to when appropriate, while more flexible and less frequent scheduling can be adapted for intermediate and senior staff. At the advanced-practitioner level, peer consultation sought voluntarily, when needed, could well become the preferred model (Kaslow, 1972). Similarly, in settings where frequent crises occur—such as acute wards of mental hospitals, foster care agencies, drug treatment programs, and prisons—access to on-the-spot crisis supervision should be available, for if a conference is not scheduled until the following week, it may simply be too late!

Most of the professions are moving toward or are already requiring continuing education credits (Kutzik, Chapters One and Two), and this is a trend we heartily endorse. Perhaps the professional organizations might consider formal individual arrangements for supervision and consultation as sufficiently meritorious to award credit for these as well as for work taken in educational programs and at institutes and conferences. This impetus for ever-increasing knowledge and competence is to be hailed.

It is likely that the trend Cohen pinpointed of private practitioners from all the helping disciplines voluntarily contracting for precepting and tutelage to acquire more knowledge and new competencies will continue, whether or not continuing education credits are awarded for such study. For we are an achievement-oriented professional culture.

In drawing to a close, we sincerely hope more "superstar" helping professionals will utilize their skills in working in and training others to work in underserved, unglamorous settings such as the prisons so accurately depicted by Brodsky or the mental hospitals mentioned by Coché. Inner-city clinics and settlements, departments of probation, and public welfare agencies are in the same category. If such positions do not provide sufficient monetary rewards and professional stimulation and satisfaction to warrant a full-time investment, then a part-time arrangement that allows such professionals to live out their own commitments to social justice is often possible. Only when supervisors, educators, and trainers have some investment in the lower-status agencies will they be sanctioning such involvement on the part of their supervisees.

We conclude this chapter as we began it—with a quote from *The Prophet:*

And a man said, Speak to us of Self Knowledge.
And he answered, saying:
Your hearts know in silence the secrets of the days and the nights.
But your ears thirst for the sound of your heart's knowledge.
You would know in words that which you have always known in
  thought.
You would touch with your fingers the naked body of your dreams.